TEILHARD DE CHARDIN
THE MAN
AND HIS MEANING

TEILHARD DE CHARDIN, 1896–
THE MAN
AND HIS MEANING

HENRI DE LUBAC, S.J.

Translated by
RENÉ HAGUE

HAWTHORN BOOKS, INC.　　*Publishers*　　NEW YORK

First American Edition, 1965

H-9070

PREFACE

"HE to whom it is given ... to see Christ *more real* than any other reality in the World, Christ everywhere present and everywhere growing more great, Christ the final determination and plasmatic Principle of the Universe, that man indeed lives in a zone where no multiplicity can distress him and which is nevertheless the most active workshop of universal fulfilment.

"Show him the inexactness or the error in the terms in which he tries to express his 'experience'—and, patiently, he will seek another formula. But his vision remains with him."

Those sentences, written on 22 December 1918, in a little room in the seminary at Strasbourg, conclude a twenty-five-page essay, significantly entitled *Forma Christi*.[1]

In disclosing the hidden source which nourished Teilhard's teaching, they also explain its strength and, for many readers, its irresistible attraction. At the same time they are thoroughly characteristic of its special quality. If Père Teilhard's "vision" is integrated in the great Christian experience, it is also clear that it expresses only one aspect of it. Similarly, the road he followed with such determination is, and cannot but be, only one of the converging roads that lead to Christ: the road, maybe, that best answers the expectations of our own days, but that must fail to reach its destination if it claims to be the only road. Père Teilhard, following up the graces given to him, explored deeply a part, but only a part,

[1]More precisely, a Note on "*L'Élément universel*" which is an appendix to *Forma Christi*. It was shortly afterwards dropped and replaced by a new *L'Élément universel*, dated 21 Feb. 1919, in which this passage does not appear.

of the domain in which are to be found "the unfathomable riches of Christ".

At the same time, this passage illuminates for us what, underlying the development of an important scientific contribution, and the many-sided activities of a life of continual movement, was Père Teilhard's constant preoccupation: always he strove to bring together within him his interior vision and the teaching he received from outside himself. Both came to him from the same God, the same Christ, and he would never make any sacrifice of one to the other. More than that, he was certain of their convergence. He had to rely on words to be the faithful interpreters of his thought, and constantly had to try and find a better way of expressing himself through them. This involved a continual effort of intense reflection and a perpetual return to the same themes, so that all newly acquired knowledge could serve to bring closer the unique Object made manifest to him, to integrate all in it and bring everything under its lordship. It was for the same reason that he would humbly and patiently listen to advice and criticism in order to achieve a more exact balance of thought. And yet all the time he clung tenaciously to the line he was following and spoke with the same note of passionate conviction, for deep within him he always retained his "vision".

Each of the two studies that follows seeks to bring out certain characteristics of Père Teilhard. Their scope is deliberately limited, and I hope the reader will not look for more in them than they attempt to give him. The first is an analysis of the principal elements that throughout his life characterized the faith of Père Teilhard, various points in his teaching being considered only in so far as they are directly pertinent. Nevertheless it may, I hope, contribute to an understanding of his work, at least on its spiritual side and in its general orientation; for, as Père Smulders has recently written, "seldom have ideas sprung so directly from a man's intimate personal life". In the second essay, in which attention is concentrated on a passage that is often quoted—often, too, in my view, badly interpreted—I have tried to define one of the central points in Teilhardian thought: the linking, with an apologetic aim in view, of the contributions of objective phenomenology and interior experience.

In both, I have made use of numerous letters and personal notes of Père Teilhard's. I am well aware of the caution with which such evidence must be used. Too much weight, even with the best intentions, should not, we know, be attributed to what may be a casual allusion. Every letter presupposes a correspondent to whom it is addressed, and who must be borne in mind if we are to interpret the way in which the letter is worded and the shades of meaning intended. We have to be careful not to take a quick reference, a tentative suggestion, a hypothesis, maybe, put forward almost at random, for the expression of a fully worked out doctrine: or an indication of a passing mood for that of a fundamental mental attitude. In fact, the nature of the texts used reduces such dangers to a minimum. Used, moreover, in conjunction with an ever-green personal memory of Père Teilhard de Chardin, they have proved the most reliable of guides.[2]

---

[2] On a number of points, I have, to avoid repetition, referred the reader to my *La Pensée religieuse du Père Teilhard de Chardin* (Paris, Aubier, 1962).

CONTENTS

TEILHARD'S
SPIRITUAL DEVELOPMENT

I

THE FORMATIVE PERIOD

FOR some time a pernicious catch-phrase has been current in some (fortunately restricted) Christian circles: people speak, with contempt, of "traditional Catholicism". For the most part, no doubt, what is meant by the phrase is a form of Catholicism that is distorted by exaggeration, a formalist, hidebound religion with no interior vitality, no personal maturity, no open-minded readiness to face new situations and new problems. There is, indeed, every reason why such a religious attitude should come under attack. It represents the dead letter that stifles the spirit. At the same time, it is an abuse of language to use such an expression; as so often happens when condemning the undesirable, it fails to preserve what is valuable. It is of the essence of Catholicism to be traditional. Tradition is its living soul. It is from tradition that it derives its strength. Every opposition made, or even admitted, between tradition and personal life, as though between letter and spirit, and from whichever angle, can be a mortal blow to our faith. Catholic tradition, with which alone we are concerned, is fruitful, and continues to draw its vitality from the most personally conditioned lives. The finest and boldest Christian effort, the freshest and most enduring, has always flourished from the roots of tradition. We find this in every order of effort, from those whose realization can be tangibly perceived, to that of sanctity, and we find it today in the adaptation of the Church to modern needs; wherever this seeks to fulfil itself, it produces, and will, we hope, continue to produce even more fully, a deeper appreciation of tradition.

This general rule is exemplified in the particular case of Père Teilhard de Chardin. If this bold Christian sometimes, as has been said, came close to the edge of the precipice, it was his roots in tradition, held firmly in place by his choice of unswerving fidelity, that saved him from a fall. We may, indeed, go further and say that it was from those roots that he drew nourishment for what we admire in him as being the most vigorously personal.[1]

His interior life, like his vocation to science, is explained in the first place by his family. His parents were Christians, with the habit of prayer. Every morning they could be seen kneeling together at Mass in the church of Notre-Dame-du-Pont. Shortly before his death, his father, Emmanuel, left an unobtrusive but finely expressed testimony to the spirit of his faith. At the age of over eighty-six he wrote, on the last page of a private notebook, "My life has been made up of sorrows and disappointments; I have had confidence in God, and now I see that it has been rounded off with a success I never hoped for or even imagined." His mother, who died in 1936, was a real saint. She was an ardent and intelligent apostle of the Sacred Heart, and it was from her daily meditation, based on the classic spiritual writers such as the Venerable Louis Du Pont, that she drew the strength she needed for a life made up of devotion and yet in no way shut off from her own

---

[1] Teilhard himself said that he wished to unite "the spirit of tradition and the spirit of adventurous research": *La Parole attendue* (1940); *Cahiers Pierre Teilhard de Chardin*, 4, p. 28; cf. p. 26, the ancient motto he was so fond of, *Nova et Vetera*. Towards the end of the 1914 war when he was billeted by chance at Chavannes-sur-l'Étang, on the borders of Alsace, he wrote (20 Sept. 1918), "It turns out that the presbytery of this out-of-the-way village used to be a Jesuit house in the days of the old Society (1720). . . . Everything in it is 'ours'. . . . Like the men who lived here before me, I am committed to God's work, in itself and as adapted to my own time, and I have the feeling that a whole accumulated store of strength is around me, within these old walls." (*Making of a Mind*, pp. 309–10).

family. On more than one occasion Pierre paid her a deeply felt tribute. In technical matters she was quite unable to keep up with him, but at the same time he always felt that it was to her that, basically, he owed the best of his thought.

We can see a little more clearly, too, how much he owed to his family environment by recalling his long and intimate relations with his sister Marguerite-Marie, an invalid, bedridden for so many years, who had acquired a "remarkable power of soothing attraction, radiating like a halo".[2] When he heard of her death in 1936 he wrote: "Her loss has created a sort of universal solitude around me, that affects all the aspects of an interior world of which I had gradually made her a part." "She and I", he said, again, "used to think together in everything to do with spiritual activity and the interior life."[3] One should read, too, the life of another of his sisters, Françoise, who died at Shanghai in 1911 as Superior of the Little Sisters of the Poor.[4] Pierre was Françoise's favourite, and the religious vocation they shared was to bring them even closer together. Shortly before joining the Little Sisters of the Poor, Françoise wrote to him in words whose vigour shines through the sometimes conventional expression: "Ask every day of him, whose heart has so loved us, that he may allow us too to love to the very end, without faltering and without weariness, trusting to our succour from on high, which will never fail us—and, as reward, in return for our sufferings and efforts, simply to grant that we may see springing from the furrow that every apostolic soul should plough across the world, the harvest of some little good brought to fruition."[5]

[2] *L'énergie spirituelle de la souffrance*, 8 Jan. 1950 (preface to the life of Marguerite-Marie by Monique Givelet); *Œuvres*, VII, p. 257

[3] Quoted by André-A. Devaux, *Teilhard et la vocation de la femme* (1964), p. 13.

[4] There are two editions of this: *Soeur Marie-Albéric du Sacré Cœur* (Little Sisters of the Poor, Rennes, 1914), and *Françoise Teilhard de Chardin, Petite-Sœur des Pauvres*, by her sister Marguerite-Marie (Clermont-Ferrand, L. Bellet).

[5] *Françoise Teilhard de Chardin*, pp. 61–2; cf. p. 48, Françoise's prayer to the Sacred Heart, "always hidden, yet always present in the Host".

In these words, dated as they are, it is not difficult to re-
cognise a plan that was to be followed by Pierre himself. In
1903 Françoise wrote to her parents from the novitiate of the
Little Sisters of the Poor: "Every day I am feeling more
strongly what Pierre always so rightly says, that the more God
asks us for the sacrifices entailed by separation, both in large
matters and in trifles, the more, in return, he increases our
affections and preserves them in all their freshness for eternity."
The correspondence between brother and sister has been
almost entirely lost, but the little that remains is sufficient to
show how close was their mutual trust. Pierre had once been
a source of strength to Françoise, during a time of severe
trial, when she was tormented with doubts about her vocation, by reminding her of the sweetness to be drawn from the
crucified Christ;[6] and later Françoise, dying of the sickness
she had contracted when nursing the aged Chinese in her
care, would ease the agony she suffered with the strains of
Jesu dulcis memoria. One of the last things she said was, "I
hope Pierre will pray for me. I shan't forget him in heaven."
Nor did Pierre forget her on earth. She had written to him, in
1907, about their eldest brother Albéric, whose memory he
had been recalling: "You see, the life of a Little Sister, if it is
really to be lived fully, demands too complete a sacrifice of all
the joys of this world to leave us any time to linger over the
delights of memory. We should seek souls in God, for that is
the real present for them, and will be ours too, one day. . . .
A Little Sister must detach herself from everything that is not
God, and God alone." Some years later, with these confidences
in mind, Pierre wrote, "My greatest happiness would be to

---

[6] Cf. *La Pensée religieuse du Père Pierre Teilhard de Chardin* (1962), p. 342. A
little while before, Françoise, intelligent and individualistic, had started on
reading the whole of Plato in Greek. At the age of twenty-one she was writing
twenty- or thirty-page essays on Descartes, Pascal and Malebranche, and was
thinking of tackling the German philosophers in the original. At that time she
used to say, "There are two things I shall never give up, my books and my
freedom."

know that I really helped her to be a little more for God and in God"; and again, when noting down one of the memories he drew from the depth of his being, "I have been recalling some things that Françoise said to me in days gone by— when she was a Little Sister—about the unique and beatifying importance that the reality of God had assumed in her life;— and I felt that I understood that we were fundamentally more alike than I had hitherto thought. There was this difference, however, that she was following a road on which the realities of this world were far more obscured or left behind than was the case with me." In his lasting memory of Françoise, this conviction remained with him until the very end.

The training he received in his family was completed at school. At Mongré (Villefranche-sur-Saône) where he received his secondary education (from second to sixth form) Pierre soon joined the Sodality of Our Lady, and before long became its prefect. It was then, no doubt, that he began, with the freshness of childhood, to turn his mind to the mystery of the Immaculate Virgin Mother, a subject which he was to treat from time to time, with exceptional ardour and depth, with subtlety and with a sure theological touch. This we shall see later. Although there was nothing exceptional in his letters from school, they show us a level-headed, quiet boy, who applied himself as earnestly to prayer as to his studies. It can hardly have come as a surprise to those who knew him when, in the year after he left school and after a few months studying mathematics at Clermont, he went to Aix-en-Provence to enter the Jesuit novitiate, on 19 March 1899.

2

THE DECISIVE EXPERIENCE

A LONG period now began for Pierre, his training for religious and apostolic life. It followed the normal pattern. Those who shared his life from 1899 to 1912 retain the memory of an endearing colleague, gay and open-hearted, putting everyone at his ease; of a young religious, devoted to every aspect of his duty, a keen worker, with great gifts but without any marked originality—apart from his scientific tastes, in cultivating which he was still an amateur. He was a good Greek and Latin scholar, but he had found no real master to introduce him to philosophical thought, and his theological studies, solid though they were, only partly filled this gap—and this in spite of the careful introductions with which one of his teachers, Père Xavier Le Bachelet, prefaced each dogmatic treatise; in spite too of the close companion-ship of such friends as Pierre Rousselot (killed at Éparges, near Verdun, in the spring of 1915), Pierre Charles (later professor of dogmatic theology at Louvain, who did much to popularize the *Milieu Divin*) and Auguste Valensin, who re-mained until the end his trusted friend and spiritual adviser.[1]

[1] In a letter written in the summer of 1954, Père Teilhard speaks of the recent death of his two friends, "The great Auguste Valensin" and "Pierre Charles, who opened my eyes for me". Of Auguste Valensin he wrote, on 5 Jan. 1954, "It was he who taught me to think" (*Letters from a Traveller*, p. 348). Cf. *Auguste Valensin, textes et documents inédits* (1961). Père Teilhard and Père Rousselot spent only one year together at Ore Place (1908–9), but they were to meet again in Paris from 1912–14, where Rousselot was professor of dogma in the theological faculty.

In between his three years of philosophy at Jersey and four years of theology at Ore Place, Hastings, he had spent three years in Cairo, teaching physics and natural history.[2] He was ordained priest on 24 August 1911, and finished his theological studies in the summer of 1912. Immediately before the war of 1914 he was given two years in Paris as a preparation for the scientific career for which, in view of his increasingly evident talents, he was destined. But what concerns us most at the moment is that while working for his doctorate in natural science, the priestly ministry played a great part in his life.[3]

However, when war broke out in 1914, Pierre Teilhard de Chardin had not yet found his real place. His scientific ideas had already matured. In contrast with the mental attitude that predominated in his environment, generalized evolution was already to him a matter of conviction, and this view was to govern the whole later development of his thought. Evolution appeared to his mind "not so much as an abstract notion, as a *presence* . . . that occupied [his] whole interior climate". "I was thirty when I abandoned the antiquated static dualism and emerged into a universe in process of guided evolution. What an intellectual revolution!"[4]

A different type of experience, of a more intimate order, which brought with it some conflict, had been added to the thought of his mother and sisters, though "without diverting or dissipating his energies". This had revealed to him the "illuminating and inspiring influence" that woman can supply,

[2] His *Lettres d'Égypte*, written to his parents from 1905 to 1908, give a realistic picture of Père Teilhard as he then was (Paris, Aubier, 1963).

[3] Every Sunday he was at Le Bourget, engaged in apostolic work for young glass-workers. In 1913 he preached the Lenten Sermons at Gap, and in 1914 at Lyons. For his scientific work, see *La Carrière scientifique du Père Teilhard de Chardin*, by Pères L. Barjon and P. Leroy (1964).

[4] Matter and spirit are no longer for Teilhard "two compartments", or "two things", but "two directions". This certainly does not mean, as some have concluded, that he no longer distinguishes between matter and spirit, or even that he blurs the distinction (*Le Cœur de la Matière*, 1950).

and the essential part of what he later called the "universal feminine" in the "salvation and perfecting of the human soul".[5] Nevertheless, he was still not completely certain of himself. Since his earliest childhood, a "burning bush" had been glowing in the depths of his soul, but the tall flames had not yet burst out from the "initial point of kindling". Before that could happen, there had to be the long, serious, patient process of initiation whose stages have just been noted, with day to day constancy both in the effort of thought and the abandonment of prayer. And then, with specially favourable circumstances to encourage it, there came the sudden explosion. During the war years of 1914 to 1919, Pierre Teilhard reached full maturity. At the front, in the shadow of death, far from the conventions of ordinary life, in the solitude of nightwatches, or, during intervals of rest a little behind the lines, he thought, and prayed, and, looking ahead into the future, he made the offering of himself. The presence of God possessed him.

We can to some extent follow the development of the work that went on within him during this "period of headlong creation",[6] in the letters he wrote to his childhood friend, his cousin Marguerite Teillard-Chambon. Here we see him as a well-tried spiritual director, already full of the experience that cannot in itself bring understanding of life unless it is

[5] Letter of 29 August 1916: "The ancient French view (rather narrow, of course, and jealous) that saw in woman a luminous and inspiring influence, and set her apart from the tumults and trivialities of everyday activity, is, in my eyes, the most perspicacious of all: we must preserve it by giving it fresh vitality" (*The Making of a Mind*, p. 121). Cf. also 8 Sept., "I also asked our Lord, through her whom he chose to set above the world as a neverfading nimbus, that woman may become among us all that she should be, for the perfecting and salvation of the human soul". (*Ibid.*, p. 123).

[6] André-A. Devaux, *Pierre Teilhard de Chardin d'après ses lettres de guerre*, *Cahiers universitaires catholiques* (Oct. 1962), p. 22. A passage in a letter written at this time has been the subject of psychological analysis, denigratory in intention, and quite without foundation. The passage has been quoted as though it originated from Teilhard's notes: in fact it was written by one of his correspondents. See *The Making of a Mind*, pp. 135–6.

accompanied by familiarity with the divine.[7] Even so, his own life of prayer can be discerned only through the veil of modesty and self-effacement that continued to be characteristic of him. It can be seen more clearly in some of the many essays he wrote at that time. Their very number, more astonishing still when one considers the conditions in which they were written, and the lyrical form in which they are often expressed, are already an indication of the internal excitement from which they, so to speak, boiled over. As Teilhard wrote them, he sent them off, either to his cousin or to some trusted adviser, such as his Provincial, Père Claude Chanteur, or the novice-master of his Province, Père Vulliez-Sermet, a man deeply versed in the spiritual life, in whom he had "absolute confidence". In the four years from 1916 to 1919 inclusive, he produced some twenty essays. Some of the earlier ones were lost, and he never had back or re-read the majority of them. From his letters we can see that he was not always completely satisfied with them and that he generally did not intend them for publication[8] or even for "limited circulation". In fact, the writing, though careful, is sometimes clumsy.[9] This clumsiness persisted (at least such is my view, which I believe Teilhard himself shared) even in his later writings, when he had more leisure to work on them and express them in a less personal form. Throughout his whole life, and as each new intellectual impulse was at work within him, Père Teilhard, with patient and attentive care but with the feeling that he could never fully achieve his purpose, strove to adjust to the demands of dogma and its accepted expression, his description or translation of an interior experience.[10] He knew that this con-

[7] Cf. René d'Ouince, S.J., *Vivre dans la plénitude du Christ, Christus*, 34 (1962). pp. 239–47.

[8] Details will be found in the forthcoming edition of these essays.

[9] See below, p. 97. At the same time, although the wording is sometimes awkward, at other times (as Teilhard himself said about *Mon Univers*, written 1924) it "needs to be carefully weighed if it is not to be misunderstood'.

[10] "Without distorting it or *weakening* it"; 3 Oct. 1918 (*The Making of a Mind*, p. 244).

tained a novel element, but he could not but believe that it was given him by God; moreover, it drew its strength from the most orthodox and the most obediently lived Christian ascesis.

The nature of this experience, the various ingredients of which it was woven, the inspiration that lay behind it, whether marginal to or an extension of his other work, the whole spiritual teaching it contained and the whole apostolic work it forwarded, these are subjects we have attempted to deal with elsewhere,[11] and there is no need to go over all that ground again. It will be clearer when the relevant texts have been published.[12] We will content ourselves with, so far as it is possible, following Père Teilhard through the course of his life, not to disclose the daily vicissitudes of his prayer or the crises of his religious life (it is too soon to attempt that), nor to analyse the nature of the mystical substratum that had evidently been given him at birth, but simply to note some of the basic characteristics of his religious life and prayer.

[11] *La Pensée religieuse du Père Teilhard de Chardin* (1962). It is not, I should emphasize again, the purpose of the present book to explain or systematically reconstruct the whole of Teilhard's thought.

[12] Some have already been published, among them the important correspondence (Dec. 1919) with Maurice Blondel (*Archives de Philosophie*, 1961).

3

"THE PERSONAL GOD"

ONE of these characteristics is so fundamental, and even of such elementary importance in the life of every Christian, so indispensable, too, to all true prayer, that I rather hesitate to refer to it. It must, however, be mentioned, since Père Teilhard was more than once at pains to explain his view of it, believing that it was his duty to add his testimony on this point for the benefit of his own generation.

There are, in fact, many today who believe that they should deny the attribute of personality to the Supreme Principle. For his part, Père Teilhard knew that when he prayed he was addressing himself to a personal Being. It was with Him that, in all humility, he made contact. He knew that He saw him, heard him and loved him. With the eye of faith Teilhard saw that God was in real truth "some-body". "The ocean that gathers up all the spiritual currents of the Universe is not only 'some-thing' but 'some-body'. And that somebody has a face and a heart."[1] This was not for Teilhard some esoteric or contingent truth, nor was it a pragmatic concession to the spontaneous anthropomorphism of the human mind or heart; neither was it a commonplace platitude soon to be forgotten

[1] Note, dated 28 Sept. 1923. The original was written in English (see Claude Cuénot, Teilhard de Chardin, 1962, pp. 48–9). Cf. L'Atomisme de l'Esprit, 7 (Œuvres, VII, p. 54), etc. In this connection a remark of Père de Tollenaere, in answer to a misguided criticism, should be noted (Bijdragen, 1960, p. 257, note 30): "How this critic can maintain that, for Teilhard, the transcendent lacks the personal character it should present to the created subject, is a complete mystery to me." See also Pierre Smulders, La Vision du Père Teilhard de Chardin, p. 132, notes 23–4.

in speculation. The whole trend of Teilhard's thought, all that is most central to his mental and spiritual effort, lies behind what he asserts as a believer, and reinforces his prayer. The more God is seen as "what lies beyond" all the objects we can apprehend, the more forcibly concentrated shall we see the mystery of his Personality. God is not a "faceless Infinite".[2] The real Infinite is not an infinite of dispersion, but of concentration; the more it is limitless and unconditioned, the more is it qualitatively determined. Not for one moment did Père Teilhard allow himself to be intimidated by mistakenly critical denials that wither the life of prayer— however constantly they appear in new and different forms and with whatever air of being the last word in wisdom they are put forward. Not for one moment, as he tells us himself, did he break away from what his mother taught him in his infancy; not for one moment did he feel the least constraint in addressing himself to his God as to a supreme "Somebody". In this connection Paul Claudel's *Magnificat* comes to mind: "Lord, I have found you! . . . You have cast down the idols . . . and now, suddenly, I see you as a person!" This is a remarkable coincidence (and not the only one) between two men of genius, very different, and even contradictory of one another, and with little mutual understanding.[3] Claudel's cry was a prophetic utterance. Teilhard's analyses sought to provide scientific justification. Thus, the two come together and complement one another. The prayer of each, like the prayer of the millions of faithful with whom they are happy to identify themselves, is the perpetual victory of faith.[4]

[2] "An infinitely determined 'superfigure'," says Hans Urs von Balthasar, *Herrlichkeit*, I (1961), part 3.

[3] Teilhard thought Claudel "a great man" but with a quality of mind quite opposed to his own. On one occasion, meeting in the U.S.A., they made rather an unfavourable impression on one another.

[4] Teilhard's emphasis on personality in general and on that of God in particular, is partly to be explained, I believe, by the influence (which he himself

This is a point that should be emphasized again, for if this evidence is misconstrued, or even if we fail to attach to it the prime importance that Teilhard himself did, his mind, will be a closed book to us, as will his philosophy, his religious life and his faith. For Teilhard, everything rests on the primacy of the person.[5] The concrete Presence at the heart of the Universe, dominating it, animating it, and drawing it to him—the presence of a personal God—super-personal, i.e., ultra-personal[6]—of a loving and provident God, of a God who can reveal himself, and has in fact revealed himself— of a God who is all Love—this was for Teilhard the supreme truth. He always sought to be "the adorer of one greater than the world",[7] and it was his ambition to lead his fellows along the road to that adoration. Starting from the "evolutionary views" which had at first led them astray, he wished to bring them back to the "traditional concepts of a God who exercises an intellectual influence on immortal monads, distinct from himself". To posit an impersonal All, he explained, is, whether you like it or not, to succumb to a "spatial illusion".[8] He urged them, moreover, to understand that "a world conceived as drifting towards the Impersonal ... would become at once unthinkable and unlivable",[9]

acknowledged) of Père Auguste Valensin. Cf. *Auguste Valensin, Textes et documents inédits* (1961). It is primarily, however, the fruit of long and concentrated thought. Cf., among others, this letter dated from Pao-te (Shansi) 15 July 1926: "In my view of the world, after the idea of the Spiritual, that of the Personal is rapidly assuming an extraordinarily increasing importance. I am rediscovering these values, after a long and roundabout journey, in a way that brings them to me completely new, consistent, and what I can only call 'appetising'. So you see I was completely sincere, on the human plane, when I said that we cannot give our allegiance to a 'faceless' world."

[5] M. Barthélemy-Madaule, *Bergson et Teilhard de Chardin* (1963), p. 325.
[6] *Esquisse d'un Univers personnel (Œuvres, VII, p. 89), etc.
[7] *La Mystique de la Science, Études* (20 March 1939) (Œuvres, VI, p. 223).
[8] *Comment je crois* (1934).
[9] *Le Rebondissement humain de l'évolution et ses conséquences* (1947); Œuvres, V, p. 265.

for from such a world we could draw neither the warmth of attraction nor the hope of irreversibility (immortality) without which our own selfishness will always have the last word".[10]

Teilhard realized that this twofold concept, of "the Personality of God" and "the survival of souls", was "probably the notion the most opposed to and, in appearance, the most antipathetic to, contemporary scientific thought".[11] Thus the greater part of his effort was directed not only to defending this concept but to winning wider acceptance for it. He was never tired of explaining that "the term of universal convergence", the "final summit of the completed world", which is "primordial Transcendence" must also inevitably "possess (in eminent degree) the quality of a Person": "the supremely Personal God, from whom we are the more distinct, the more we lose ourselves in him".[12] He continually sought to show that in God—"the ultra-personal God"—lay the "ultra-personalizing centre".[13] He traced the conflict that ravaged the world in 1940 primarily to "the inner fact that men have despaired of the personality of God".[14] Answering the pseudo-mystical concepts of Aldous Huxley, he noted in 1943 that "a personal God must inevitably be accepted for reasons based on the structure and dynamism of the cosmos". At the same time he rejected any prejudice or exaggeration,

[10] Comment concevóir et espérer que se réalisera sur terre l'unanimisation humaine (1950).

[11] See also Esquisse d'un Univers personnel (1936): "God is almost inevitably conceived by a modern positivist as a shoreless ocean in which all things, losing themselves, are made one whole" (Œuvres, VI, p. 85).

[12] Le Phenomène spirituel (1937); Œuvres, VI, p. 136. Un seuil mental sous nos pas, du Cosmos à la Cosmogenèse (1951); Œuvres, VII, p. 271. Comment je vois (1948), no. 20. Cf. La Pensée religieuse, pp. 260–3.

[13] Le Sens de l'espèce chez l'Homme (1949); Œuvres, VII, p. 210.

[14] Peking, 18 Oct. 1940 (Letters from a Traveller, p. 269). Claude Soucy echoed Teilhard perfectly when he wrote (Études, March 1964, p. 400): "The world will never be emancipated from the anthill and disintegration until there is a collective rediscovery of the sense of a personal absolute."

such as too often provides an obstacle to intellectual conversion. "To nine-tenths of those who see him from outside, the Christian God appears as a great landowner administering his estates." This, he said, "is a conventional figure" which, even if "justified by too many apparent resemblances, in no way corresponds either to the basis of dogma or to that of a true evangelical attitude". How right, indeed, he was! It was with the same object in mind that he criticized—at the risk of being misunderstood when the terms he used should become more widely known—a certain "creative paternalism". This only served to strengthen him in his assertion that "the message of Christ . . . is completely summed up in the announcement of a 'divine fatherhood'—which means that the Christian God, a personal Being, is to man the term of a personal union".[15]

By this he made it clear that the word "Father", which the Christian, following the example of Christ, uses in prayer, is not the same thing as (in the words of a theologian, Fr Karl Rahner): "The projection into the infinite of childish ideas designed to govern existence in a pre-rational manner, and which he justifies to himself because God, to whom all things are possible, introduces his creature to his freedom and his love."[16] For Père Teilhard, then, true religion is a link with a Father-God.[17] It is a "religion of the Personal", and, as

[15] *L'Énergie humaine* (1937); *Œuvres*, VI, p. 193. *L'Étoffe de l'Univers* (1953), VII, p. 405. Cf. M. Barthélemy-Madaule, *Bergson et Teilhard de Chardin* (1963), p. 463. It will be appreciated that in spite of a coincidence of expression, the thought is radically different from that of Harnack.

[16] Address at the Hanover *Katholikentag*, 1962: *La Foi du Prêtre, aujourd'hui*. Travesties, such as those denounced by Fr Rahner, are not infrequent. Thus, Paul Souday recently went so far as to compare the Father-God or God-Love of Péguy with Béranger's naïve "good-fellow" God, simply because in each case there is a naïve element in the literary style. On the divine fatherhood, in Christian teaching, cf. Stanislas Lyonnet, S.J., *Initiation à la doctrine spirituelle de saint Paul*, (1963), Ch. 3, "La Prière au Père".

[17] We might even add, with André-A. Devaux, "Teilhard was very conscious of the almost *maternal* fatherhood of God" (*Teilhard et la vocation de la femme*, 1964, p. 58).

he was fond of repeating, "Christianity is first and foremost the religion of the person." [18] It is through Christ's message, and through his operation, that the "personifying depth of Love" is both revealed and realized.[19] Occasionally he expressed it with a touch of exclusivism—though it should be borne in mind that the passage that follows is taken from a private letter and does not claim to give a complete or fully considered definition:

> The essential core of Christianity, in my view, is certainly none of the humanitarian or moral ideals so dear both to believers and unbelievers: it is to maintain and preserve "the primacy of the Personal", extended analogically to the whole—and also positively to bring the World into contact with the supreme Person, that is to say, to give him a name.[20]

It was with this conviction that in 1940, writing to Père Schurmans, Vicar-general of the Society of Jesus, Teilhard expressed his desire to engage wholeheartedly in "The battle for a personal God". We should read again the final sentence of his *Réflexions sur le Progrès*, written at Peking on 30 March 1941. It brings out the continuity of his plan, and the strength of the conviction that inspired it. "Ultimately we must seek the generative principle of our unification not simply in the contemplation of one and the same Truth, nor simply in the desire aroused by *Something*, but in the attraction, common to all, exercised by one and the same *Somebody*." In the first essay he wrote, *La Vie Cosmique*, he had said, our term is "a living, loving Being, in whom our consciousnesses, when once they are lost in him, are finally enabled to attain their fullest degree of accentuation and

---

[18] *L'Esprit de la Terre* (1931), 6; *Esquisse d'un Univers personnel* (1936), 7; *Œuvres*, VI, 52-7, 110-14. On Christianity as revealing personality, there is a passage that matches Teilhard's view in F. von Hügel's *The Mystical Element of Religion* (1909), I, pp. 25-6.

[19] *Pour y voir clair* (1950); *Œuvres*, VII, p. 235.

[20] Written from Peking, 15 Aug. 1936.

illumination, right up to the extreme potentialities of their personality".[21]

[21] "Pascal indeed said that the Jesuits tried to combine God and the world but he never foresaw that a Jesuit would try to merge the world in God." That choice remark is quoted from M. André Thérive, *Écrits de Paris* (1964), p. 100. According to one writer, Teilhard argued for "a cosmic God, and therefore de-personalized" (the last two words in bold type); according to another, "Teilhard's teaching . . . divinizes sacred Matter . . . what, then, remains of a personal God?" See also Mgr André Combes, *Teilhardogenèse?* (*Ephémérides Carmeliticae*, 14, 1963, p. 180): "But would not Père Teilhard, maybe, divinize this very earth itself, and does that not explain why, as he says, 'its enchantments are powerless to do him harm'?" Such, we are asked to believe, is the "obvious meaning" of the *Milieu Divin*.

4

THE DIVINE PRESENCE

PÈRE Teilhard was far from divinizing the Cosmos, the world known to us by experience, "this very earth", nor did he in any way bury the Divinity in it, or dilute the Divinity with it, as some critics have persisted in accusing him. Such accusations have been based on occasional expressions that have been misunderstood, and are made in spite of very many passages, written at all periods of his life, in the most explicit terms, passages, too, that are the most central and integral to his thought. In fact, Teilhard protests against those who endow the Universe with "divine attributes". In his view, on the contrary, "far from pointing to the discovery of a new God, Science will only be able to show us the Matter which is the sheath of Divinity"; once again in our own day Nature is revealed to us (as it was to St Augustine) not as divine and to be adored, but as humble and suppliant. He rejects "a 'naturalist' cult of the world" and recognizes a "love of the earth" as legitimate only when it is based on God-the-Creator.[1] The whole of creation is seen by him as answering to the attraction of the Creator, with whom there can be no final rejoining except through a sort of inversion, of turning back, of excentration.[2] In apologetics his aim is to

[1] *Les fondements et le fond de l'idée d'évolution* (1926); *Œuvres*, III, p. 76. *The Making of a Mind*, pp. 62, 235–6. On the "unique grandeur of God" see *Letters from a Traveller*, p. 83.

[2] *La Messe sur le Monde* (*Hymne de l'Univers*, pp. 19 and 30); cf. p. 30: "The task of the world consists not in engendering within itself some supreme Reality, but in consummating itself through union with a pre-existing Being".

win the admission that, "In the final reckoning, above Man's rediscovered grandeur, above the newly discovered grandeur of Humanity, there reappears—not doing violence to but preserving the integrity of Science—in our universe seen through the most modern eyes, the face of God".[3] And the progress of Teilhard's dialectic, in its final stage, consists in the passage from the "Noosphere" to the "Theosphere", so that man can adore and love God "not only with his whole body and with his whole soul, but with the whole universe".[4] As he wrote in one of his first essays, he seeks to direct "the whole life-sap of the world into an effort towards the divine Trinity".[5]

We know that in his formulation of the Christian faith Père Teilhard, seeking for greater fidelity to the thought, the tactical sense, and the very words of St Paul, would have liked to win acceptance for the expression "Christian pantheism",[6] as opposed to all the "false pantheisms", whether new or old, Eastern or Western, crude or subtle. Sometimes he risked using the words, explaining them, however, in a way that made any wrong interpretation impossible. Occasionally

[3] *La Place de l'Homme dans l'Univers* (1942); *Œuvres*, III, p. 324.

[4] *L'Énergie humaine* (1937), conclusion; *Œuvres*, VI, pp. 194-8. For a fuller treatment of Teilhard's concept of the cosmos, see the second essay in this volume.

[5] *La Conquête du Monde et le Règne de Dieu*, ch. 3: "Who then will finally be the ideal Christian, the Christian at once new and old, who will solve in his soul the problem of the vital equilibrium by directing all the life-sap, etc.?"

[6] Cf. Mgr. Lucien Cerfaux, *Le Chrétien dans la Théologie paulinienne* (1962), p. 212, on 1 Cor. 15. 28: "The ancient Stoic formulas, pantheist in tone, the identity of the one with the whole, God all in all, are Christianized. Personal monotheism asserts itself. ..." Or again, Edgar Haulotte, S.J., *L'Esprit de Yahwé dans l'Ancien Testament* (in the symposium *L'Homme devant Dieu*, 1964, I, p. 28) on Acts 18. 24-9: Paul "puts the language of the Bible into words that can be understood by the Epicureans and Stoics to whom he is speaking. ... He relieves 'the whole', 'the one', 'the origin', 'life', 'breath', from the implication they have in Stoic thought with impersonal cosmic forces; instead, he brings these realities into the same circuit, so to speak, as the personal creative force of God." Cf. Jacques Dupont, *Gnosis* (1949), pp. 431-5, *Pierre Benoit, Exégèse et Théologie* (1961), II, pp. 138-53.

one feels that it went against the grain to have to refrain from doing so. There are other passages in which he simply contrasts the Christian or the "guest of the divine milieu" with pantheist.[7] In any case, quite apart from the actual terminology, there can be no doubt that of all contemporary thinkers it was Teilhard who was the most outspoken opponent of pantheistic concepts of Godhead. He vigorously rejected every type of "pantheist bliss". In every doctrine, whatever might be said for it in other respects, that describes the "final state" as "a faceless organism, a diffuse humanity,—an *Impersonal*" he denounced its "betrayal of the Spirit".[8] On one occasion he spoke of the "triumphant joy", retained even in his "worst hours", that he drew from his faith in the transcendence of God.[9] At the same time he held that "we must love the World greatly if we are to feel a passionate desire to leave the World behind".[10] He knew also that "the false trails of pantheism bear witness to our immense need for some revealing word to come from the mouth of Him who is".[11] He sought, too, to do more than reject or refute pantheism: by establishing the "differentiating and communicating action of love",[12] he neutralized its temptation.[13]

[7] *Le Milieu Divin*, p. 116, etc. In *L'Élément universel* (1919) the "Christian solution" is openly contrasted with the "pantheist solution".

[8] *L'Énergie humaine* (1937); *Œuvres*, VI, pp. 187–8.

[9] *The Making of a Mind*, p. 98.

[10] Forma Christi (1918).

[11] *Le Milieu Divin*, pp. 129–30.

[12] *The Phenomenon of Man*, p. 309, etc. In *La Vie Cosmique* (1916) we already find "the cosmic temptation" (p. 3), "the temptation of pagan, naturalist pantheism" (p. 19), etc.

[13] Cf. *La Pensée religieuse*, pp. 219–27. One cannot help seeing here a kinship of thought with Maurice Blondel. In the same year as Père Teilhard was writing *Le Christ dans le Matière*, Blondel was writing to Père Auguste Valensin: "I can no longer remember very well the arguments you remind me of in connection with the Catholic antidote (through the Eucharist) for the terrible evil of pantheism. I was trying, no doubt, to show the strength of that pernicious doctrine, precisely because of the profound sense it shows of the problem of in some way getting the finite and the infinite to cohere and live together. And it is to

What perhaps introduces some confusion into this subject is that too many people in our modern West, even including some who are extremely firm in their faith and heedful of the spiritual life, are apt to forget the divine Presence and the divine Action in all things—even indeed at the natural level. It is here that a superficial cult of the spiritual has done a great deal of damage. Just as many, when they have to consider their final end, can only oscillate "between the concept of an individual survival that leaves beings isolated from one another, and a reflection that absorbs them into the one",[14] so the divine transcendence is too often conceived, or rather imagined as itself, too, being purely exteriorized. As Père Abel Jeannière has said,[15] "Among many who are opposed to the thought of Teilhard we find an underlying mental attitude which allows no possibility of distinction except in separation and mutual exteriority." It was of these people that the author of the *Milieu Divin* was thinking when he said: "Of those who hear me, more than one will shake his head and accuse me of worshipping Nature." In fact, "however absolute the distinction between God and the world (since everything in the world—and the world itself—exists, even at this present moment, only by divine creation), God is

---

escape both a baneful immanentism and a frigid, unintelligible, incommensurable, transcendentalism that one can find (as a Catholic, not spontaneously as a philosopher) an illuminating sweetness in the *Verbum Caro*, which affirms the distinct absolute reality both of God and of the creature, and their most intimate union" (5 April 1916). Earlier, on 30 Oct. 1915, Blondel wrote: "It is the first and last temptation of all who refuse to receive the word of God." Cf. 11 July 1904, writing to J. Wehrlé: "The problem of the simultaneity, and of their relation in him (= in Christ), of human knowledge and divine science is linked with the problem, is an aspect of, is the key to the problem, of the co-existence of the infinite Creator and the finite created world" (in René Marlé, *Au cœur de la crise moderniste*, 1960, p. 235). On Blondel's "panchristism" see his letter to Père Valensin, 5 Dec. 1919, with the note (*Archives de Philosophie*, 1961, pp. 127–33).

[14] Cf. Henri de Lubac, *Catholicisme* (1938), p. 266.

[15] *Approches christologiques*, in *Essais sur Teilhard de Chardin* (*Recherches et Débats*, Oct. 1962, p. 93).

present in the world and nothing is more present in it than the God who creates it: for 'it is in him that we live, and move, and have our being'".[16] *Deus non creavit, et abiit* (St Augustine.)

Père Teilhard de Chardin lived, with great intensity, this prime truth, constantly recalled in Scripture and Christian tradition, by the Fathers of the Church and the great scholastic theologians, no less than by the mystics. With all these, he held that God is both "further than everything and deeper than everything".[17] His master St Ignatius Loyola, in particular, had taught him to "contemplate God as existing in every one of his creatures. He 'venerated an omni-presence', resting on and losing itself in the peace a deep intimate union."[18] St Teresa would have been delighted to meet him on her road, to save her from the "half-baked doctors, always so ready to take exception" who would not leave her in peace, as she entered into her mystical life, to believe that God is present in all beings; Teilhard could have set her mind at rest by assuring her that God's intimate presence is not an impossibility but a solid fact.[19] He could have told her, in the words of St Thomas Aquinas, that "God must be present in all things, and that in an intimate manner".[20]

Here, again, is what a Thomist theologian has to say, whose only concern is to state the most fully traditional teaching:

> Many of the objections and difficulties we meet in connection with our relationship to God, arise from our considering God as a stranger, as someone other than ourselves. This, to put it plainly, is simply untrue. Our habitual concepts tell us only about personalities exterior to and therefore foreign or strange to our own.

---

[16] Mgr Bruno de Solages, *Initiation métaphysique* (1962), p. 253, quoting Acts 17, 28 (St Paul's speech to the Areopagus).

[17] *Le Prêtre* (1918).

[18] *The Making of a Mind*, p. 300

[19] St Teresa, *Interior Castle*, 5, Ch. I, *Autobiography*, Ch. 18.

[20] *Summa Theologica*, I, q. 8, art. 1: "*Oportet quod Deus sit in omnibus rebus, et intime*"; III, q. 6, art. 1, *ad primum*.

When we are concerned with God, we must realize that we are concerned with a being who is certainly distinct from us, but who is at the same time the reason for our own being. . . . If I take myself, suppressing all my imperfections and magnifying to infinity my own poor perfections, even those most personal and peculiar to myself, the most incommunicable, then I have God. That is why theologians can say, "God is not another, he is virtually and eminently myself, he is an infinite myself, pure act." *Deus est virtualiter ego ipse*, as John of St Thomas puts it. It is thus that, while completely rejecting pantheism, we retain anything legitimate that may be contained in its tendencies.[21]

If this is indeed bold doctrine, which of the two writers expresses it the more boldly? However, St Thomas, too, was already accused of pantheism,[22] and for this same reason. Some contemporary critics of Teilhard's thought accuse him of a "deception", on the ground that beneath his repeated affirmations of the personality of God there lies an "unacknowledged pantheism"; without realizing it, they are continuing to bring forward last century's accusation against scholasticism in general and St Thomas in particular of an "implicit pantheism", the reason behind which was an inability to envisage any true personal monotheism except in the position of a God who is "cut off from the world". The only difference is that the earlier critics did not put forward their objection in the name of orthodox Catholicism; they maintained, on the contrary, that such a "cosmic pantheism", the fruit of all "metaphysical theology", was "essential to

---

[21] Pierre-Thomas Dehau, O.P., *Divine intimité et Oraison*, in *La Vie Spirituelle*, May 1942, pp. 412–13. See also J. J. Surin, *Guide Spirituelle* (ed. M. de Certeau, 1963), pp. 138–9.

[22] The half-truth that explains, though it does not justify, this accusation has been pointed out by M. Étienne Gilson (*La Philosophie au moyen âge*, 1922, II, p. 144; 1925 and 1930, p. 302): "In Thomism itself there is a sort of virtual pantheism that a mere relaxation of strict doctrine would allow to come out into the open but that would thence cease to be Thomism. On the other hand in Eckhart, we find, if not a deliberate, avowed, pantheism, at any rate what is in fact, though disavowed and denied, pantheism". (In the 1944 edition, pp. 698–9, this view is less forcibly expressed).

consistent Catholicism".[23] Their unconscious disciples might well bear that in mind.

Père Teilhard might, again, have said with St John of the Cross, "the centre proper to each of us, the centre of the soul, is God".[24] His own words, indeed, are better and more accurate, "The centre of centres", and, again, "*Centrum super centra*".[25] Such was for him, "at the heart of the world, the heart of a God". No doubt he was more familiar with *The Book of St Angela of Foligno*, which he had read before 1916, since he quotes it freely in *La Vie Cosmique* and refers to it again in the *Milieu mystique*. He was later to quote it again in the *Milieu Divin*, probably after re-reading it in the translation his friend Père Paul Doncôeur[26] brought out in 1926. "I saw", says St Angela, "that every creature was filled with him"; and again, "I see him who is being, and I see how he is the being of all creatures."[27] He translated this classic doctrine into his own words when he spoke of the "transparency of the universe", to the eye of faith—which is for him the "*milieu divin*". He placed it, of course, in its proper perspective, too, when he explained that it is impossible to set God "as a focus at the summit of the Universe without, in doing so, simultaneously impregnating with his presence even the most insignificant evolutionary movement";[28]

[23] Charles Renouvier, *De l'idée de Dieu* (*L'année philosophique*, 1897, pp. 3–15); *Philosophie analytique de l'histoire*, vol. 3 *passim; Histoire et solution des problèmes métaphysiques*, p. 166; *Correspondance avec Charles Secrétan*, p. 11. Cf. Marcel Méry, *La critique du Christianisme chez Renouvier* (1952), I, pp. 308, 361, 399; II, pp. 218, 226–8, 380, 405.

[24] *The Living Flame*, I, 3.

[25] *La Centrologie* (1944), no. 26, *Œuvres*, VII, p. 120.

[26] *La Vie Cosmique*, p. 57; "God is everywhere, God is everywhere (St Angela of Foligno)." *Le Milieu Divin*, p. 116; "The Creator and, more specifically, the Redeemer have steeped themselves in all things and penetrated all things to such a degree that, as St Angela of Foligno said, 'The world is full of God'." Cf. *The Making of a Mind*, p. 130.

[27] "*Et tunc videbam quod omnis creatura erat plena Ipso.*" Similar passages will be found in Henri de Lubac, *Sur les chemins de Dieu* (1956), particularly in ch. IV.

[28] *L'Énergie humaine* (1937); *Œuvres*, VI, p. 183.

it is impossible, therefore, to see in this "supreme consciousness" a "higher pole of synthesis" without at the same time
asserting its "omnipresence" and "omni-action".[29] This
means that the immanence of God is seen as deriving from
his transcendence, and is thus the exact contrary of immanentism.

Elsewhere Teilhard adds, "God the eternal being in himself, is everywhere, we might say, in process of formation for
us".[30] Here, every word should be weighed. One should not
concentrate only on the second half of the sentence, and,
above all, the words "for us" should not be overlooked. It will
be noted, too, that, in the correlative assertion of a dynamic
immanence, the idea of divine transcendence is in no way over-
shadowed. "The majesty of the Universe" does not obscure
for him "the primacy of God."[31] While Père Teilhard, in the
hope of rousing the Christian of today from a lethargy he
believes hostile to the spread and even the maintenance of his
faith, urges him to "discern, *below God*, the values of the
world, at the same time he is careful to urge the humanist of
today to "discern, *above the world*, the place held by a God".[32]
And it is with the same care to maintain the correct relation

[29] *L'Atomisme de l'Esprit* (1941); *Œuvres*, VII, p. 61. Cf. Robert Bellarmine,
De ascensione mentis in Deum, gradus 2: "Were another world to be created, God
would fill that, too; and if there were to be more worlds, or even an infinite
number of words, God would fill them all. . . . with his omnipotence and wisdom,
he is present everywhere" (Montpellier ed. 1823, pp. 40–1).
[30] *Trois histoires comme Benson, La Custode* (14 Oct. 1916), etc.
[31] g. *Esquisse d'une dialectique de l'Esprit*, (1946); *Œuvres*, VII, p. 158.
[32] *Quelques réflexions sur la conversion du monde* (1936), p. 2. *L'Énergie humaine*
(1937); ". . . above creation . . ." (VI, p. 196). In 1952, a San Francisco news-
paper printed a report from a French newsagency to the effect that "the God of
Père Teilhard was becoming a God immanent in the evolution of the world".
On 3 Aug., Teilhard wrote from New York to Père André Ravier, "What annoys
me in this business is the offhanded way it makes me jettison a divine 'transcendence' that I have, *on the contrary*, spent all my life in defending—though
seeking at the same time, it is true (like everyone, but by using the new properties of a universe in process of cosmogenesis) to reconcile it with an immanence
which everyone agrees must be given a progressively more important and more
explicit place in our philosophy and religion."

between immanence and transcendence that he speaks of Christ: "The risen Christ of the Gospel can never hold, in the consciousness of the faithful, his primacy over the created world that, by definition, he is to consummate, except by incorporating in himself the evolution that some people seek to oppose to him." [33]

Here his teaching echoes his prayer: "Lord, grant that I may see, that I may see *You*, that I may see and feel You *present in all things* and *animating all things*." [34] "If so many souls have been touched by his message", writes Jean Lacroix, "it is perhaps primarily because he knew how again to make of the universe a Temple." [35]

If man, as Teilhard understands him, is to fulfil his destiny, he must add the voice of his consciousness and, throughout all his activity, of his freely given homage, to the hymn that rises up to God from all creation. That is why we may speak of "Père Teilhard's cosmic liturgy": [36] and why, too, *The Hymn of the Universe* was a happy choice of title for a miscellany of prayers and meditations selected from his writings. [37]

[33] *L'Énergie humaine* (1937); *Œuvres*, VI, pp. 196-7.

[34] Peking, 20 Oct. 1945.

[35] *Le Sens de l'athéisme moderne* (1958), p. 28. Cf. letter of 7 Aug. 1923: "With himself, Man brings back to God the lower beings of the world. Sin consists in falling back among them;—virtue in carrying them along with him."

[36] M.-D. Chenu, O.P., *La Foi dans l'intelligence* (1964), p. 288.

[37] Some hasty readers have referred to this as "Hymn *to* the Universe", a mistake that points to a serious misunderstanding of Teilhard's thought. I have also seen it called "Hymns to the Universe". A similar mis-reading is referred to later (pp. 95, 188).

5

THE COSMIC CHRIST

THE face that God assumes for us in his revelation, the heart he discloses to the believer, is Jesus Christ. Already, when Teilhard is thinking of the presence of God within the universe, he is thinking of the presence of Jesus. His prayer, like all Christian prayer, passes through the channel of Jesus.[1] In a surge of overpowering tenderness, he delights in addressing it to Jesus. At the same time he bears in mind, generally speaking, "the total Christ".[2] To use a word that Teilhard coined, to express the special tone proper to it, and to link it with the most personal element of his thought, his prayer is *Christic*.[3]

Teilhard professed the traditional doctrine of the mystical body with a realism that was seldom found in religious circles when he was a young man. He wrote:

> Without in any way rejecting the forces of liberty and conscience that make up the physical reality proper to the human soul, we must realize that between the Incarnate Word and ourselves there are links as strong as those that, in the world, direct the

---

[1] *In L'Élément universel,* Teilhard distinguishes explicitly between, on the one hand, the presence of the creator and his action, which is found everywhere, and, on the other, the "cosmic influence of Christ".

[2] Cf. *Le Milieu Divin.* pp. 122–3: "The divine omnipresence makes itself felt in our universe through the network of the organizing forces of the total Christ"; see also pp. 123–4.

[3] We may note incidentally (though only to call attention to the verbal similarity) that St John Damascene in the eighth century used the word *Christotes* (*De fide orthodoxa,* Migne, *P.G.,* vol. 94, col. 993A).

affinities of the elements towards the building up of natural
wholes.[4]

"The mystical body of Christ," Teilhard says again, "must
be conceived as a physical Reality, without attenuation."[5]
But the position of the human soul in the cosmos, or rather
Teilhard's own idea of the cosmos in relation to souls, led
him to take a step further. At the time of the First World War
(and before it, no doubt), when thinking about the mystery of
the "body of Christ", which includes the mystery of the "communion of Saints" and which is "bound up in the blessed
unity of a physically organized whole", he was filled with
wonder at its "so astonishingly cosmic character".[6] Then he
offered himself to God, meditating, the day after his religious
profession, on his priesthood in order (as he said in his
prayer) that "in my own humble way I may be the apostle
and (dare I but so speak of myself) the evangelist of your Christ
in the universe".[7] That, it seemed to him, was his real vocation. He made no claim to make of it a law of a universal

[4] This passage is quoted by Dom Georges Frénaud in his *Pensée philosophique
et religieuse du Père Teilhard de Chardin* (for full details of which see note, p. 170),
pp. 20–1, with the following comment: "Teilhard was to assert that the links
between Christ and souls through which the mystical body is built up are physical and *natural*"; and again, "The mystical body thus becomes *a natural biological whole*, in which the whole universe is concentrated, *in a natural way*, with
men serving as the medium" (my italics). Teilhard, as a reference to his words
will show, said nothing of the sort. To speak of "links as strong" as certain
natural links does not mean that the former are natural. Again, "natural" and
"physical" are no more synonymous for Teilhard than for the most classic
theologian: one has only to think of the "physical causality" of the sacraments
which is in straightforward contrast with "moral causality" (or again, of "physical premotion"). Cf. P. Smulders, *op. cit.*, p. 126, note. Among many other
examples, we may quote the words of Mgr Duchesne, in which he sums up the
eucharistic theology of St. Cyril of Alexandria: "Jesus Christ is truly God in us.
The Christian touches him directly, in physical, though mysterious, union, under
the sacramental veils of the Eucharist. Through this body and this blood, he
attains contact with God, for they have in Jesus Christ a union, physical too, with
the divinity" (*Églises séparées*, 1905, p. 39). See below p. 35 note. Cf. Ephes. 4.16.

[5] *La Vie Cosmique* (1916), p. 47.

[6] *Ibid.*, pp. 43–4.

[7] *Le Prêtre* (1918).

apostolate. It was simply that his own spontaneous urge, matured by his inner vision, reinforced and enriched by all his reflection, fostered, too, by the developments of his scientific thought, was leading him towards Him whom he called the "universal Christ".[8] In this form in which he loved best to express his devotion to Christ, and which so far from excluding any other, sought to integrate all forms, he found a sense of completeness, because in it what he had most intimately experienced, and what his scientific knowledge led him to foresee, coincided with the great scriptural pronouncements:

> Men are called to form a single body, within an extraordinarily intimate divinization—and the Humanity of Jesus has been *chosen* to serve as the instrument for this unification in which the scattered cluster of all the fibres that make up the Universe is closely knit. In Scripture, Christ appears to me as essentially invested with the power to give the World, in him, *its definitive form*. He has been consecrated for a cosmic function.[9]

In that passage, as in many others, can one detect the least uneasiness, the least tendency to look for some expedient that will save a faith that is threatened or cover up some shortcoming? To say, as some have said, that here Père Teilhard's "boldness" is no more than "a supreme effort to find in Scripture texts that, come what may and at the cost of no matter what ambiguities, can be made to agree with a doctrine of radical evolutionism" is to parody and completely falsify not only his thought but his personal conduct. No one could make such a statement who was not ignorant of his whole character and life. He had no doubt whatever that in so writing he was being faithful not only to Scripture but at the same time also to the surest and most trustworthy tradition, even if he had not himself studied it in much detail (which, indeed, is

[8] Teilhard's "universal Christ" or "personal universe" corresponds more or less to Blondel's "universal concrete", as explained in his *Exigences philosophiques du christianisme*, p. 185.

[9] *Forma Christi* (1918), p. 1.

true of many, including professional theologians). When he then struggled to give clear expression to what he had vitally experienced in prayer, in an effort towards synthesis that more indulgent critics have been willing to accept as insubstantial dreaming, he felt that he was giving form to some essential thing which was dimly striving to assert itself in the Christian mentality of his time:

> During the first century of the Church, Christianity made its decisive entry into human thought, boldly assimilating the Jesus of the Gospels to the Logos of Alexandria. We cannot fail to see the logical sequel to this gesture and the prelude to a similar success in the instinct which is today impelling the faithful, two thousand years later, to adopt the same tactics—not, this time, with the ordering principle of the static Greek kosmos, but with the neo-Logos of modern philosophy—the evolutionary principle of a universe in movement.[10]

"Never," he wrote again, "has Christ been found lacking in his limitless capacity of fitting in with the whole physical and psychological order of our Universe."[11] It was his dearest wish to make this plain to everyone in our present circumstances. He was not, indeed, either so foolish or so impudent as to claim that he found his concept of Noogenesis in St Paul or St John. Divine revelation was not for him a substitute or an advance understudy for Science. But he thought that if "the word is convergent", as he hoped to have demonstrated scientifically, and if "Christ occupies its centre, then the Christogenesis of St Paul and St John[12] is neither more nor

[10] *Christianisme et Évolution* (Peking, 11 Nov. 1945). Here we can trace an echo of a brilliant passage by Père Pierre Rousselot on the Logos of St John which appeared in *Christus*, edited by Père Joseph Huby (1912; 6th, revised, edition, 1934, pp. 1046–8). It was at Ore Place, during his years as a theological student, that the book was planned. Teilhard had a warm respect and affection for Rousselot.

[11] *Le Christianisme dans le Monde* (1933).

[12] That is to say, the growth of the mystical body, as pointed out by Père Smulders, who shows how well founded is Teilhard's assertion (*op. cit.*, p. 135, *note*).

less than the extension (both awaited and unhoped for) of the Noogenesis in which, as our experience has shown us, Cosmogenesis culminates."[13] And, for the work of synthesis and reconstruction that he was attempting in his belief, it was principally from St Paul and St John that, for the religious factor, he borrowed his foundations.

For a long time Teilhard carried with him a notebook in which he had collected many passages from both, in order that he might "extract the marrow of their teaching" and so provide matter for his continual meditation.[14] The words of our Lord's "priestly prayer" in St John, "that they should all be one, as we are one", polarized his thoughts on personal union in our final end.[15] It is to this prayer that he has recourse in the *Lutte contre la Multitude*, as being "the definitive Word, that gives us the key to the Gospel and to the World". At the same time, it was the apostle of the Gentiles who left his mark most deeply on Teilhard. "If there is one special characteristic," writes Père Irénée Hausherr, "in the theology of St Paul, it is an obsession with totality, which lies at its roots, in its culmination, and, between the two, in its development." Moreover, "it was not just that Christ taught Paul this universalism; in his very being, he represents it for

[13] *The Phenomenon of Man.*, p 297; "man finds himself capable of experiencing and discovering his God".

[14] *Note pour servir à l'evangelisation* . . . (1919). Cf. Letter of 2 Aug. 1935 in C. Cuénot, *Pierre Teilhard de Chardin*, 1958, p. 23, note 6.

[15] John 17. 22. One can detect Teilhard's influence, hinted at by the wording, in this fine passage from M. Jacques Perret: "Every day experience shows us that the more [Jesus] is present to us . . . the more he ennobles our effort. . . . He binds us to God with a reciprocal link. . . . Can we conceive that this work of grace should come to nothing? We have only to recall our memory of the saints. Not to go further, take St Teresa of the Child Jesus. Can we imagine an eternity in which there would be no Teresa, and in which, in consequence, Jesus would no longer know Teresa? We see that one of the most wonderful aspects of the mystery of God is that, supremely personal and supremely personalizing, to him, to unite is to personalize" (*L'Avenir*, *Semaine des intellectuels catholiques*, 1963, p. 240). Cf. above, p. 16, and, for example, *L'Univers personnel* (*Œuvres*, VI, pp. 84–5).

him. Everything is concentrated in him". St Paul, says another reliable interpreter, Père Jules Lebreton, "does not separate the role of Christ in the Church from his role in the world".[16]

Similarly, Père Ferdinand Prat, in his classic work *The Theology of St Paul*, notes that, for Paul "without Christ all creatures would be scattered, would be fragmented, and, in mutual conflict, would sink back again into nothingness. It is Christ who preserves for them, with existence, cohesion and harmony. . . . He is the all-mastering centre of creation. . . . Even, then, in so far as he is man, Jesus Christ has a cosmic role."[17] Similarly, in his classic commentary on the Epistles of the Captivity, Père Joseph Huby writes:

> In him all was created as in the supreme centre of unity, harmony, and cohesion, which gives the world its meaning and its value, and so its reality: or, to put it another way, as in the "foyer" (*the meeting-point*—Lightfoot) at which all the threads, all the generating forces of the Universe, are woven together and co-ordinated. . . . He is the dominating centre, the keystone of the Universe: "In him all subsist". . . . Of the created world he made an ordered cosmos, giving it a meaning, a value, and relating it to an end. . . . Creation is orientated towards him as to the perfection of its fulfilment.[18]

Père Pierre Benoit, O. P., again, commenting on the Epistle to the Colossians, writes:

> The person of Christ and his work are looked at from a *cosmic* point of view. Christian salvation takes on the dimensions of the

[16] *Histoire du dogme de la Trinité* (1927), I, p. 402. Cf. N. M. Wildiers, *Teilhard de Chardin* (1960), pp. 90–110; *L'Univers christifié.* Maurice Goguel: "The epistle to the Colossians insists on the cosmic role of Christ, who achieves his plenitude by becoming the *kephale* of the world". (*Revue de l'histoire des religions*, 1935, p. 77; cf. pp. 87–8). J. B. Lightfoot, *St Paul's Epistle to the Colossians* (1904), p. 154.

[17] On Ephes. 1. 9–10 and Col. 1, 17. See also 1 Cor. 8. 6, Rom. 11. 36, etc. It will be noticed, too, that Teilhard habitually translates Paul's *en pasin* (in omnibus), 1 Cor. 15. 28, as Prat does, by "in all" (*en tous*) and not "in all things". His universe is a personal universe. See below, p. 89.

[18] In *Verbum Salutis*, 8 (1935), pp. 40–2.

universe. ... To designate the whole, Paul uses the word "Pleroma". ...

The central theme that strikes one immediately is that of the *cosmic supremacy* of Christ [Paul asserts] that the *plenitude of the cosmos* lies in Christ. ... Christ, God and man by virtue of the Incarnation crowned by the Resurrection, embraces in this plenitude not only God who saves, not only men who are saved, but the whole setting of humanity, that is to say, the cosmos, including the angelic powers. ... From these views the Epistle to the Colossians acquires the *cosmic, celestial, horizon* that characterizes it.[19]

The cosmic Christ! The cosmic function of Christ—"not only moral, but physical!"[20] This, we see, is not simply something that Teilhard invented. "I find it quite impossible," he wrote in 1924 in his second draft of *Mon Univers*, "to read St Paul without being dazzled by the vision under his words of the universal and cosmic dominance of the incarnate word." And if it is true that he attributes to the risen Humanity of our Lord (as others also do)[21] "a presence in the world as vast

[19] *Les Épitres de Saint Paul aux Philippiens*, etc. (1949), p. 49 (*Colossians*, introduction). *Paul, Épitre aux Colossiens, Supplément au Dictionnaire de la Bible*, fasc. 36 (1961), col. 163–4. As Père Benoit remarks, the commentators are not all in agreement about the precise meaning of the word "Pleroma".

[20] Teilhard's realism was always hard (sometimes excessively so) on the type of theology that, in general, preferred what are called "moral" or "juridical" rather than "physical" links ("physical" here meaning "organic", and not being used as opposed either to "supernatural" or "metaphysical"). See above p. 11 and note 7. Cf. *La Vie Cosmique*, pp. 44–5; "For minds that are afraid to conceive things boldly or are filled with individualistic prejudices, and always try to interpret the connections between beings as moral or logical relations, the body of Christ is much more like a social agglomeration than a natural organism. Such minds dangerously weaken the thought of Scripture ... No, the body of Christ is not an ... extrinsic, juridical, association, etc." See also *Forma Christi*, I, etc.; *L'Évolution et la responsabilité dans le monde* (1950), *Œuvres*, pp. 219–21, where the juridical is contrasted with the organic.—Teilhard would have approved (with the alteration of an occasional word) Blondel's criticism of his friend Père Laberthonnière's *Dogmatisme moral*: "The role of the Mediator, of the Emmanuel, is treated only in its practical, restorative, empiric aspect, not in its metaphysical, essential, fulfilling aspect" (Letter to Père D. Sabatier, 12 March 1899; *Lettres Philosophiques*, 1961, pp. 175–6).

[21] For example M. Blondel, *Exigences philosophiques du Christianisme* (1950), p. 18.

as the very immensity of God",[22] can we be certain that in holding this against Teilhard our censure may not at the same time embrace St Paul? If we hold that "from the standpoint of human reason the 'cosmic Christ' is necessarily an expression tainted with pantheism and contradictory of a personal God"[23] we are even more certain to be attacking the great Apostle while under the impression that we are criticizing only his interpreter.

Omnia in ipso constant—"in him all subsist"—this sentence from the Epistle to the Colossians had long fired Teilhard's enthusiasm. Following some of his seniors, he had learnt during his years of theology to set them at the heart of Christian thought.[24] Nor could he have felt that he was introducing any innovation when he said that, "Christ is the term supernaturally, but also physically, assigned to the consummation of humanity";[25] nor, again, in saying that for St Paul, "all energies hold together, are welded deep down into a single whole, and what the humanity of our Lord does is to take them up again and re-weld them in a transcendent and personal unity".[26] It became increasingly more evident to Teilhard that if Christ is to remain himself, without diminu-

[22] Dom G. Frénaud, *op. cit.* p. 22. Cf. *La Messe sur le Monde* "... through the manifestation of the superhuman powers conferred on you by the resurrection" (*Hymne de l'Univers*, p. 33).

[23] Bernard Charbonneau, *Teilhard de Chardin, prophète d'une âge totalitaire*, p. 68. Whatever importance one may attach to the author's "reason", it is not the standard by which we judge our faith.

[24] Père Yves de la Brière, who was for some time to teach Teilhard theology and whom he was to meet later in Paris at *Études*, had, on 21 May 1907, given a lecture at Ore Place, Hastings, of which the printed summary included the following: "Thus the whole of theology may be summed up in what St Paul said of Christ, '*Omnia in Ipso constant*'" (*Lettres d'Ore*, 1907, I, p. 46). The same text appears as a colophon to a mimeographed essay by the Abbé Pierre Tiberghein, a disciple of Père Pierre Rousselot, on *La Question des rapports du naturel et surnaturel* ... (1922).

[25] *Comment se pose aujourd'hui* (1921); *Œuvres*, I, p. 37. *Le Christique* (1955), p. 8: "Christ, in his 'theandric' [God-man] being gathers up all creation".

[26] 2 Feb. 1916; *The Making of a Mind*, p. 93.

tion, at the centre of our faith, then—if the world is indeed an evolution—this cosmic Christ, the Beginning, the Bond and the Term of all creation, must now offer himself for our adoration as the "evolutive" Christ.[27] He had the insight to perceive that this new way of looking at Christ involved more than a new shade of interpretation of the Apostle's thought, but this in no way diminished his hope of continuing to "follow his line",[28] and this he thought was the price that should be paid for a fundamental fidelity. It was thus that "the great concept, so essentially dogmatic, of the Christian Pleroma" would finally be accorded its full significance. "*Descendit, ascendit, ut repleret omnia*: for the Romans, the Corinthians, the Ephesians, the Colossians, this image must have had no more than a vague meaning, since at that time the world, the 'whole' (with all the organic definition that those words imply for us), were still non-existent for human consciousness"; now, however, when that Object has acquired in our eyes such grandeur and consistence, we must not allow it to escape Christ.[29]

"*Jesus, the centre towards whom all moves*"[30]

If Teilhard realized that he was going further than St Paul, he realized, too, that others lagged far behind Pauline thought.

It is impossible [he wrote in 1940, returning to what had been a constant theme for many years] to read St Paul without being

[27] Cf. Albert Schweitzer, *La Mystique de l'Apôtre Paul* (tr. M. Guéritot, 1962), p. 25; "Pauline mysticism is historico-cosmic, and looks towards the end of all time." This again was vividly appreciated by Teilhard.—A commentator has pointed out how appropriate, in *Sagesse*, VII, 21–9, are the attributes of wisdom —which, for the Christian, is Christ—to the "evolutive Christ".

[28] Cf. Retreat of 1940: "Into the famous text of Romans 8. 38, '*Quis separabit nos a caritate Christi*'—'Who will separate us from the love of Christ'—I introduce a shade of meaning that differs from St Paul's (even though it follows his line). For St Paul, charity is the force greater than all forces; for me, it is the *dynamic* milieu that embraces and super-animates them all."

[29] *La Parole attendue* (1940); *Cahiers P. Teilhard de Chardin*, 4, pp. 26, 27.

[30] *La Vie Cosmique* (end). Cf. Crespy, *op. cit.*, p. 88: "Christ is more and more clearly him *in quo omnia constant*, because it is he *ad quem omnia tendunt*".

astonished by the fundamental importance the Apostle attaches to this concept (of the Pleroma), apprehended in its most absolute realism, and at the same time by the relative obscurity in which it has so far been left by preachers and theologians, and by its wonderful aptness, for the religious needs of our day.[31]

We should, it is true, recognize at any rate that during the last few centuries this "cosmic" aspect of Pauline teaching had become somewhat blurred in current Catholic thought. There can be no doubt that most modern theologians have devoted little attention to it.[32] Some of the best New Testament exegetes[33], both Catholic and Protestant, have commented only briefly on the passages in which it is to be found. It was this lack that Père Teilhard wished to supply: and even those readers who find themselves unable to accept what is most personal to him in his explanations, should be willing, I believe, to recognize that his attempt will prove to have been well worth while.

[31] *La Parole attendue, loc. cit.*

[32] See, however, among others, J. Fr Bonnefoy, O.F.M., *La Primauté du Christ* (Rome, 1959).

[33] In his important *Christologie du Nouveau Testament* Oscar Cullmann has hardly a word to say about the Pauline texts to which Teilhard attached such importance.

6

"O CHRIST, EVER GREATER!"

TEILHARD, however, had a further aim in view. He wished not only to harmonize or "reconcile" his Christian faith and science, but to integrate them, and at the same time integrate his work and his prayer. This was dictated by his need for a "coherence" that was far from being any sort of "concordism". Teilhard detested attempts at reconciliation that, "not discriminating between different planes and different sources of knowledge, and confusing the two distinct zones of the 'Discovered and the Taught'" succeed only in producing "arrangements that are unstable because monstrously distorted"; forcibly as he rejected these, with equal ardour he sought for the "Synthesis of the Real, which brings the peace of harmony and is the sign of truth".[1]

Thus he was glad to find in St Paul's teaching not, once again, a ready-made synthesis, but the basis for a meeting and

[1] *La Pensée du Père Teilhard de Chardin par lui-même* (April 1948): "The objection has been raised that this 'philosophy' is no more than a generalized concordism. To this Père Teilhard answers that we should not confuse concordism and coherence. Religion and science can be seen as representing two different meridians drawn on the mental sphere, and not to keep the two separate is a falsification (the concordist error). Both these meridians, however, must necessarily meet somewhere at a pole of common vision (coherence): otherwise the whole structure, in the domain of thought and knowledge, collapses on us". (*Les Études philosophiques*, 1955, p. 581). *Comment je vois* (1948), preface; *Mon Univers* (1924); *Le Phenomène spirituel*, *Œuvres*, VI, p. 118. Cf. *The Phenomenon of Man*, p. 68; *Le Christique* (1955), p. 14; *L'Activation de l'Énergie*, *Œuvres*, VII, pp. 426–9.

a "coalescence"[2] between scientific and theological thought. To seek for this was a fine and noble enterprise that was certainly worth attempting. It may be, however, that Teilhard was a little too hasty in his search for "coherence" and increasingly looked for it along roads that were rather too direct. We may perhaps say, at least, that, being in a hurry to translate his unifying vision into intellectual terms, he made use of over-abrupt short cuts. "We may wonder," writes Père Pierre Smulders, "whether in his writings there are not some hasty and premature ways of reconciling things."[3] It is true that he understood that the truth of science and that of revelation "lie on different levels"; that "in no field and at no point do science and Revelation encroach on one another— they never duplicate one another"; in seeking, as he says again, to bring about their "conjunction",[4] he wished only to correct a separatism whose effects appeared to him baneful. The question is, whether he took sufficiently into account the full complexity and all the aspects of the real.

It was an undertaking that, theologically too, was not without risk. One can, and indeed even must, regret that occasional expressions that Père Teilhard used in this connection were less happy than they might have been: for example, when he spoke of the "cosmic nature" of Christ as a sort of "third nature" of the incarnate Word. This has, quite rightly, been held against him,[5] although one would have to be very literal-minded to fear that it might lead "straight to heresy". Here, then, a correction is called for, though it is one easily made and in no way contrary to the spirit of what he wrote. Teilhard was careful to put "nature" in quotes, and he wished to

[2] The word used by Pastor Georges Crespy in a lecture to the C.C.I.F.— a Teilhardian word, cf. Œuvres, V, p. 370, and La Grande Monade.

[3] Op. cit., p. 35.

[4] The Phenomenon of Man., pp. 283 ff.

[5] In an unsigned article in the Osservatore Romano, 1 July 1962. See the second essay in this volume.

put forward the idea only, he said, "in a true sense".[6] This shows quite clearly that he recognized that his paradoxical expression could also be taken in a wrong sense. Again, using deliberately tentative language, he spoke only of a "sort of 'third Christic nature'", adding, further, the words "if I may express it so".[7] He perhaps put it better, though rather imprecisely, in an earlier article, when he compared the "cosmic being of Christ" to an *aura*.[8] We can only agree again with Père Smulders that, wishing to give a jolt to a "narrow, formalist" theology that neglected the full scope of the humanity of Christ, he risked a "somewhat thoughtless"[9] expression. In his anxiety to remind us of an element that is not only compatible with orthodox doctrine but necessary to the integrity of the faith—an element that "he could read in all St Paul's writings" and which seemed to him to have taken on a character of extreme urgency in our own day—he gave insufficient thought (here as elsewhere) to the precision of his language and to the respect due to accepted formulas, which are something equally necessary. It would, however, be unfair to bear too heavily on a paradoxical expression in which there was no intention of attacking dogma.[10] It is better to uncover the underlying intention.

A passage from a letter Teilhard wrote from New York (14 January 1955) to Père André Ravier will help us to see what he meant. He was looking for a new way of expressing himself that would leave intact the traditional terminology used in connection with the two natures. This passage brings out the amplitude of the problem he was trying to solve and the

[6] *Le Christique* (1955), p. 9.

[7] *Comment je vois* (1948), no. 31.

[8] *Forma Christi* (1919), I, p. 4. "The cosmic being (the Aura) of Christ." Cf. *L'Élément universel* (end).

[9] *Op. cit.*, pp. 249–50.

[10] No more could one quarrel in the St Thomas for having on one occasion spoken of three substances in Christ. *In Joannem*, c. 10, lectio 4, n. 2; "Sed cum in Christo sint tres substantiae, sc. substantia Verbi, animae et corporis ...", (*Opera Omnia*, ed. Fretté, Vivès, XX, p. 136).

extreme importance he attached to it, and at the same time shows us the spirit in which he was making the attempt. He cannot admit that on any principle the universal influence of Christ should be limited to the horizon of the earth we live on. No "spiritual substance, created or still to be created in the Universe", can escape his lordship:

> It seems to me that we are living again, at a distance of fifteen hundred years, the great battles of Arianism: but with this difference, that the problem today is not to define the relations between the Christic and the Trinitary—but between Christ and a Universe that has suddenly become fantastically big, formidably organic, and more than probably poly-human (n thinking planets— perhaps millions. . .).[11]—And, to put it crudely (but expressively) I can see no noble or constructive outcome for the situation apart from theologians of a new Nicaea introducing the sub-distinction, in the human nature of Christ, between a *terrestrial* nature and a *cosmic* nature. What do you think?

Earlier, in 1945, Teilhard had written:

> We may say that the dominant concern of theologians in the first centuries of the Church was to determine the position of Christ in relation to the Trinity. In our own time the vital question has become the following: to analyse and specify exactly, in its relations, the existence of the influence that holds together Christ and the Universe.[12]

Writing on 17 November 1947 he was even more precise:

> I cannot explain to you how these worthy theologians of ours, faced with such an enlargement of the Universe, would react. But I assert that the most sacred and most essential requirements of Dogma insist that we must say: if the Universe is pluri- noospheric, its centre can only be, once again and always, Christ.

> *Neque longitudo, neque latitudo,*
> *neque profundum . . . .*

[11] Teilhard raised this question in 1944, in the last paragraph of *La Centrologie*, 33, *Les autres sphères?* (*Œuvres*, VII, pp. 113–14). It had been occupying his mind for a long time, as we learn from a short unpublished note dated 1918.
[12] *Christologie et Évolution.*

It was, we see, a series of attempts, of tentative gropings, of inquiries—and of consultations: and all, continually, with a view to according to Christ his full grandeur and to looking deeper into his inexhaustible riches. In this connection we may say of Teilhard what Père Benoit says of St Paul: The essential thing in his eyes, what he really had at heart, was "to maintain the absolute primacy of Christ",[13] and Teilhard's preoccupation with stars that may possibly be inhabited is an apposite reminder, *mutatis mutandis*, of Paul's preoccupation with the angelic powers in the Epistle to the Colossians. Occasionally, one can note a slip in Teilhard's wording, but in his thought we find the very opposite of any "Minimism".[14] We can see, too, that all Père Teilhard's Christology is for him the living bond between prayer and action. It is from the very heart of his mystical life that springs the apostolic flame with which he is afire. "The majority of men who learn to read nowadays learn that Christ is a thing of the past." That judgment is taken from a recent book.[15] In some intellectual circles such expressions as "post-Christian thought", "post-Christian culture", "the post-Christian era", are freely used. Père Teilhard had noted this, with distress. But he did not lose heart. He did not "seek in the heavens some other star than Christ".[16] Following the example of St Paul in his mission to the Gentiles of the first century, Teilhard—the modest but eager disciple of the great Apostle—sought to preach Christ, the same Christ, to the dechristianized Gentiles of his own day. Instead of taking refuge in some illusory figure greater than Christ, he cried, "O Christ, ever greater!"

In the shape of a "little one" in his mothers' arms—in harmony with the great law of birth—you have taken root in my infant soul

[13] *Les Épitres de Saint Paul, loc. cit.*, p. 49. Cf. Origen, *In Rom.*, v. 10 (Migne, *P.G.*, 14, 1053 B).

[14] See below, p. 180.

[15] Joseph Comblin, *La Résurrection* (1959), p. 152.

[16] *La Conquête du Monde*, end. Cf. M. Blondel, writing to Victor Delbos, 6 May 1889, "As humanity grows greater, so Christ is exalted".

—Jesus. And now, repeating and extending in me the circle
of your growth in the Church—now that the humanity you
put on in Palestine has gradually spread to all parts, like a halo
of countless colours, in which your Presence penetrated
every other presence around me, super-animating it, never
destroying . . .

. . . The more the years pass, my Lord, the more I seem to know
that, in me and around me, the great, hidden, care of modern
Man is much less to quarrel over possession of the World than
to find some way to escape it. The anguish of feeling not spatially
but ontologically imprisoned in the cosmic Bubble! The anxious
search for an outcome—no, a focus—for evolution! There—the
price we have to pay for a still-growing planetary infolding—is
the grief that, dimly discerned though it be, weighs heavy
on the mind of Christian as of gentile, in this world of
today.

Beyond and above itself, Humanity, now emerged into consciousness of the movement that draws it along, has ever-increas-
ing need of some Direction, some Solution, to which at last it
can give its allegiance.

And so—this God, no longer only the God of the old cosmos,
but the God of the new cosmogenesis (precisely in as much as the
effect of a mystical work now two thousand years old is to show
us in You, beneath the Child at Bethlehem and the Crucified, the
Beginning and the collective Kernel of the World itself)—this
God, so longed for by our generation—is it not You, You,
indeed who are this God—and you who bring him to us—
Jesus?

Lord of Consistence and Union, You whose distinguishing
mark and essence are that You can grow indefinitely, without distortion or break, in time with the mysterious Matter at whose
heart you lie and of all whose movements You are the final con-
troller—Lord of my childhood and of my end—*God, fulfilled
for himself, and yet for us, God whose birth has no end*—God who,
since You offer Yourself for our adoration as "evolver and
evolutive", are now the only God who can bring us satisfaction—
tear away at last all the clouds that still veil You—and
tear away the clouds, too, of hostile prejudices and false
beliefs.

And grant that, in diaphany and in flame, your universal
presence may spring forth.

O Christ, ever greater! [17]

This passage has been quoted because it belongs to Teilhard's later period, and because it includes several expressions
that have made some readers fear that Teilhard did not
believe sufficiently in the eternal present-ness of God or in
the initial divinity of Jesus of Nazareth. The ambiguity of the
wording in some places—which is almost inevitable and will
be found in other writers [18]—arises from a twofold cause: the
transition from the order of being to the order of knowledge,
and the transition from the personal Christ to the Christ, whom
following St Augustine, we call the "total Christ". The
passage itself, however, contains expressions that remove the
double ambiguity: the God to whose birth for us there is no
end is the God "fulfilled for himself", and the "evolutive"
Christ is first, in himself, Christ "the evolver". [19] "So far, my
God, from our conferring on you this plenitude, as parts are
added to a sum, it is we who experience it." [20]

We should, therefore, make no mistake. Any misunderstanding would be fatal, and Père Teilhard would have protested against it with all the ardour of his faith. "Alpha and
Omega, Beginning and End, Foundation Stone and Keystone" [21]—even in this cosmic role Christ was still for him the
one and only Jesus of history and dogmatic tradition [22]—

[17] *Le Cœur de la Matière.* Cf. 15 July 1952, to Marguerite Teillard-Chambon,
"I have absolute trust in Him, whose greatest possible exaltation is my only
care" (*Letters from a Traveller*, p. 329).

[18] We see it, for example, in the classic phrase *Deus semper major.*

[19] Our italics in the quotation. See also above, p. 6 and note. Already in 1933
Teilhard was speaking in his letters of the "necessity for a greater Christ for
a greater world", but his thought is given greater precision by the words he
himself underlined in another passage: "What must Christology become *if it
is to remain itself?*" (Letters of 25 July and 9 Dec. 1933).

[20] *Le Prêtre* (1918), p. 7.

[21] *Science et Christ* (1921), p. 13.

[22] Cf. letter of 6 Nov. 1916 (*Making of a Mind*, p. 142).

"the historic and trans-historic Jesus", the Jesus of the Gospel
the son of the Virgin Mary, he whose hands "were pierced",
the "Jesus" whose name comes so often in his prayers. It
was the Risen of Easter, he of whom it is written in the Epistle
to the Philippians, "... *secundum potentiam qua possit Ipse
omnia sibi subjicere*":[23] "By ascending into heaven after having
descended into hell, You have so filled the universe in every
direction, Jesus, that henceforth, to our joy, it is impossible
for us not to be within You: *Quo ibo a spiritu tuo, et quo a facie
tua fugiam?*"[24] It was Jesus, incarnate God, who had made
himself "evolving" that he might be "evolver".[25] For
Teilhard it was indeed always, as he was to write once again
in the evening of his life, "He whom the Society [of Jesus]
taught me to love".[26] He whom he had learnt to follow by
practising the *Spiritual Exercises* of St Ignatius. He of whom
he said one day, laying bare his soul, "I find myself in the
state of not being able to breathe outside our Lord, and of
understanding that without an historical and traditional
revelation, our Lord simply disappears."[27]

This "ever-greater Christ" was, again, the Sacred Heart,
devotion to whom he had learnt from his mother, and to
whom he sometimes used to address the prayer of an old
sixteenth-century Jesuit: "*Tu, Domine, include me in imis
visceribus Cordis tui*".[28] In the Sacred Heart he found "above
all the Master of the spiritual life", and of the Sacred Heart

[23] Phil. 3. 21. The words are given as Teilhard quoted them, in the colophon
to *Forma Christi* ("so effective is his power to make all things obey him"). Cf.
Comment je Crois (1948): "Every element in the Universe is (physically as well
as metaphysically) an elementary centre in relation to the totality of time and
space. But in Christ this co-extension of co-existence has become co-extension
of domination." Cf. Joseph Huby, *Saint Paul, Épitres de la captivité* (1935), p. 42.

[24] *Le Milieu Divin*, p. 127. Cf. pp. 116–17.

[25] Retreat, 1945 (second and third days).

[26] Letter to Père J. B. Janssens, 12 Oct. 1951, in *Letters from a Traveller*, p. 42.

[27] Letter of 31 Dec. 1926, Cf. *La Pensée religieuse*, pp. 82–6 and 142–7.

[28] This prayer, with its conclusion, is repeated in *La Messe sur le Monde*
(*Hymne de l'Univers*, p. 32).

he wrote to his cousin in 1917: "Our Lord's heart is indeed ineffably beautiful and satisfying: it exhausts all reality and answers all the soul's needs. The very thought of it is almost more than the mind can compass." [29] With the freedom that the Church has always allowed to her children in their spiritual life, Teilhard dispensed with certain features that in his view were too personal, too restrictive, though retained by the devotion of recent centuries; at the same time, it was, indeed, as he says, "under the sign of, and filled with wonder by, the Heart of Jesus", that his religious life developed, "to what depths, with what vigour and continuity" it would be difficult, he adds, to explain. More and more, for Teilhard, the Heart of Jesus was the "Fire", bursting into the cosmic milieu, to "amorize" it. [30] He always carried a picture of the Sacred Heart in his breviary, a link between the invocations he had been taught and those which he now found better nourishment for his prayer. He turned his eyes towards its rays, carrying radiance to all parts: "At the centre of Jesus, no longer the spot of purple, but a burning hearth, drowning all the contours in its glow." [31] Thus the concept that was so dear to him and that in the end was supreme in him, of the "universal Christ" was born from "an expansion of the Heart of Jesus". [32]

This universal Christ, a living synthesis of the "Above"

[29] *Making of a Mind*, pp. 107, 203, 192. "Why must this devotion be ruined by so much mawkishness and false sentimentality? . . . I may be mistaken about this, I fear (for our Lord urged the love of his heart as something very popular, open to all, and therefore, like the Holy Eucharist itself, exposed to the excesses of false devotion), but my own natural inclination is to look on the Sacred Heart as an object of love worthy of such respect, so sacred, that it should be the centre of an almost esoteric cult reserved for those who wish to be real Christians through and through." The passage should be read in its context, which is explained by over-zealous propaganda that accompanied the distribution of Sacred Heart badges to the troops.

[30] *Le Cœur de la Matière*, part 3, 1, Cf. Pierre Smulders, *La Vision du Père Teilhard de Chardin*, p. 248.

[31] *Le Tableau* in *Le Christ dans la Matière* (1916). Cf. *Making of a Mind*, p. 192.

[32] *La Parole attendue* (1940). *Cahiers Pierre Teilhard de Chardin*, 4, p. 28.

and the "Ahead", mastering the world and imposing his form upon it, was also for Teilhard "Christ the King".[33] He was overjoyed, accordingly, when the feast was instituted by Pius XI. And finally, even in his glory, as he stretched out his arms to the furthest extremities of creation, the source of a "prodigious spiritual energy", Christ remained always for Teilhard, "Jesus", "crucified Jesus".[34]

"What the world now awaits from the Church of God," wrote Père Teilhard in 1952, "is a wider and deeper appreciation of the meaning of the Cross." In the light of the prospects he opens up for us "the Cross is taking on a new gravity and new beauty".[35] This is because they enable us to realize better that "it is not the gospel of the Cross that brings the Cross to this world, but that it alone can reveal its potential fruitfulness, in him who, through the Cross he accepted, leads us towards the only Kingship over the world that is, in the end, not the Kingship of death but of life." "Only these," ends Père Louis Bouyer, "to whom faith in the mystery of the Cross has revealed the final realization of the cosmic kingship of Christ, can love the world as he loved it, with the love that seals and saves."[36]

[33] Letter of 4 Dec. 1947, etc. Cf. Louis Bouyer, *Royauté cosmique* in *La Vie Spirituelle*, April 1964, p. 396.

[34] *Le Prêtre* (1918); *Forma Christi* (1918); *L'Énergie spirituelle de la souffrance* (1950). Cf. *La Parole attendue, loc. cit.* "Nor is there any danger that, forgetful of heaven, the faithful, drawn by him (the universal Christ) may let themselves be captured by a pagan naturalism and be diverted to a materialistic conquest of the world. Does not the Universal Christ, in all his glory, never cease to emerge from the Cross?"

[35] *Le Christ évoluteur* (1942), p. 7.

[36] *Royauté cosmique*, in *La Vie Spirituelle*, April 1964, p. 396.

7

SPIRITUAL ANCESTRY

Père Teilhard belonged to the generation that had felt in its youth that it was being "stifled in the prison of a religion that concentrated on morality", and had escaped by "re-learning from St Paul and St John the living foundation of Christianity".[1] He knew that, in the main lines of his thought, he had been faithful to St Paul and St John, and there are many competent exegetes today who would be inclined to agree with him.[2] He felt, too, that he was carrying on the speculative effort of the Greek Fathers, in particular St Irenaeus and St Gregory of Nyssa, to whom he more than once alludes, though in a general and rather inexact way.[3] He believed also that his concept of Christ the evolver should have the effect of "giving traditional Christianity a new reinforcement of up-to-dateness and vitality".[4] We may wonder, too, how far he realized that he was thus, in a new context conditioned by new scientific advances, forging a more exact bond with an ancient tradition running through so many long centuries. We can well picture the enthusiasm that

[1] Paul Doncoeur, S.J., *Études*, 20 June 1923, p. 708.
[2] The following is from a letter, signed by several members of the faculty of Fordham University, that appeared in *America*, 9 Nov. 1963: "Speaking of the 'few selected verses of St Paul' which were especially dear to (though by no means exclusively cited by) Teilhard, the real question is whether his insistence on them does violence to St Paul's thought. Some serious Pauline scholars are inclined to think he simply focused attention on an oft-neglected aspect of the Apostle's doctrine."
[3] In the 1940 Retreat, for example, contemplation *ad amorem*.
[4] *Le Christ évoluteur* (1942), p. 4.

would have possessed him, had he visited the catacomb of Calixtus, when he saw the lovely ceiling of a cell, on which Christ is represented at the centre of a cosmos symbolized by the winds blowing from every quarter of space. Even more, perhaps, would he have loved this litany from an old sermon on Easter, attributed to a disciple of St Hippolytus, which pays tribute to the Cross of Christ: "Strong bulwark of the Universe, bond that holds all things together, foundation of the world we live upon, framework of the cosmos, from all sides straining together in its vast hands the manifold spirit of the aether!"[5] And his joy would have been overflowing, had he learnt these are but the two first links in a chain that runs through all the centuries of Christianity.

Thus, Origen in his commentary on the Psalms, speaks of Christ, "of whom all human kind and, maybe, the whole universality of creation, is the body".[6] And in his commentary on the Epistle to the Romans, he brings out "the strength of the Cross" by explaining that "it brought salvation not only to all present and future centuries, but to all past centuries, and not only to this earth and our human world, but to all the heavenly orders".[7] In the next century, St Ephraem the Syrian, in his *Hymns on Paradise*, puts forward Christ, in whose humanity the premordial order was restored, as the second Adam, the cosmic Christ, the total Christ.[8] Speculations, mythological in origin, on the cosmic Adam, have in fact brought in the imagination to help in according proper value to Pauline thought on the cosmic role of the Incarnate Word. St Gregory of Nyssa, again, is constantly relating to the symbolism of the Cross to the divine presence that fills the Universe. He says that "God dominates and gathers up

[5] *Homélie paschale*, c. 51 (*Sources chrétiennes*, 27 d., Paul Nautin). See de Lubac, *Catholicisme*, end, text 48.
[6] *In psalmum* 36 (Migne, P.G., 12, 1330 AB).
[7] *In Rom. comm.* v. 10 (Migne, *P.G.*, 14, 1053 B). Cf. *In Joannem*, frag. 89 (*C.C.S.*, 4. pp. 552–3). Similar passages quoted in *Pensée Réligieuse*, pp. 84–5.
[8] Cf. M. Lot-Borodine, in *Romania* (1957) p. 143.

all things with the image of the Cross". On several occasions, commenting on the text from the Epistle to the Ephesians, "the breadth, the length, the height and the depth", he shows "the great Apostle distributing adoration in the shape of the cross". He is no less ready than Paul himself to transpose Stoic speculations and use them to magnify Christ.

Even if it is not always completely successful, such a procedure betrays not a deviation from, but what one might call a superabundance of, faith. For Gregory, "the Cross of Theology", at the deepest level of its mystery, proclaims "the all-powerfulness of him whom we see nailed upon it", the all-powerfulness of him who "unites firmly and fits to himself the whole Universe, bringing back into óne single concord and one single harmony, through his own person, the different natures of the world"—he "who is all in all".[9] Here, surely, we have the Teilhardian concept expressed in *Forma Christi*. In the seventh century, St Maximus the Confessor celebrates in less inspired language the "blessed end for which the Universe was conceived and brought into being".[10] Later again, in our nordic West, Rabanus Maurus constantly repeats the same theme. His rather heavy-handed ingenuity recalls the lofty poetry of the disciple of Hippolytus:

In its four arms, the Cross of Christ contains all: all that is in the heavens, on earth, under the earth; all the visible and invisible, the quick and the dead. Thus the four arms of the Cross, with their four quarters, show forth the mystery in which all creatures find their

---

[9] Homily I on the Resurrection (Migne, *P.G.*, 46, 621–5). *Contra Eunomios* (ed. Jaeger, 121–3). *Great Catechism* (ed. L. Méridier, pp. 146–57). Cf. Jean Daniélou, *Le Symbolisme cosmique de la Croix* in *Maison Dieu* (1963) pp. 23–6. See also Robert Gillet, O.S.B., *L'Homme divinisateur cosmique dans la pensée de Saint Grégoire de Nysse*, in *Studia Patristica* (1962), pp. 62–83. Following the lead of St Paul, Christianity in the first centuries assigns to man, and in a more complete form to Christ, the role attributed by the Stoics to the "elements of the World".

[10] *Quaestiones ad Thalassium* (Migne, *P.G.*, 96, 249–50). On the similar tradition in Eastern theology, see N. M. Wildiers, *Teilhard de Chardin* (1960), pp. 90–110.

being, rational, celestial, terrestrial, infernal, and supercelestial . . .
The Passion of Christ holds up all the real, it rules the world, it
bursts asunder Tartarus . . . It maintains that which exists, preserves that which lives, animates that which feels, enlightens that
which thinks . . . By its power, the Holy Cross encircles, enfolds,
unites one to another, all realities, on high and below, in veneration
of Christ.[11]

Père Teilhard's cosmos, it is true, is no more the cosmos of
Rabanus Maurus than it is that of Ephraem or Gregory of
Nyssa. Certain naturalist overtones are more foreign to him.
Even so, had Teilhard known that extraordinary poem, with
its series of cosmic diagrams, he would certainly have recognized with respect, as did a number of Renaissance Christian
humanists, one of his spiritual ancestors in the man who
taught so much to Germany, Rabanus Maurus. On one occasion, we know, as Teilhard left the Museum at Naples, he
exclaimed, "What great men the ancients were!" Greater
familiarity with Christian tradition would not have made
him cling to the antiquated forms of past ages, but might
well have led him to exclaim, "What great men our own
ancients were!"

There is another book, not so old, that he might have read,
and perhaps did. It is by an author by no means to be underestimated, Cardinal de Bérulle. In his tenth discourse on the
"condition and dignities of Jesus"[12] de Bérulle writes that at
his "third birth", by which he means his Resurrection,
Jesus Christ received from his Father a body "far more
glorious than the sun", a body that "contains within its
immense grandeur both earth and sun, all the stars and all
the expanse of the heavens, a body that rules all bodies and
all heavenly spirits", etc. In his second discourse, again, de
Bérulle writes: "The Earth on which mankind lives in Jesus
Christ . . . is a new centre of the universe, to which every

[11] *De laudibus sanctae crucis* (Migne, *P.G.*, 107, 157–8).
[12] 5th ed. (Paris, 1639), pp. 536, and 152–3.

spiritual and bodily creature tends. At once Centre and Heaven, etc." Had Teilhard read de Bérulle's *Life of Jesus*, he would have found a similar exaltation, "Earth and Heaven, Grace and Nature, look to you and tend towards you, as to their whole and their Centre".

With this in mind, and feeling that such assurances confirmed more solidly than ever his interpretation of St Paul, would it have disturbed Teilhard at all had he foreseen that a theologian of standing would one day confront him with a contradictory doctrine?—as has been done by Père Philippe de la Trinité. In his view, "the sacred humanity assumed by the Word is, in its nature, exactly as ours" and hence "it is not endowed with mysterious cosmic powers".[13]

> When he was living on earth, when he died on the Cross, and lay in the sepulchre, when he arose in glory and sat in triumph at the right hand of the Father, the Man Christ Jesus (the Word in and through his humanity) never exercised, never exercises, and never will exercise, as such, any influence of the "natural" order, of the *cosmic* order, on the consistence and evolution of the world, whether it be cosmos or cosmogenesis. . . .
>
> The resurrection of Christ magnified humanity to the dimensions of the cosmos. What exactly does that mean? It is simply an expression peculiar to a preacher-poet. We cannot grasp its doctrinal meaning, whereas Col. 1. 15–18 is and remains completely intelligible, in the line of tradition, without Teilhard's distortions.[14]

Even if Père Philippe de la Trinité does not explain what he means by "in the line of tradition",[15] one thing at any rate is clear, that he denies to the glorified humanity of Christ the cosmic role which a number of commentators, such as Père Ferdinand Prat, Père Joseph Huby and Père Benoit saw, as did Teilhard, in St Paul's statement: a role which some first-rate theologians of today still attribute to him. A quotation

---

[13] *Teilhard et Teilhardisme*, in *Quadrani de Divinitas*, 1962, p. 52.
[14] *Rome et Teilhard de Chardin*, 1964, p. 172.
[15] Even though he adds, "in the light of the teaching of St Thomas".

from Père François-Xavier Durrwell's *La Resurrection de Jésus, mystère de salvation*, will suffice to illustrate the point.

> During his first periods of imprisonment, the Apostle had leisure to appreciate the import of the exaltation of Jesus, and to follow up its effects throughout *the whole cosmos* . . . For Paul, Christ is the *very principle of the cosmos* . . . That prerogative is derived, no doubt, from his divinity, but the Christ of the Resurrection is wholly and completely divine . . . The *pleroma* (plenitude) which, according to contemporary biblical and theological opinion, means "the Universe filled with the creative presence of God, is, with all its being and all its dynamism, present first in him." It is "In him" that God calls all things into existence and maintains them in it . . . The world is recalled and resumed in him and becomes a cosmos. . . .[16]

To this Père Philippe de la Trinité may retort, "the concept of a cosmic activity of Christ . . . is not admissible. Could one more obviously confuse the natural and supernatural orders?" He may criticize Teilhard's expression "the total centre at which all is resumed" as pure "confusion" or ask, "Christ, the organic centre of all participated being? In sound theology, what exactly does that mean?" He may remark that the Word assumed "only a *single* human nature" and that we cannot "in any way speak of a universal cosmic centre (even in virtue of the Humanity of Christ) without involving ourselves in the corollary of a God who is *cosmicized* and *cosmicizing* through his Incarnation".[17] Whether such denials and condemnations may not in some way impugn the Scriptural texts themselves is a question we need

---

[16] 7th ed., revised and enlarged, 1963, pp. 145-7. Père Durrwell adds on the next page, "that in this there is an 'anticipation', but that even if 'cosmic lordship' is an eschatological end of Christ, it is nevertheless a paschal reality". With this, I believe, Père Teilhard's thought is in agreement.

[17] *Rome et Teilhard de Chardin*, pp. 91, 97, 101, 173, Cf. p. 134. "In seeking to make the transcendent mystery of the Incarnation that redeemed us, cosmic, and hence more human and more efficacious, Teilhard is obliged to make it natural".

not discuss here.[18] We need do no more than note that Père Philippe de la Trinité's contradiction, however categorically expressed, is not in itself sufficient to refute Père Teilhard's opinion.

[18] For a discussion of the influence of the humanity of Christ on the sensible world, see Gaston Fessard, S.J., *La vision religieuse et cosmique de Teilhard de Chardin*, in *L'Homme Devant Dieu* (1964), pp. 223–48.

8

THE "EXTENSIONS" OF
THE EUCHARIST

IT was perhaps in the mystery of his Eucharist that Jesus Christ was most often the subject of Père Teilhard's meditation.[1] With the consecrated host as his starting-point, and remaining always "under its domination"—"in the radiance of the consecrated host"—he would contemplate with the eyes of faith the effulgence of the divine Presence through the Universe, "drawn from its outward semblance". Such is the theme of two of the three "stories in the style of Benson" that he wrote on the Verdun front, at Douaumont, in 1916. "The picture" is a picture of the Sacred Heart, but the titles of the "Monstrance" and "The Pyx" announce their eucharistic symbolism.[2]

"The Pyx" originated from the days that Teilhard, as a priest-stretcher-bearer, spent "literally heart to heart with our Lord", when, during the First World War he carried

---

[1] On 20 Sept. 1915 he urges "union with our Lord, sought for with faith and perseverance in the Eucharist". (*Making of a Mind*, p. 70.)

[2] See Étienne Borne, *De Pascal à Teilhard de Chardin* (1963), pp. 79–80. "Both in Pascal and in Teilhard, we find the symbolism of fire in their most inspired passages, on the border-line between the human and the divine; it is this that gives the same quality of tone to the original confidences of the *Memorial* and to this little work, modestly entitled 'Three Stories' in which a young Jesuit serving on the Verdun front, as he meditated on the central dogma of Catholicism, the eucharistic presence, disclosed a Christ . . . gathering up to himself the universe of nature and history, and so giving to the whole world its fullness and consistence".

upon his person the sacred species.[3] During those war years and later during his expeditions in the deserts of Mongolia and Central Asia, there were many days, again, when Père Teilhard found it impossible to say Mass. Distressed by this "prolonged fast", he formed the habit of recollecting himself so that he might offer Mass in spirit, just as the laity are urged in similar circumstances to make a spiritual communion. He would turn his mind to the sacrifice that has never, since the upper room and Calvary, ceased to be offered on the face of the earth. From this intense prayer and the meditation it developed into, we owe the two parallel writings of "The Priest" and "Mass on the Altar of the World", to which a passage in the *Milieu Divin* provides a complement.[4]

It is only by completely misunderstanding these texts in a way that would be impossible for anyone who had read them properly, that some critics have thought to detect in them the echo of some purely natural mysticism or sacramentalism: as though, in Teilhard's eyes, "the Mass were no more than the oblation of a cosmic evolution continually in progress".[5] It would be much truer to say that these writings are an admirable and well-ordered version and extension of what the faith teaches about the fertility of the mystery of faith once it has been accepted in its full realism.[6] In considering this, as any other, mystery, Père Teilhard would not be satisfied by that sort of "narrow common sense" which is ready to "take

[3] *Making of a Mind*, p. 196.

[4] *Le Milieu Divin*, pp. 126–8, 136–7.

[5] Dom Georges Frénaud, O.S.B., *op. cit.*, p. 29. A contrary view is expressed by Père Édouard Boné in the *Nouvelle Revue Théologique*, Jan. 1964, p. 94: "Reading these pages gives one a better understanding of the solidity and precision of his faith in the eucharistic mystery: the fertility of his thought might overflow into extensions of the Eucharist, but (whatever may have been said to the contrary) he was completely clear in his mind about the absolute orthodoxy of the direction they took."

[6] Letter of 7 Aug. 1923, from the eastern Ordos: "As I travel by mule, for whole days on end, I repeat, as of old—for lack of any other Mass—the 'Mass on the altar of the world' that you know" (in Claude Cuénot, *Teilhard de Chardin*, 1962, p. 46). Cf. *La Pensée religieuse*, pp. 87–8.

the words literally", because our faith tells us we must do so, and leaves it at that.[7] Anyone, it is true, who looked in the record of his thoughts for a didactic exposition would be disappointed: but how could Teilhard have guessed that any of his readers—should he ever find readers—would think of such a thing? In any case Père Teilhard, in his "boldness" sought no more than to be faithful to the "boldness of Revelation". He believed, as St Augustine believed, whose formulas he revives, in the "devouring power of the Eucharist"—"the little host, as devouring as a glowing crucible"—which, far from being assimilated by him who receives it, assimilates him itself. Similarly he considers the further consequences of the act of consecration. Here, true theologians make no mistake: "It is not a lack of respect for the sacramental celebration that leads him to extend it, but real respect and love. He sees that it is the prototype, the source and the centre that make possible cosmic consecration and communion."[8] "Through the attractive force of his love and the efficacy of his Eucharist, Jesus Christ gradually gathers to himself the whole unifying power scattered throughout the universe."[9] There we have what he calls the "extensions" of the eucharistic Presence:

> The Host is like a burning hearth from which flames spread and radiate. As the spark thrown into the briars is soon surrounded by a circle of fire, so, throughout the centuries, the sacramental Host (for there is but one Host, growing ever greater in the hands of priests as one follows after another),[10] the Host of bread, I repeat, is continually more closely surrounded by another Host, infinitely greater, which is nothing less than the universe itself— the universe gradually absorbed by the universal Element.[11]

[7] *La Vie Cosmique* (1916), p. 55.
[8] Pierre Smulders, *op. cit.*, pp. 255–6.
[9] *La Lutte contre la Multitude* (1917).
[10] Cf. letter of 2 Feb. 1916, where he says that he has just offered up in the little cellar-chapel at Nieuport "the one unique Host of the World".
[11] *Mon Univers* (1924). I hope the reader will allow me the pleasure (for some have reproached me for my habit of pointing out such parallels) of comparing

Whatever greater precision we may think should be introduced into such a concept before it can become a thesis suitable for didactical exposition, it cannot be denied that it stems from the purest faith in the Sacrament of the altar. The "consecration of the world", a concept that the writings of Père Pierre Charles have helped to make widely known and that is now becoming generally accepted in the Church, is a Teilhardian concept,[12] and it is the concept of consecration by the Eucharist.

Further passages will help to make this clear:

When the priest says the words *Hoc est enim corpus meum*, what he says falls directly upon the bread and transforms it directly into the individual reality of Christ. But the great sacramental act does not stop short at that local and instantaneous event. . . .

Grant, my God, that when I approach the altar to make my communion, I may now and henceforward see the infinite vistas hidden beneath the littleness and nearness of the host in which you are disguised.[13]

Is not the infinite circle of things the final host which you desire to transmute?[14]

Thus, as Teilhard once wrote to his friend Père Auguste Valensin, who agreed with him on this point, he contemplated "the vast horizons opened by the concept of a Eucharist understood as an essential mechanism of spiritual transformation".[15] "In the radiance of the consecrated host, all nature is set in motion . . . . From the cosmic element in which it is enclosed, the Word acts to dominate and assimilate all the

---

this with Claudel's comment on the "cellar of wine" of the Song of Songs (2. 4): "It is not only the Tabernacle in which the sacred species are reserved. It is the altar at which the voice of the priest operates transubstantiation. There the consummation of the whole universe is achieved in the sacrifice" (*Paul Claudel interroge le Cantique des Cantiques*, 1948, p. 58).

[12] *Hymne de l'Univers*, p. 24.

[13] *Le Milieu Divin*, pp. 123, 154–5. Cf. *Letters from a Traveller*, p. 86.

[14] *Le Prêtre* (1918). *Le Christique* (1955): "To the amazed eyes of the believer, it is the eucharistic mystery itself that stretches out into infinity."

[15] Paris, 2 Feb. 1920.

rest." [16] And thereby, "to the amazed eyes of the believer, it is the Eucharistic mystery itself that stretches out into infinity." [17] It is this that Teilhard had tried to express symbolically in the second of the "three stories", "The Monstrance".

> Then, as I gazed at the host, I had the feeling that its surface was gradually spreading out, like a drop of oil. . . . The flood of whiteness was enveloping me, passing over and beyond me, swallowing up everything. And everything, drowned in that flood, still retained its own shape, its own free power of movement, for the whiteness did not efface the features of anything, changed no nature, but penetrated things more and more intimately. . . . In the mysterious expansion of the host, the World became incandescent, until the whole of it was like one great host. . . . The white glare was active. . . . After giving life to all, after purifying all, the vast host now began slowly to contract, and the treasures it gathered within itself were ravishingly clasped in its loving light.

The symbolism may not, perhaps, appeal to us—that is a matter of literary taste. But no one who can read could possibly doubt the exact realism of the dogmatic thought that lies behind it, "the Realism by which mysticism lives", as Teilhard wrote.[18] It may, then, be well to continue to quote. The paragraph that follows immediately will help us to understand him still better, because it brings out the full spiritual significance and weight of a line of thought that did not shrink from adding, as a contrasting background, the dark, forbidding aspect of the mystery:

> When the wave falls back or the flame dies down, flecks of brilliance or sparks of fire mark the surface that for a moment was occupied by the sea or the conflagration. Thus, too, as the Host closed in again upon itself, like a flower closing around the calix,

---

[16] *Le Prêtre*—thoughts on analogous "extensions" of baptism. Cf. *Le Milieu Divin*.

[17] *Le Christique* (1955).

[18] *Making of a Mind*, p. 195. He used the phrase in connection with the essay he was writing on "the mystical milieu".

some rebellious elements of the Universe remained behind, in the outer darkness. Something still shone upon them: but it was a soul of perverted light, corrosive and poisonous. These rebel elements burnt like torches or glowed like braziers.[19]

[19] These reflections on hell were to reappear in the *Milieu Divin*. In a shorter and more theoretical form, the possibility of damnation is referred to in more than one later essay, in connection with the essential choice on which man's destiny depends. In *La Vie Cosmique* (1916), p. 69, we already read: "It is no surprise to the believer that here, as elsewhere, a Hell should be the natural corollary of Heaven, and he learns to fear it." *La Lutte*, end. *Forma Christi*, p. 17. *Le Prêtre* (1918): "Christ is the sword that separates, without mercy, the unworthy or corrupt members."

9

THE VIRGIN MARY

ALL truly Catholic piety is also piety towards the Virgin Mary. Père Teilhard never wrote of set purpose about her, any more than he did about any other particular dogma. Few contemporary writers, however, have spoken of our Lady with so personal an emphasis.[1] He sees her, raised above the world, as "a perpetual aurora".[2] When the day of the Virgin came, he says in *La Vie Cosmique*, "the profound and gratuitous finality of the Universe was suddenly revealed". By a process of analogy which is also, as we find in the first generations of Christianity, a process of both assimilation and contrast, he hails in Mary "the true Demeter".[3] One Sunday, in October 1918, when he was in rest-billets with his regiment in a village of the Haut-Rhin, Teilhard, at the invitation of the parish priest, preached on the devotion of the rosary. This is how, writing to his cousin, he summarizes his sermon:

> The rosary is an expansion, a further explanation, of the Hail Mary. . . . The Hail Mary is first of all a manifestation, primarily instinctive, of love for our Lady, a manifestation that is

[1] Père Philippe de la Trinité has a very poor opinion of Père Teilhard's Mariology. This is hardly surprising since he appears to be unacquainted with any of the passages quoted here (or to have deliberately overlooked them). It is not fair to judge Teilhard, as he does, from a few phrases in a letter, obviously designed to meet his correspondent's point of view.

[2] Cf. Song of Songs, 6, 9, "*quasi aurora consurgens*".

[3] *La Vie Cosmique* (1916): the earliest of Teilhard's writings to survive from the First World War. Cf. *Œuvres*, V, p. 396.

"interested". It turns into a need to know our Lady better, to "sympathize" with her: in some way, the heart of the Blessed Virgin becomes transparent, and in it we relive the mysteries, so that the whole of dogma becomes familiar, concrete and real, in *Mary*. Finally, we understand that the mysteries have their parallel and their extension in the alternations, often indeed mysterious, of our own joys and sorrows. So our whole life is Christianized, in a way, in the development within us of the Hail Mary.[4]

Here we see the interiorizing process of Christian prayer, and what Teilhard says follows the pattern handed down by spiritual tradition. There is no parade of learning, and no parrot-like repetition: it is no more than simple fidelity to common tradition, but we feel that the tradition has been assimilated, has been lived, under the guidance of the Spirit of Christ. To this we owe a deep personal analysis of the mystery of Mary, in which he sees first and foremost a mystery of purity. It was in the light of Mary and her mystery that he reflected on woman's vocation and the part she will have to play in the civilization of the future. He wrote of this more particularly in connection with the Immaculate Conception, and again in connection with the Annunciation. He loved to meditate on St Luke's account:

The Immaculate Conception is to me the feast of "action in immobility", by which I mean action that is exercised simply by transmitting the divine Energy through us. Purity, in spite of appearances, is essentially an active virtue, since it concentrates God in us and on those who are subject to our influence. In our Lady, all modes of lower, disordered, activity disappear in this single, luminous, function of attracting and receiving God and allowing him to pass through her. To be active in such a way and to such a degree, the Blessed Virgin must have received her being in the very inmost heart of grace—no later justification, however immediate, could replace this constitutive, inborn, perfection of

---

[4] *Making of a Mind*, pp. 246–7. Until the end of his life, we learn from a witness who was at various times in a position to be well informed, Père Teilhard was faithful to his habit of reciting the rosary daily.

the purity that watched over the birth of her soul. It is thus that
I see the Immaculate Conception.[5]

Consider for a moment—as many of us must have done at times
—the meaning of the mystery of the Annunciation. The moment
having come when God had decided to make his Incarnation
visible to us, he had first to create in the world a virtue strong
enough to draw himself down to us. He needed a mother who
would bear him in a human setting. It was to meet this need that
he created the Virgin Mary, that is to say he caused to appear on
earth a purity so great that, in its translucency, he concentrated
himself into the semblance of a little child.[6]

These words about the Blessed Virgin, it will be realized,
have a wider application. In particular they introduce us to
the concept of spiritual activity, or of "action in immobility"
as Teilhard, who attributed great importance to it, understood it.[7] They can help us, too, to correct another misunderstanding which also has turned out not to be simply potential.

It is, no doubt, easy to see, from the very plan and from the
titles to the various sections of the *Milieu Divin*, the predominating and favoured role that Teilhard attributes to the

[5] *Ibid.*, p. 149.
[6] *Le Milieu Divin*, p. 134. In his article *Finalité et Animisme* (*Aquinas*, 1963,
reprinted in *La Pensée Catholique* [1963], p. 72) Père M. L. Guérard des Lauriers
rightly remarks: "The Christian faith holds that the Word of God personally
assumed a Humanity that issued ... from a human creature personally pre-
destined by God for this mission. *Et Verbum caro factum est, Natus ex Maria
virgine* ..." He adds the solemn warning, "Whoever maintains any deviation
from this doctrine is, like Satan, a liar from first to last". Such an anathema,
whatever his own view of it might have been, could never fall upon Père
Teilhard. It is worth re-reading the passage from *La Vie Cosmique* quoted earlier,
with its conclusion: "When the day of the Virgin came, the profound and
gratuitous finality of the Universe was suddenly disclosed: ever since the time
when the first breath of individualization, passing over the expanse of the lower
Supreme Centre, stimulated upon it the smile of the original monads, everything
moved towards the Infant, born of Woman". *Ibid*: "*Et Verbum caro factum est.*
It was *the Incarnation*" (p. 45).
[7] Cf. 1940 Retreat: "First meditation (fourth day): The Annunciation:
'Passive' or immobile energies: the transparence of purity and the 'ancilla
Domini'. (Fedility.) Faith, too: 'Virtus Altissimi.'—'Non impossibile omne
verbum'."

Christian's "passivities" as compared with his activities. One may, however, fail to appreciate equally that, in his view it is passivity, in its highest and most detached forms, that is ultimately the highest form of activity: that it is virtues and situations commonly regarded as passive, and less esteemed by most men, that are or can be the most truly active, that is to say the most effective in being directed towards the Kingdom of God.[8] To use Teilhard's own words, it is the passive that releases the energy needed to form the Theosphere. He repeats this constantly, and it is this that he here points out in connection with the purity that has, in its perfection, the power to draw the Word of God down to our earth. "One can only be terrified at the crying need for purity the Universe suffers from, and almost beside oneself with longing to do something to supply it."[9] On another occasion, with our Lady in mind, on the eve of the feast of the Purification, he writes: "May our Lord create in each of us a leaven of purity, in that universal and age-old operation by which Mankind is so mysteriously, through the action of the Child-God, divided into the chosen and the rejected."[10]

Whether in external action or in solitary recollection, purity is always, in itself, the operative force of unity:

Like a sweet sound, or a scent, that moves us without our knowing why, purity, by its very name, and still more by its appearance, awakes in our soul a sense of attraction, quite sure of itself, but indefinable. Purity, we somehow feel, touches the deepest, hidden fibres of our most intimate being. It appeals to

[8] In normal conditions, Teilhard would nevertheless say that "true passivity is legitimate, and is achieved, only at the term or at the maximum, of activity" (To the Abbé Gaudefroy, Peking, 14 July 1934). "It's Jacob and the Angel, again," he adds.

[9] *Making of a Mind*, p. 252. Cf. "You know what, particularly on this feast, is my dearest wish: that God, through our Lady, may grant us so to share in her purity that we may really be able to serve, in our own small way, to regenerate the world" (8 Dec. 1918, *ibid.*, p. 262).

[10] *Making of a Mind*, p. 178. "Mary's position is at once unique and a model": G. Crespy, *Pensée Théologique de Teilhard de Chardin*, p. 92.

the most subtle hopes that our make-up can entertain. We live purity. But from what angle should we try to understand a little the creative function it exercises in us through the grace of God?

Perhaps from that of the Multitude.[11]

The pure heart is the heart which, loving God above all things, can see him, too, spread throughout all. Whether he rises up, above every creature, until he attains an almost direct apprehension of Divinity, or whether—as it is every man's duty to do— he casts himself upon the world that he may perfect and master it, the just man has his eyes only upon God. Objects have, for him, lost their superficial multiplicity . . . the pure soul, as is its natural privilege, moves within a vast higher unity. So enclosed, can anyone fail to see that it will be united right to the very marrow of its being? and who can fail to see, then, the inestimable reinforcement that the progress of Life will find in that Virtue?

Whereas the sinner, who surrenders himself to his passions, scatters and dissociates his spirit—the saint, by an inverse process, escapes from the complexity of affections, the complexity which is responsible for retaining in beings the memory and the mark of their original plurality. By that very fact the saint becomes immaterialized. For him, everything is God; God is everything for him, and Jesus is for him at once God and everything. Upon such an object, which, in its simplicity exhausts— for the eyes, for the heart, for the spirit—the truth and beauties of heaven and earth—upon such an object, the faculties of the soul converge, make contact with one another, fuse together in the flame of a unique act in which perception becomes one with love. The specific action of purity (its formal effect, as the scholastics would say) is thus to unite the inner powers of the soul in an act of unique passion, rich and intense beyond words. Ultimately, the pure soul is the soul that, rising above the multiple, disorganizing, attraction of things, tempers its unity (which means matures its spirituality) in the furnace of divine simplicity.[12]

Thus, following St Francis of Assisi and St Paul, Teilhard burns to live only for Christ "seen in all things"; at the same

---

[11] The choice being dictated by the subject of the essay.

[12] *La Lutte contre la Multitude* (1917). Cf. *Making of a Mind*, p. 176. On Teilhard's views on virginity, see André-A. Devaux, *Teilhard et la vocation de la femme* (1964), pp. 41–53.

time he knows that this flame, "which can come only from on high" cannot be kept alive "except by the force of purity and humility".[13] He pays tribute to the "operative virtue" not only of faith and recollection,[14] but also of humility and gentleness.[15] Speaking of silent contemplation, he compares its indispensable function and sovereign action in the life of the Church and the world to that of the snow-covered peaks of nature.[16] These, again, are so many "passive energies", which are the highest form of energy. "Under the appearance", he says again, "of a gentle and humble moral system, the law of purity and Christian charity hides an operation that is pure fire: in this the original plurality of being is re-cast and fused together until its unity is perfected."[17] The same should be said of suffering, which is "transformable—provided it be *properly* accepted—into an expression of love and a principle of union".

O Marguerite, my sister, while I, in dedication to the positive forces of the Universe, was traversing continents and oceans, passionately absorbed in watching all the tints of the earth take on a fuller colour, you, motionless, laid low by sickness, were silently, in the deepest depths of your self, converting into light the darkest shadows of the world. Which of us, tell me, as the Creator looks down on us, will he say has chosen the better part?[18]

Like the contemplatives and those whose life is spent in prayer, the sick and the suffering have a special function, which they alone can fulfil. Being, "as though driven out of themselves, forced to emigrate from the present forms of

---

[13] *Making of a Mind*, p. 307.

[14] Cf. "The tranquil recollection that I love more than anything" (*Ibid.*, p. 175).

[15] *La foi qui opère* (1918).

[16] *Le Milieu mystique* (1917). *Le Milieu Divin*, p. 134. Cf. *La Pensée religieuse*, pp. 318–20. Similarly, to Père Lucien M. de St Joseph, contemplation "is an indispensable organic function of the mystical body" (*L'impatience de Dieu*, 1964, p. 71).

[17] *La Lutte contre la Multitude*, (1917), p. 16.

[18] *L'énergie spirituelle de la souffrance* (1950); *Œuvres*, VII, pp. 255–7.

life", they are thereby "chosen for the work of making the world rise above immediate enjoyment towards an ever-loftier light". It is they whose part it is "to supply air that their brothers may breathe, working like miners in the depths of matter". Bearing "in their wasted bodies the weight of the world as it moves forward, they become, by an admirable counter-stroke of Providence, the most active agents in the very progress that appears to sacrifice and crush them".[19]

The supreme energy is that of the Cross of Jesus "the symbol and focus of an action whose intensity is beyond all words. The crucified Jesus, who "takes away the sins of the world" is also, and even more, he who takes up the burden and continually leads upward to God the forward steps of the advancing universe. In this Cross, the absolute synthesis of all passivities, lies the supreme Activity."[20]

[19] *La signification* ... *de la souffrance* (1933); *Œuvres*, VI, pp. 64–5. Cf. Blondel, *Carnets intimes*, p. 85 (10 Oct. 1884): "I want to show that the highest mode of being is action: that the most complete mode of action is suffering and love: that the true mode of loving is adherence to Christ."

[20] *Op. cit.*, p. 66. Cf. in Teilhard's "note on evangelization of a new era" (1919), the third period of the "complete cycle of the interior life": "To *sublimate* human effort by making it attain (by extension of itself) the higher forms of activity—purity, contemplation, death *in God*."

SPIRITUAL LIFE

PÈRE Teilhard loved another essential form of Christian prayer, that found in liturgical prayer. He loved—this we know from his own words—ceremonies well carried out, and for this reason he confessed that he was ill at ease when he had to officiate himself in rough and ready conditions, without the "supreme decency" the liturgy calls for.[1] During the occasional holidays he spent with his family in Auvergne, he liked every evening to give a short spiritual talk on the next day's Mass. He loved the feasts of the Church: Easter and Christmas, too, the Epiphany, the Transfiguration . . . and, above all, the Ascension. No doubt, working as a Jesuit and an explorer, the externals of the liturgical life occupied little place in his life. But he enjoyed the Divine Office, which he read in a spirit of interior recollection. I may, I hope, be allowed a personal memory: some time after my ordination as a priest—this must have been about the end of 1927, on one of the occasions when Père Teilhard was back from China— he gave me some excellent advice on how to avoid routine and mechanical repetition when reading my breviary. In particular he urged me to underline certain passages, or words, whenever I should first appreciate their flavour, so that I might later recapture it. Although no one could have been more on his guard than he was against an abuse of ritual forms, at the same time he recognized, in acts of private prayer as in

[1] Cf. *Making of a Mind*, pp. 175-6.

the practical organization of life, the value of external discipline, which in fact he interpreted somewhat strictly. His fellow Jesuits are definite on this point: both in Paris and New York they noted "the extreme punctiliousness" he observed in carrying out the duties of the religious life, obeying the most trifling details of the rules "not with ordinary correctness but most fastidiously".[2]

Teilhard's most intimate letters often allow a glimpse of a sustained life of prayer. No doubt there were passing periods of less intensity,[3] and it went through phases of great distress, but it always ended in strengthening him in his supernatural detachment and forgetfulness of self, releasing him for the single effort towards "the greater glory of God". Those, of course, who met him only incidentally, as a pleasant companion in work or recreation, in a laboratory or a reception at some embassy, or as a chance travelling acquaintance, cannot speak with any authority on this point: nor can correspondents who consulted him on their own problems, whom he answered to the best of his ability:[4] nor even those who enjoyed his delightful friendship. Teilhard was frank and open to all; he had too, a great power of being able to adapt himself to others, and could, by "an exquisite gift of sympathy",[5] allow those around him to share, as he did in his writings, his feelings and experiences. Even so, he had a secret side to him. "How I wish you were here", he wrote one

---

[2] J. Lafarge, S.J., in *The World of Teilhard*, ed. R. T. Francœur (Baltimore, 1961); Cf. from Peking, writing to his cousin, 24 Jan. 1940: "Nothing really new to tell you about my existence here; it goes on in the same routine, and with the same exemplary regularity. I must admit that thought is the gainer up to a certain point, and the interior life, too" (*Letters from a Traveller*, p. 255).

[3] Cf. letter of 18 Jan. 1936: "My life of 'prayers' is tending to become more regular and more intense."

[4] A remark he made about one (29 Oct. 1949) might be applied elsewhere: "I had written two pages of critical comment for him, but without having the heart to discourage him. . . . Anyway, I still don't understand why he relies on me."

[5] Pierre Leroy, in *Letters from a Traveller*, p. 46.

day from Tientsin to a friend who enjoyed his full confidence. "There are plenty of confessors, as St Teresa said, but where can you find anyone who really knows you? You only meet him once or twice in your life." [6]

He knew, as we noted earlier, what it is to go through an interior crisis. Sometimes he felt "desires", "revolts", and "passions"[7] enter into him, and this inspired a need to lay bare his soul. This was always that he might beg in the name of God for some sure guidance, so anxious was he to know where, for him, lay "the most perfect". It is impossible to read without as much admiration as emotion such a cry as burst from his heart on an occasion when he was faced with a choice of extreme gravity and difficulty. "Yes, I believe that I shall drink, *with deep joy*, from this small cup: but let me, at least, be *sure*, that it is the Blood of Christ!"[8] And, in another similar situation, "If you knew how bitter it is to give way, when you have not the interior evidence that it is right to give way—and when in spite of everything, you still fear that, if you do so, you may be false to true courage and true renunciation!" However, thanks to his integrity, his intimate self-searching, and to prayer, he made his way through to the light, and then his serenity returned. The crisis would be overcome in a sort of "renaissance". He understood that the "wrenches" asked of him opened "the road to a zone where God would be at hand to supply, with his saving power, all that was most dear to him".

Speaking of certain "present forms" of the Church, certain examples of narrow-mindedness or short-sightedness in the body of theologians, etc., Teilhard more than once confidentially described his "uneasiness", immediately, how-

[6] To Père Auguste Valensin, 13 Oct. 1933.

[7] "But", he continues, "it has all evaporated" (27 June 1926). It would be a great mistake to take these passing feelings as temptations that he allowed to become rooted in him.

[8] To Père Valensin, 19 May 1925.

ever, adding that it did not induce in him any "lively reaction"
—"not the least prospect of a break, nor even of an interior
slackening of spirit".[9] In the same letter as that in which he
anxiously consults his friend about the "cup" he is asked to
drink, he outlines the ground of his interior debate as follows:
"In telling you this, I do not feel that I am describing a practical problem ... I am only submitting to you a difficulty of
the intelligence, of the mind, which prevents me from acting
with complete tranquillity." He had once and for all taken his
stand on obedience. "I have absolute faith", he had written,
"that our Lord will see to it that the sacrifices I might have to
make for obedience work for the spontaneous success of any
good there may be in my aspirations." He had really, in circumstances that more than once made it heroic, built into his
life the attitude that he had once described:

> Blessed are they who suffer at not seeing the Church so fair as
> they would wish, and are only the more submissive and prayerful
> for it. It is a profound grief, but of high spiritual value. It can
> never be repeated too often: the Catholic is the man who is sure
> of the existence of Jesus-Christ-God, for a number of reasons,
> and *in spite of* many stumbling-blocks.—Why is it that so many
> minds see nothing but the stumbling-blocks and wait until they
> are removed before they look at the reasons?[10]

Père Teilhard was quick to express his regret for some
rather over-pessimistic touches that escaped him in some of
his essays.[11] A friend could truly write of him that he "never
gave way to bitterness".[12] He had himself made a resolution,
"to smile", at everybody and everything, "and always without

[9] Letters of 19 May 1925, 31 Dec. 1926 and 16 Jan. 1927.
[10] *Making of a Mind*, p. 59, Cf. p. 156.
[11] Letters of 30 Dec. 1929 and 31 July 1930.
[12] Pierre Leroy, S.J., in *Letters from a Traveller*. Cf. letter to L. Zanta, from
eastern Mongolia, 20 May 1924, after a harrowing experience: "We must
simply ask our Lord to help us to maintain this attitude without bitterness, by
showing us that his action can be made incarnate even in the most distasteful
schemings of dull or pharisaical minds."

bitterness".[13] With his superiors he was always completely frank, with the absolute frankness of which he said that it is "one of the Society's most precious treasures". So, too, his spirit of obedience was absolute. "What do you think of this situation, *in Domino*? You know that you can say anything to me, and I shall do anything you say."[14] These were not simply empty words, as the event clearly showed. He made a point of behaving with punctilious correctness, so that there could be no room for any misunderstanding.[15]

His loyalty as a religious, again, was recognized by his superiors, and on more than one occasion they testified to it, at the very time when they were obliged to impose restrictions upon him.[16] To another of his superiors he wrote, after receiving a particularly distressing order, "You know that these administrative frictions do not weaken my ever more profound attachment to a Church without which I can see no way of 'valorizing', or 'amorizing' a 'hominization' to the forwarding and advancing of which I have definitely dedicated my life."[17] Many outside the Society have been similarly impressed by this loyalty. It is in itself sufficient

[13] 1940 Retreat. He added, " = the fruit and factor of Omegalization".

[14] To Père André Ravier. (Père Ravier has in preparation a study of youth in the Universe of Teilhard de Chardin.)

[15] For example, on accepting a laboratory appointment at the Wenner Gren Foundation, he wrote to Père Ravier, "A nice letter, very 'paternal', from the Father General (received a little before Christmas), approves—almost warmly— subject to your approval—of the idea that I should work for the time being in New York, and the New York Father Provincial has written me his approval also". (5 Jan. 1952).

[16] Cf. Letter of 9 Nov. 1948: "At Rome I met with a great deal of sympathy and trust (especially from Father General). If the Society is not backing me up— on the other hand she has been ready to make it known that she recognizes me as one of her legitimate children. And it appears that, by Roman standards, even this little is a great deal." In Rome, "the Christic pole of the earth", Teilhard rejoiced to find "the security of a faith that will not be side-tracked" (*Letters from a Traveller*, pp. 299, 300).

[17] To Père Ravier. In 1944, at Peking: "Try when back in Europe, to treat differences in ideas 'in a spirit of affection'."

evidence that behind it lay a regular practice of prayer and self-denial from which it drew nourishment.[18]

Strong in this loyalty, Père Teilhard never allowed himself to be cast down. He knew that he was working not for himself, nor for a purely human cause, but for God. Here, for example, is what he wrote from Peking, on 8 February 1940, at the time he was engaged on *The Phenomenon of Man*:

> *The Phenomenon of Man* progresses at the rate of a page or two a day. I am beyond the half-way mark in the draft. What its value will be, I don't know. But I long so much to finish it properly. I feel that I have seldom worked so entirely for God alone. I am sure that he will give me the light and the strength to complete as it should be completed what I wish to say *only for him*.

And again, on 7 March:

> The whole interest and point of the book is concentrated towards the end, which must be particularly lucid and carefully written. I hope that the Lord will help me, since it is entirely in an attempt to make his countenance seen and loved that I am taking such pains, which sometimes I'd like to be spared.[19]

As Père Teilhard was bold in research, so there was nothing timid or half-hearted in his spiritual life. "We must", he said, alluding to the faith of St Peter, "courageously and in a filial spirit, constantly go forward. If we make our way towards our Lord, the waters will hold us up."[20] It was thus, too, that he could say with complete sincerity, and sometimes in "a sort of intoxicated lucidity", "I am exclusively and

[18] This aspect of Père Teilhard has been more fully studied in Père Louis Barjon's article in *Foi Vivante* (Brussels, no. 15, 1962, pp. 70–82), *Fidélité chrétienne et religieuse du Père Teilhard de Chardin*. See also *Pensée Religieuse*, pp. 327–32, and, above all, René d'Ouince, S.J., *L'Épreuve de L'obéissance dans la vie du Père Teilhard de Chardin* (in *L'Homme devant Dieu*, 1963, Vol. 3, pp. 331–46).
[19] *Letters from a Traveller*, pp. 257, 260.
[20] 17 Dec. 1922. Again on 22 Aug., to L. Zanta: "I think that, as in the Gospel, the moving waters will hold us up in so far as we have the courage to walk upon them, providing we walk towards God and in his love!"

madly in love with the divine influence that guides the world."[21] This belief was behind the almost gay resilience with which he recovered whenever he had met with a disappointment that would have made many other men lose heart. "It's one more case", he thought, "of triumphing over events by trusting to them."[22] It would be a great mistake to see in this no more than the optimistic reactions of a well-adjusted temperament, even if with a sincere admixture of supernatural considerations. All who knew Père Teilhard at all intimately can testify that he was as sensitive to suffering as any other man, and that even before the sickness in 1947 that made him more easily moved, he experienced "the dizziness of anxiety and instability".[23] They know, too, that he often had to make an effort to get back into the "divine milieu", and that he felt the severity of the sacrifice all the more that the plans or wishes that were denied him came from a completely disinterested heart. Yet there was in Père Teilhard not a grain of rancour:

> I feel that I have never been more profoundly indifferent to what may happen to me personally or to what in the world is pettily "human". . . .
> All the pettiness of things is vanishing for me, almost perceptibly, in infinitely grander vistas.[24]

Once he had got over a few "moments of irritation", to which he admits, he forgot these "pettinesses", as he launched

[21] Letter of 31 July 1930. Cf. to L. Zanta, 15 Oct. 1926; and to Claude Rivière, 1942: "To be in communion with the future, in so far as, at every moment, the future expresses the totality of God's loving action on us through the universe."

[22] Letter of 18 Feb. 1934. Cf. 13 Nov. 1918: "It's useless for us to want or regret things over which we have no control. Once again it's God's will manifesting itself; all we can do is to abandon ourselves to it in all peace and openness of heart". (*Making of a Mind*, p. 251).

[23] On 16 Feb. 1953 he wrote from New York to Père Ravier: "Externally, my work is going well, almost better than ever. But interiorly, for the last month I have been going through a phase of anxiety like those that on several occasions since 1940 have been periodically making any effort extremely trying."

[24] Letters of 30 Dec. 1929 and 31 July 1930.

himself again on to the "ocean of the unum necessarium"—
the one thing that is necessary,—and continued to practise
"that gesture, essential not only in death but in life too, that
consists in allowing ourselves to rest, as upon an invisible
support, on him who sustains and upholds us right outside
all the tangible things to which we feel so strong an instinct to
cling".[25] Thus it was that at the end of 1924, on the very day
when he learnt what he might well have regarded as catas-
trophic news—the decision from Rome that dealt him a terrible
blow, forced him to solve an extremely difficult case of conscience, and brought with it the abandonment of his Chair and
exile from Paris[26]—even then he wrote to an intimate friend,
telling him what had happened and adding, "Fundamentally,
I am quite at peace. Even this is one more manifestation of
our Lord: it is his work, so why should I worry?"[27] To
appreciate the full significance of these words, one should
understand, as Newman did, how hard it is to "realize"
what one believes, how hard it is to accept trials as what they
are meant for, that is, as real blessings.[28] This was something
that Père Teilhard knew how to do. Thus, even in a period
of trial he retained the "joyful consciousness of being in the
embrace of a Universe super-animated by God our Lord",[29]
seeking both to work and to suffer *only for him*.[30] "Whatever
happens," he said on another occasion in a letter of conscience

[25] *Letters from a Traveller*, pp. 262, 264. Cf. "Fundamentally, I am experiencing with new intensity the intense joy and longing of clinging to God through
everything". (*Making of a Mind*, p. 141).

[26] Père R. d'Ouince describes this incident, *op. cit.*, pp. 334-6. See also Barjon
and Leroy, *op. cit.*, pp. 29-34.

[27] Letter of 13 Nov. 1924. Cf. letter to his cousin, 7 Nov. 1915: "Deep down
in your soul, set above all things, immovably, as the basis of all your activity, as
the criterion of the value and truth of the things that enter your mind, the peace
of God". (*Making of a Mind*, p. 80).

[28] Cf. Letters, ed. A. Mozley, vol. 1, p. 183.

[29] Letter, Easter 1927.

[30] To Max and Simone Bégouën, 8 Feb. 1940 (when working on *The
Phenomenon of Man*), *Letters from a Traveller*, p. 257. Cf. letter to his cousin 7
March 1940, *ibid.*, p. 261.

in which he opened his soul, "never have any doubt but that my only passion has for a long time been the glory and radiance of Christ Jesus."[31]

[31] To his Superior-General, Paris, 25 Sept. 1947 (quoted by Père d'Ouince, *op. cit.*, p. 342).

11

ANNUAL RETREATS

P ÈRE Teilhard used to make a number of notes during his annual retreats; some of these, covering his last years, have been preserved, and from these we can derive a certain amount of information.

As we all know, every Jesuit has once a year to drop his work and spend eight days in retirement, devoting himself to prayer and meditation. Père Teilhard set great store by this time of retreat. So far as possible, he arranged it every year for the same date, at the beginning of autumn, his favourite season.[1] "Its two great effects", he thought, "should be to 'make God real to him' and to 'immerse him in the pure Divine'."[2] Instead of eight days, Père Teilhard spent nine, the last being devoted to drawing up a "plan of life" for the coming year. He noted subjects for meditation that had particularly attracted him. In short, and often elliptical, phrases, in which we find some of his favourite themes and expressions—there are continual references to Omega and Omegalization, Pleromization, evolver and evolving, super-communication, etc.—he tried to focus his reflection and interior life. He

[1] "I have always been particularly fond of autumn" (*Making of a Mind*, p. 236). "Autumn has always been the best season for my soul".(p. 241).
[2] 1940 and 1943 Retreats, Peking. After his 1939 retreat he wrote to his cousin, on 3 Dec.: "Rather an austere time, but one feels the need of it more as one gets older in an increasingly disturbed world. Let us hope that this stock-taking may have brought me back to the axis, to the one, which increasingly seems to me to be the only, Necessary". (*Letters from a Traveller*, pp. 249–50). 25 Jan. 1940: "Since my last retreat, I have a sort of feeling of being closer to our Lord". (p. 255).

made a certain number of definite resolutions for each new year, not hesitating to enter—or, shall we say descend—into the details of external practices.[3] Further, he chose, as a young novice might have done, a motto which he promised himself he would constantly call to mind and apply both in directing his researches and in his daily behaviour; the care with which he later copied out the list confirms that he attached considerable importance to this practice. Thus until the end of his life we find traces of habits of care and application that date back to his youth.[4]

During his retreats, Père Teilhard meditated as much on sin as on the mystery of God or of our divine vocation. "The past is one with us: and it must be purified *in se* (not simply in the new surge of time) ... Miserere! Amplius lava me!" On one occasion he is distressed and self-reproachful, at feeling too little moved by sin, or at being habitually too ready to justify his own conduct in everything: he humbles himself, in the knowledge that he is "the lowest of the low beside the adorable purity and transparence of Christ-Omega".[5] Even were it possible, we have no need to inquire to what degree these self-accusations correspond to practical reality. One point, however, emerges that is worth recording: There must be some truth in the charge that has been made against Teilhard of not fully understanding the nature of the evil constituted by sin, since he accuses himself of it—but at the same time the fact that he does accuse himself suggests the thought that his failure to understand sin was not so marked as appears. We may note, too, that the passion he discloses for absolute purity, echoes exactly what we read in 1917 in the *Milieu mystique*: "That no blemish, then, may separate him, were it but by an atom of himself, from the

[3] Thus, among the resolutions for 1940 and 1942, we find: "Our Lady: angelus: rosary", etc. In 1943, "Better prepared meditation".

[4] He made his last retreat in New York (Aug. 1954) when he returned from his last visit to France.

[5] 1940 and 1944.

essential limpidity, he ceaselessly purifies his affections, rejecting even the slightest opacity in which the light might falter or be dimmed."

Similarly, he sometimes notes what he believes to be his shortcomings in his exercise of his apostolate, in particular (this recurs on several occasions) a certain lack of gentleness, innate in his temperament,[6] that might have repelled a number of souls. On another occasion (during his 1943 retreat) he wonders "by what sign" he will be recognized "as having come from God"; and this sign, he answers, is first and foremost "gentleness".[7] From various remarks in his letters and other writings, since the First World War, this was a point on which one suspects he often questioned himself. Thus in 1915, "May our Lord be seen in all that we do, in his kindness and great love, that is what I ask of him"; and in 1916, "My need is great to steep my soul in him again, so that I may have more faith, more devotion, more kindness";[8] and again in 1934, "May the Lord preserve in me a great gentleness."[9]

It is not surprising that he should have felt the necessity for this insistent prayer—even though it was of him that it has been said that he was "good, good beyond the ordinary standard",[10] and again that he indeed loved his neighbour in the Gospel sense, since he knew how to forgive.[11] The

[6] Cf. letter of 4 Aug. 1916: "I can't help realizing that my own nature is much more that of the drill that bores a way for the advance of progress rather than the oil that eases it". (*Making of a Mind*, p. 117).

[7] "1. Gentleness, peace, before everything. 2. To love better, to fear less. 3. Disinterestedness."

[8] *Making of a Mind*, pp. 75, 105. Cf. May 1915: "Gentleness is our first source of strength, the first also, perhaps, of the visible virtues. I have always been sorry when I have allowed harshness or contempt to show—and yet it is so agreeable a temptation". (p. 55).

[9] *Letters from a Traveller*, p. 206. On 7 Feb. 1930, he wrote from Tientsin, to say that he would soon be returning to France: "Morally, I think you'll find me (in the autumn, I hope) exactly the same—perhaps more gentle."

[10] Pierre Leroy, in *Letters from a Traveller*, p. 15.

[11] Mme Solange Lemaître, *In Memoriam, Cahiers*, II, p. 151.

fact is, that he had too lofty and just a concept of the meaning of charity, in its various forms, to believe, as some do, that all one needs to practise it is to surrender to the kindly promptings of an affectionate nature, or to trust to the mysterious affinities of human love. Teilhard knew that this left the door open to an extremely insidious and serious difficulty, since "our Lord's essential precept", of which he has given us an example in his Incarnation, is something very different. It is more like the "revelation of a mystery".[12] "Purity", he had written in 1917, "lies at the base of renunciation and mortification. And Charity, still more."[13] This was something that Teilhard continued to understand ever more clearly.[14]

As the years went by, Père Teilhard asked himself more urgently whether the constant tension of his being towards him whose coming he desired through all and above all, was not turning into too intellectual a form of search. He was afraid that it might be damaging to "communion", by which he meant recollection in the presence of God already present in a hidden form.[15] He then reminded himself of the necessity to "progress from speculation to practice"; though this did not prevent him, in a "contemplation *ad amorem*" from crying out in wonder, "Omega = The Great Coherence!" At one point he notes that "overflowing faith in being" is still strong in him, and gives thanks for this.[16] At another time

[12] Cf. *Le Milieu Divin; Making of a Mind*, pp. 117, 118, 134.

[13] *La Lutte contre la Multitude.*

[14] See M. Barthélemy-Madaule's short but careful study, *Teilhard de Chardin et l'amour du prochain*, in *Foi vivante*, 1964, pp. 44-9.

[15] As a parallel, we may note the advice he gave in a letter of 25 Jan. 1924: "Your true strength will always lie in the spiritual tension you can contrive to maintain in yourself, through thought and through contact with God."

[16] On 24 Jan. 1929, he wrote from Obock: "After a period of eclipse in physical restlessness, I feel that I am in good form. By which I mean that I am conscious, with sufficient intensity, of the 'appetite for being'. Once again, the great animating Providence, to which it is such a relief to resign oneself, seems, like a mother, to have harmonized around me the interior and exterior forces of the world." (In this, as in other passages, the care taken in the use of a capital or small initial for "being" will be noted.)

he wonders, with some distress, what can be the source of the "weariness of God" that even those who believe and pray the most ardently sometimes experience, and he prays that he may be allowed to emerge "beyond this weariness". He notes that he finds it impossible to live without "the appetite for God", and records the "distress" he sometimes suffers at the moment he "embarks on the pure Omega", by which he means "withdraws into God alone".[17]

This, in fact—"re-entry into Christ Jesus"—was the purpose of the first day of the retreat. It was characterized by a new "effort to know more deeply, or at least to recapture the Presence". It was a "day of re-establishment in the Presence", and during the subsequent days he immersed himself so far as he could—in a spirit of faith—in that "Sacred Presence".

Day of re-establishment in the Presence. This, for me, is the real Foundation.[18] Really to believe that you exist, my God. That's where the whole difficulty lies—for everyone, I imagine. If you're "lukewarm", it's because you refuse to take a chance on what's uncertain or insubstantial. Oh! who will give us back the real, *consistent* God! . . .

The specific strength of a Retreat, lies in *making God real again* in life.[19]

The true Foundation is not a logical relationship . . . that relationship is evident. . . . What we lack is the sense of the Reality

[17] 1939 and 1940 Retreats. Letter of 13 Oct. 1939. Cf. 30 July 1918 (*Making of a Mind*, p. 223). 1950 Retreat: "I am still circling around the Presence without feeling myself possessed by it. This is, of course, largely my own fault. For some months research has been more important to me than communion. But can I love without 'understanding'? . . . All the same, I must find some line of advance . . . within the Presence." Cf. Blondel, 8 Feb. 1891: "Because I now feel . . . a sort of weariness of God . . ." (*Carnets intimes*, p. 387).

[18] The "Principle and Foundation" serve as a sort of introduction to the *Spiritual Exercises* of St Ignatius, and normally provide the subject for the opening meditation of the retreat.

[19] It is to be hoped that no reader will conclude that Teilhard puts forward retreats as being "God-producing", as Blondel has recently been accused of doing for "action".

of God, it is complete Faith. . . . *Domine, fac me videre,—fac me Te videre!*[20]

Thus, beyond—never normally this side of—all the intellectual fabric he built up, all his hypotheses, all the roads he sought to make plain for his fellow men, Teilhard tried always to adhere to the "one thing that is necessary", the *unum necessarium*—for which he used a number of synonyms: the "Unique Necessary", the "Unique Interest", the "Omnipresent", the "Pan-consistent" (or "Pan-substantial"), the "Pan-sufficient", He without whom man can do nothing ("*sine me, nihil potestis facere*"). One of the means he used to penetrate more fully this primal truth was what he called "the exercise of inconsistence".[21]

Completely dependent on him; in my cohesiveness, in my action —in my very perception of Him and passion for Him. If the beam[22] turns away I fall back into dust and darkness. The total, the limitless dependence: to "founder in it", so that one may expand one's being in *abandonment*, and strive in an effort of *purity* and *fidelity*. . . .

My God, from whom I depend even in such yearning as I can have for you. . . .

Maybe it is inevitable, maybe it is well, and necessary, that I should feel at every moment as though I can advance no further, never sure of the next step. . . .

To accept and love the feeling of total inconsistence.

O Creative Flow, Consolidating, expanding, with all deliberation I dedicate and abandon myself to your universal and deep-seated influences! O God, my consistence![23]

[20] 1939, 1944, 1954 Retreats. Letter of 30 Oct. 1943. Cf. 13 Nov. 1916: "The Realities of faith are not felt with the same solidity as those of experience" (*Making of a Mind*, p. 145) 9 May 1940: "to give to God, as his Saints do, the true value of reality". (*Letters from a Traveller*, p. 264).

[21] Inconsistence: In 1918 Teilhard had described this (in *La Foi qui opère*) as "fragility" and "contingence".

[22] A little earlier he had compared the illuminating action of God to a "beam of light" which shines "wherever He wishes: *Domine, illumina me!*"

[23] 1940 and 1945 Retreats. Cf. St Augustine, *Confessions*, I, ii, c. 30, n. 40: "Solidabor in Te, in forma mea" ("I shall take on consistence and solidity in You").

"Without our Lord", he said to himself elsewhere, "—if he lets me fall, I become a cipher".—"Without *Him*, nothing". Thus, during his retreat, Teilhard sought a more intense and "pure" union with Him for whom alone his intelligence worked: *Jesus solus*, *solus Jesus*, Jesus alone, only Jesus was for him, the "unique essential".

> Jesus, in fuller consistence, be to me peace, appetite, serenity!
> Oh yes! The dizziness of fragility, of instability! . . . And yet there is still the all-embracing Hand and Heart of the Universal Christ: "Come to me once more, walking on the insubstantial and moving waters! Why are you afraid, *modicae fidei*"?[24]

Thus Père Teilhard engaged, as St Ignatius recommends the retreatant to do, in an intimate dialogue with Jesus, after having first meditated on him in a Gospel scene—in the temptation in the desert, for example, or in the Transfiguration, the visit to Bethany, or the last interview with St Peter—or in one of the grand visions of the Apocalypse, or perhaps after once again quietly probing the teaching of the prologue to St John's Gospel or of some great Pauline text. He was particularly fond of the Gospel account of Peter walking on the waters to meet Jesus.[25] Often, too, his thoughts about our Lady recur in brief notes, associated with a reminder of the importance of purity, prayer, and trust. At the end of his 1945 retreat, the concluding offering-up to our Lord, "*Sume et suscipe* . . ." is prefaced by a "consecration to the Blessed Virgin": "*O Domina mea* . . ."; and as, when meditating on the Incarnation of the Word, he would associate Mary with Jesus, so he would associate with him this other mother, *Mater Ecclesia*, to whom he clung, from whom he "depended",

[24] 1939, 1945, 1948 Retreats. Cf. 22 Jan. 1916: "What should we not be able to do, to give up, if we believe in Jesus Christ?" (*Making of a Mind*, pp. 91–2).

[25] Cf. H. Urs von Balthasar: "With no more than the hope of a believer, we can dare to leave the ship with St Peter and so make our way to the living infinity of the Spirit of God" (*Le Saint-Esprit, l'inconnu au-delà du Verbe*, in *Lumière et Vie*, 1964, p. 121).

as he says, like a "phylum of love", in spite of many "tangible, modern, manifestations that conflict with what, thanks to her, I adore".[26]

Meditating on the Epiphany, he notes that the Wise Men were faithful in following the star that shone before them; so, too, he thought, should he be faithful in following his "special vocation".[27] "My incentive", he says, "(self-given and so continually unsatisfied) is the passion for Omega, for Omegalization", the passion to reveal and make known Omega.[28] He then asks himself how he stands on the spiritual road— for so many years he has been striving to define this *via tertia*, driven to do so as much by an imperative interior need as by his apostolic zeal, and linking it ever more closely with his view of cosmic evolution; already, too, he had explained this "third road" to Maurice Blondel and defended it, at the same time expressing it more precisely, against the objections or doubts that had become apparent to him.[29] As he was now seeing it, as he would like to find it, it is a road of "emergence". He traces it without hesitation between the Charybdis of "minimizing" and the Scylla of "involvement": "not a timid, neutral, middle way, but a bold higher way, in which the values and properties of the other two ways are combined and correct one another".[30] He has no anxiety about his principle; he well knows that it is no easy principle, and he has always been aware, ever since he put it into words in *Forma Christi* in 1918, that "already the effort of spiritual attachment to the natural Universe is a matter of pressing urgency, and imposes strict austerity on the faithful". He cultivates the "appetite for renunciation". He continues to seek to "centre himself for Christ" that he may be "excentred

---

[26] 1944, 1945 and other Retreats.
[27] 1940 Retreat, fourth day: "Epiphany. *Stella : Jesus-Mary.* Grace: to follow *my* light, my special vocation".
[28] 1940, second day.
[29] Cf. *Archives de Philosophie*, Jan.–March 1961.
[30] *L'Atomisme de l'Esprit* (1941); *Œuvres*, VII, p. 63.

on Him".[31] Teilhard has never changed since the day when
he described the dispositions in which his meditations
on Verdun and the Chemin des Dames had confirmed
him:

> I am now more sharply aware that for the rest of my life my
> task is to develop within myself, humbly, faithfully, doggedly—
> and at the same time to impart it as much as possible to others—
> the sort of mysticism that makes one seek passionately for God in
> the heart of every substance and every action. Never have I so
> clearly seen how God alone, and no personal effort, can open
> our eyes to this light and preserve this vision in us. And never,
> on the other hand, have I understood so fully how much the
> practice of this particular science of divinizing life calls for the
> diligent co-operation of every form of activity I engage in. It
> needs the sacraments, and prayer, and study: all these directed
> to the same concrete, very precise, end.[32]

The difficulty, however, lies in realizing what he has conceived. How is he to follow this road, of which he is certain
that it is God's road? With sharp clarity, he asks himself
whether in practice it may not develop into "a perpetual
compromise". Hence his criterion: does it lead, as effectively
as the road of total separation, "to renunciation and peace"?[33]
He does not believe that he is entirely safe from being side-
tracked, nor that he is always sure of his position. At the same
time, his self-examination reassures him, and he perseveres
along his road.[34]

[31] Cf. *Le Cœur de la Matière* (1950), p. 28. Here we have the basic pattern of
activity and passivity, corresponding to that of attachment and detachment.

[32] *Making of a Mind*, pp. 190–1. In his last essay, *Le Christique*, Père Teilhard
repeats this in more categorical, and hence more debatable, terms: "To coin-
cide, with all one's heart and all one's strength, with the Focus, still diffuse and
yet already in existence, of universal unification".

[33] 1944, fourth day.

[34] Père Philippe de la Trinité (*op. cit.*, p. 113) condemns this *via tertia* only
because, instead of trying to understand it, he "logically", or "in sound logic",
derives from it all sorts of "roads". He is good enough to admit that this conclusion does not meet "the author's intentions". To put it, however, more
simply, Teilhard taught nothing of the sort.

Similarly, Père Teilhard turns his attention to the allied responsibilities of his priesthood and his intellectual work. Remembering that St Ignatius and his first companions, as St Francis of Assisi earlier, had already "caught the attention of the world by 'Gesture'," he prays humbly and lovingly to our Lord: "Jesus, teach me the gesture that reveals the Omega!"—"Jesus, help me to make the gesture, to find the word, to give the example that will most clearly reveal you!" —"O Jesus, grant that I may end well, that I may end in a gesture of witness sealing my life's affirmation and faith in a Pole of Love to which the Universal current flows!" Again, and with even greater humility, we find this pathetic cry— which may encourage some of Père Teilhard's critics, though I should be happier to believe that it will help to silence them: "Jesus, take me to you in good time, before I spoil anything for you!"[35] And the prayer he said in secret forgot none of those whom Divine Providence had, in any capacity, put in his path:

> Why did I feel distress this evening for all those I love, and have lost, or who are growing old, or are far away? Have I done enough for them? ... I confide them to You, Lord. Bring *all* close to You, and give life to us all.[36]

Again, when he felt his strength was failing, he prayed, "*Usque ad senectam et senium ne derelinquas me, Domine.*"— "He must grow greater in my life, in my Reality, and my interior World, *as I grow less.*"[37]—"To accept, to love interior fragility, and old age, with its long shadows, and the ever-shrinking days ahead. ... To love diminishment and decline".—A final aspiration, in which so many others

---

[35] 1940, 1948, 1949 Retreats. Cf. 1945: "If I make the 'gesture', it will be because our Lord, by a gracious intervention, makes me do so".

[36] 1939 Retreat. These words bring to mind what he wrote on 24 Dec. 1915, speaking of the "blessed oneness of God, in which all things and all persons are embraced, with absolute certainty and permanence" (*Making of a Mind*, p. 84).

[37] 1939 and 1944 Retreats.

are echoed: "To plunge into the bottomless depths of Faith!"[38]

Père Teilhard's last resolution, made on the last day of his 1954 Retreat (26 August) was, "Abandonment to the End".[39]

[38] 1944, 1945, 1946 Retreats.

[39] "This retreat", he wrote on 29 Aug., "will, I hope, have brought me closer to Him, who draws ever closer". (*Letters from a Traveller*, p. 352).

12

DEFENSIO FIDEI

WE have just seen how Père Teilhard, first and foremost a religious, lived and prayed. And yet some critics, not content with completely rejecting his thought, as they are perfectly entitled to do, on the ground that it is "primary evolution", and expressing their fear of its influence as being "to the utmost degree pernicious", carry their attack to the heart even of his faith. Their zeal to protect the deposit of the faith is no doubt entirely laudable, and we share it. But they go too far, or rather the line they follow is completely mistaken.

One critic seems to regard it his duty to convince us—in somewhat roundabout, but nevertheless unmistakable terms—that according to Père Teilhard God did not really exist, since he could only become a personal God, as he understands Père Teilhard's teaching, at the term of the Universe's cosmic process of personalization! Refusing the evidence of countless absolutely explicit and clear passages available to everyone—not bothering to consult those best qualified to interpret Père Teilhard's thought[1]—blind to all the psychological improbabilities he thereby piles up—he claims to detect some more or less hidden contradiction in the simple words "personal Universe".[2] We should bring to the notice of this

[1] For example, M. Barthélemy-Madaule, *Bergson et Teilhard de Chardin* (1963), pp. 492 ff.

[2] Mgr André Combes, *Teilhardogenèse?* (*Ephémérides carmeliticae*, 1963, p. 172 note 41); *La Pensée Catholique*, 1963, p. 60, note 41. The same conclusion must be drawn from a passage by M. Claude Cuénot: '*Enfant terrible!*' If the

critic just one of many passages, taken from Teilhard's most important and best-known work:

> Neither an ideal centre, nor a potential centre, nor anything of that nature, could suffice. A present and real Noosphere must have a present and real Centre. To be supremely attractive, Omega must be supremely present. . . . If by its very nature it were not outside the Time and Space it brings together, it would not be Omega.—Autonomy, actuality, irreversibility, and finally transcendence, those are the four attributes of Omega.[3]

The same critic adds that if anyone wished to "convince him that this controversial Jesuit believed in Jesus Christ", he would feel himself constrained to answer, "I should be very glad to be reassured on that point"; and yet he apparently does not feel it necessary to give any indication of a positive reason for his doubt.[4] Everything that Père Teilhard wrote before his sixties, unless it can be given an objectionable interpretation, is rejected in advance, as prior to what is mysteriously called "the inexorable unfolding of his destiny", and as having little importance compared with what is taken

---

personal-Universe is God, if the personal-Universe is the final point attained by this 'universe on the road to psychic concentration' which is 'identical with a Universe which is being personalized', God is personal only at the term of the Universe's personalization." We know the significance in French of 'enfant terrible'. In making so grave an accusation against a Catholic priest, not a single passage, not a single word he wrote has been quoted in justification. Rather than trying to force an objectionable interpretation upon a few lines written by a so-called 'enfant terrible', would it not have been better to have gone back to what Père Teilhard actually wrote? In a letter of 18 Jan. 1936 he explains what he means by the title Univers personnel: '[I am thinking of getting on paper] when I have time, the essay I'm dreaming about at the moment: A personal Universe (I can't manage to find as short an equivalent in French).' This essay was printed at Peiping in 1937 (in English) under the title, A personalistic Universe. (My English friends tell me that Le Cœur de la Matière [The Heart of Matter] is a more characteristically English than French title.)

[3] Cf. The Phenomenon of Man, pp. 269–71; Du Cosmos à la Cosmogenèse (1951); Œuvres, VII, p. 271, etc.

[4] Ephémérides . . ., p. 189; La Pensée Catholique, p. 77: "[Attempts have been made] to convince us that this controversial Jesuit believed in Jesus Christ. We should be very glad to be reassured on that point, but we do not see him living."

to be his "essential message", or, even more, as being simply an example of "novice's Thomism" or "the fervour of a young priest".[5]

Others believe that they can confront Père Teilhard with the proud profession of faith, "For us, the babe of Bethlehem, in as much as he is the Word made flesh, is to be adored"[6]— as though they, too, had never been able to read any of the texts—all openly published, and all unmistakably expressed— in which the man they accuse said exactly the same thing with equal force. As though Teilhard had not written of the mystery of the Annunciation and the Incarnation of the Word with peculiar precision and beauty![7] As though he had not celebrated the humano-divine contact manifested in the Epiphany of Jesus![8] Yet neither these words nor others equally clear are given any weight against a few lines, taken out of their context, that might be made to lend themselves to a systematically hostile interpretation.[9]

[5] *Op. cit.*, pp. 188–9, 192, 191 and n. The author, after saying, "We need pursue the matter no further", goes on to point out "all the same" that "after November or December 1946 Père Teilhard de Chardin entered into friendly relations with Julian Huxley". Into what mysterious depths is the reference to so simple a fact supposed to introduce us? We know that Père Teilhard's *Singularités de l'espèce humaine* was written as an "indirect reply" to Huxley and other scientists (G. Simpson, Charles Galton-Darwin, J. Rostand—Cf. letter of 16 Jan. 1964). See also *Le Christique*, p. 7, where Huxley's utopian views are directly discussed: also letter of 11 July 1951, *Letters from a Traveller*, pp. 304–5.

[6] Mgr Charles Journet, *Nova et Vetera*, 1958, pp. 227–8; *ibid,.* 1962, p. 226, where he expresses his surprise that his accusation should have been contested.

[7] See above, p. 64.

[8] *Milieu Divin*, p. 116 and context. Cf. Introduction to *La Vie Chrétienne* (1944): "To suppress the historicity of Christ, that is to say the divinity of the historic Christ, would mean that all the mystical energy accumulated in the past two thousand years in the Christian phylum immediately evaporates into the unreal. Christ born of the Virgin, and Christ risen from the dead: the two are one indivisible whole." Letter of 1 Jan. 1917: "I was surprised to find Péguy so close to me (he would be too modest to put it the other way round). His care to defend and exalt the "fleshly cradle" of Christ corresponds with what interests me most intimately."

[9] "Why should we look to Judaea of two thousand years ago? . . . No, what I cry out for, like every being, with all my life and even all my earthly passion, is

Another accusation, again in contradiction of the evidence, is that this dangerous man was a tempter who offered the masses "an immediate, seductive, intoxicating, solution, a sure means of reuniting 'all the kingdoms of the earth and all their glory'"; the suggestion is that he invites mankind to "hope for salvation ... by trusting to the resources of its will for power": a pathetic appeal is accordingly made to mankind to "turn its back on the temptation" as Christ did in the desert; and men are reminded of the dogmatic truth that "their supreme hope comes not from themselves but from God"![10] As though this new Prometheus, this Nietzschean, as they accuse him of being, this second Satan had not more than once himself anathematized the "ancient pride of the Titans", and denounced the temptation of Prometheus as that of "Babel" and "Faust"! and as though, with all the clarity that words can convey, he had not, addressing his Lord—and this in the very essay to which exception is taken—written: "From you, all enterprises derive, and of

---

far from being an equal to cherish: it is a God to adore." Had the beginning of the paragraph from which this was quoted been included, it would not have been so open to misrepresentation: "There are some who think they can increase your attraction in my eyes by extolling, almost to the exclusion of all else, the charms and excellences of the human form in which you were clothed of old. ..." (*Milieu Divin*, p. 127). Cf. *Messe sur le Monde* (*Hymne de l'Univers*, p. 33). Similar expressions can be found in writers whose faith has never been under any suspicion. They derive from a spiritual current that has continually been present in the Church since St Paul's famous saying, "I seek not to know Christ according to the flesh." One can recognize that it sometimes appears in various exaggerated forms, but it is a far cry from so doing to bringing an accusation of such gravity. Particularly appropriate in this connection is a fine discussion in Père Victor Poucel's *Le Sacrament de Jérusalem* (1919), pp. 58–67—he was a colleague and friend of Père Teilhard—in which he comments on St Paul's words, and, in essentials, echoes Père Teilhard's thought.—Apart from that, one can well imagine the sort of insipid and doctrinally unsatisfying piety Teilhard met in his youth, and which could have stimulated the reaction expressed in the lines quoted.

[10] *Id.*, *La vision Teilhardienne du monde*, *Divinitas*, 1959, p. 344. Cf. Matthew, 4. 8.

those the first is my prayer." [11] As though, again, he had not, precisely in connection with salvation, often expressed in many different ways the conviction that: "all that human activity can do, is to cultivate humility of disposition and accept in humility". "The attitude that brings us fully into the truth is that of the Presentation, by which we humbly expose ourselves to the radiance of the Infinite Being." If we are to desire God, he said, "God must first give us the wish to do so; and even our desire is powerless: 'the soul will never see God unless God looks to the soul'; and then again the soul is still powerless to raise herself up to the beam that plays on her and to bathe in its radiance. For it is written: No one comes to me unless I take him and draw him into me." [12] During his last years, Père Teilhard was constantly returning in his meditation to the saying of Jesus, "Without me you can do nothing."

To turn now to a writer who claims to have made a strange discovery in Père Teilhard's work: he sees in it an indication that in our day "the desire to imitate God we find in Aristotle has given way to the desire to find a substitute for him". Has not Teilhard written that, "only Man can enable Man to read the secret of the World"? Has he not prophesied that the time is approaching when we shall "master the hidden laws of Biogenesis"? This is sufficient to justify M. Jean Brun in associating Teilhard with Feuerbach in the assertion that "there is no God for man, other than man himself". At first, anyone who reads such a criticism would think that he must be dreaming—and blame himself for taking it seriously—until he realized that it was put forward by a writer of repute and

[11] *La Foi en l'Homme* (1947), *Œuvres*, V. p. 238; *La Mystique de la Science* (1939), *Œuvres*, VI, p. 233; *La Messe sur le Monde* (*Hymne de l'Univers*, p. 21); *Science et Christ* (1921); Letter of 2 Feb. 1916 (*Making of a Mind*, p. 92); *La Lutte contre la Multitude*, p. 19: "It is not the pride of strength, but evangelical sanctity, that preserves and keeps in motion the true effort of Evolution."

[12] *Le Milieu mystique* (1917). Cf. 1948 Retreat, fourth day: "The Supreme Virtue: total trust."

appeared in a serious review, the *Revue d'histoire et de philosophie religieuse*.[13] One can only hope that if M. Jean Brun
becomes more fully acquainted with Père Teilhard's writings,
he will have no difficulty in understanding the truth of the
matter: the explanation of the universe by man "the spearhead
of the world in growth" is not an attempt to substitute man
for the Creator; it is a reassertion, in answer to materialistic
science or to what is simply a superficial and unenterprising
classification, of "the unique value of Man", and, in Père
Teilhard's thought, it represents, as it does in actual reality,
an essential stage on the road that leads, or leads back to,
God.[14] In making us realize "the extraordinary singularity
of the human event" and thus enabling us to see in man "the
key to evolution", Père Teilhard begins by pointing out to
us "the higher Term which directs the progress of hominization".[15]

Other criticisms have, indeed, been less unbalanced, but
are still far from being fair. One writer begins by admitting
that the passages he quotes might possibly be regarded as
"cases of clumsy or exaggerated expression"; to justify that
view of them, he adds, however, "we should be able to produce other passages that explicitly re-state them in the correct
light of tradition".[16] In point of fact, such passages, although
this writer never seems to have suspected it, were ready to
hand and unmistakably evident. The passages on which his
criticism is based were, in the first place, so mangled that they
do in fact produce an almost disturbing effect.[17] Thus, again,

[13] 1964, p. 126: *Technique et Aliénation*. Cf. Teilhard, *Œuvres*, VI, p. 26, and
Le Groupe Zoologique humain, p. 147.
[14] Cf. *Pensée religieuse*, pp. 106–12 and 233–47.
[15] *L'Hominisation*, *Œuvres*, III, pp. 75–111.
[16] Dom Georges Frénaud, *op. cit.*, p. 38.
[17] *Loc. cit.* Why should passages be picked out and mangled, unless the critic is
anxious to destroy the writer's reputation? On 12 Dec. 1919, Père Teilhard had
written, in answer to Maurice Blondel: "In the first place, there are two essential points on which M. Blondel and I are completely in agreement. (a) Most
important of all (as is obvious), on the fact that Christ must be loved as a World,

he assures us, on the evidence of these distorted quotations, that the "essence of the spiritual approach" of this grievously misguided Jesuit is "to go to the world", and to "go to Christ only because he is the centre of the World's evolution". One wonders how anyone can be so blind to so much that Père Teilhard wrote: in this very letter, for example, whose meaning is so misrepresented, we find a sentence that entirely contradicts what Dom Frénaud says: "So long as Christ is a World to me, the only definitive World, it matters little to me, in short, that his omnipresent action on me is characterized by a break-up, an extinction,

---

or rather as the World, by which I mean as the physical centre of final determination and true 'consistence' imposed on all of Creation that is destined to survive. (b) But also [. . .] on the capital and definitive role (by no means 'simply penitential') of renunciation and ascesis in the construction of the new Universe, etc." (*Archives de Philosophie*, 1961, p. 135). Dom Frénaud begins his quotation with the words "Christ must be loved, etc." but ends before (b) without giving the least suggestion of the context. It is rather as though someone said, "Man is (a) animal, and (b) rational" and was quoted as saying simply, "Man is animal". The words introduced by (b) specify what is said in (a). Moreover, has Dom Frénaud realized, or does he allow his reader to realize, that Teilhard is here summarizing the points on which he is, "as is obvious", in agreement with Blondel, an agreement that Blondel would not dispute? If that is so, the same accusation should be made against Blondel. Finally, the prejudice that has induced Dom Frénaud to mangle the text blinds him to the meaning of the words he quotes. He thinks that Teilhard means that Christ should be loved "as the World", i.e. as this World, the World of experience, the World we refer to when we simply say "the World"; going further, he even thinks that it is this World itself that would be loved for itself, Christ being but a means. Teilhard, in fact, immediately expresses his thought more exactly, and it can be seen without a shadow of doubt that he is speaking of what St John calls "the new heaven and the new earth", of what Teilhard himself, a few lines later, calls "the new Universe", and, even more precisely, of Him, who is its "physical centre of ultimate determination and true consistence". This completely upsets the order of precedence that Dom Frénaud claims to read into the text. It is not in this perfectly legitimate sense that he speaks of "going to the world" as being, he says, "the essence of Teilhard's spiritual approach". This, indeed, is the extreme of distortion. It is, accordingly, hardly surprising that Dom Frénaud has been so governed by his prejudice as to be unable to find other passages (among the many that are available) to contradict his interpretation— nor that, misquoting the title of *Hymne de l'Univers*, he makes of it a hymn *to* the Universe.

of the visible World,—or, conversely, of a transformation." [18]

There is something distasteful in having to bring up such matters. But these attacks on Père Teilhard have been published so widely and so insistently, and have reached so large an audience, that to be silent would be a disservice to our faith: for many souls, I fear, may well be tormented by doubt.

From the examples we have given, the prayer and practice of Père Teilhard give a sure indication not only of an uncommon spiritual life but also of a profoundly Catholic spirit. For anyone who really knew him or reads him with an open mind, this goes without saying; and there would be no need to insist on it, had it not been violently challenged. On one occasion (during his 1940 retreat) Père Teilhard was questioning himself about his spiritual life and the orientation of his thought: he noted the twofold "primordial condition" that, in his view, should ensure that they were basically sound— "(1) to be intimately united with Our Lord, and (2) to be intimately united with the Church." This will not automatically produce miracles, and it would, indeed, have been a miracle if a task in many ways so new, should never, in its effort to meet a sudden new situation, have led to a false step. It would have been even more of a miracle, if, in the particular perspective Père Teilhard adopted, which was completely governed by the initial approach to the problem, he had succeeded in solving all the problems, clarifying all the aspects of the real, and embracing all perspectives in a complete synthesis. Perfect Catholicity is an orchestra in which the different instruments complement and, if necessary, correct one another. Those who would seek to appraise Père Teilhard's work, whether to accept it or contest it, in a totalitarian spirit that was completely foreign to the man himself, cannot but distort it. It is the work of one who was no more than human,

[18] *Archives de Philosophie* (1916), p. 137.

and while its influence is wholesome, there can sometimes, and for some people, be some danger in it. The expression is sometimes too compressed, sometimes perhaps over-emphatic, and these, I think, are indications of a thought that is too one-sided.[19] Much that he wrote, accordingly, calls for some corrective; it often needs to be made more precise, it needs something to complement it: and that again is no simple matter, for what complements another, we should remember, is itself incomplete.

Père Teilhard himself was the first to recognize this. He said, for example: "I am trying out this road as a possible line of approach to one of the aspects of truth"; and again: "A spiritual tendency has been trying to shape itself in me, that others, later, will define more successfully than I." Throughout all his life, his modesty and sincerity constantly prompted such remarks. Of a Note, the draft of which he had been obliged, unwillingly, to surrender, he wrote: "All it contains is a number of rough pointers, certainly impracticable as they stand."[20] Of a hastily written essay, which is now freely quoted and which some even consider capital to his thought, he wrote himself, "I know that in this form it is not yet practicable."[21] Of another, one or two sentences from which have been used against him, he said that he had "realized that it needs pretty serious revision".[22] He was perfectly aware, too, that he had not yet, in spite of several times "thinking better of it", found a completely satisfactory way of formulating a hypothesis that might well have been prompted by a correct intuition. It was thus that, without any false shame, he would speak of his "clumsy efforts", his "blunders in research", regretting that there were "so few people" who "were not frightened off" by such things, and wishing that he

[19] I have dealt with this in an earlier book, and need not discuss it here in detail.
[20] Holy Saturday, 1922.
[21] Letter of 7 Jan. 1934.
[22] Letter of 2 Feb. 1940.

could be helped to "see it clearly", wishing, again, that in what he wrote might be distinguished "the elements that could be integrated into a common Summa".[23] The practical results of this spirit of self-questioning were not always, unfortunately, as considerable as we should have wished; but it should be remembered, too, that the points in which his writings are most open to criticism play a very small, and never a central, part in his work.[24] Moreover, he never achieved a definitive formulation of his thought, nor did he ever claim to provide a complete theological or dogmatic exposition. What we look for in Père Teilhard is something quite different.

[23] Letters of 4 July 1940, 18 Feb. 1942, etc.
[24] No serious student of Teilhard could conceive of "teilhardism" as a system whose "meaning" stemmed from a number of mistaken metaphysical principles.

13

LIMITATIONS OF TEILHARD'S WORK

ANY shortcoming or, to put it more fairly, any limitation, should be particularly noted, since it affects the whole body of work; it marks out its boundaries for us, and so explains the chief gaps and onesidedness in his thought of which Père Teilhard has been accused.

If we leave on one side the directly religious or mystical writings, the universe of Teilhard—by which I mean his basic universe, not the universe he is constructing but that from which he starts and is analysing—is the universe of science. Teilhardian man is first and foremost technical and social man. He is not man considered immediately in all his dimensions. Nor is it the concrete universe of naïve consciousness. Initially, then, such a man and such a universe lack a certain depth. In principle, Teilhard is concerned to use his dialectic to restore this to them, but without undertaking himself to probe it to the bottom. Thus, we might say, he forces the order of science and technique to outstrip itself, by attaching man to a higher order, that of reflective consciousness and liberty: this in turn obliges him "to define his attitude to religion" [1]—but his culminating point still bears the marks of his point of origin. Already, in his concept of an "inside" of beings and in the duality which—while excluding any "dualism"—he sees in the cosmic stuff, he preserves intact

---

[1] *Place de la technique*, etc. (1947); Œuvres, VII, p. 169.

total reality;[2] so he arrives again at a universe which, he says, is that of modern science "exactly in reverse"; he re-introduces, or makes it possible to re-introduce, all the values of aesthetics, ethics and religion. However, in studying this "inside", even at the highest level of being, and even when it comes to speaking of "introspection",[3] he adheres to his objective "phenomenology". He leads the reader to the conclusion that the "outside" cannot ultimately be explained except by the "inside", and in all that he writes he seeks to provide a "key" which will make it possible "to explore from the inside the Universe that Physics has hitherto attempted to grasp from the outside."[4] For his own part, Teilhard, true to his point of view as a "physicist", generally stops at the threshold of this interior universe; he is quite content to have opened the door and to look at it and show it from outside, as though he were showing the promised land.

In this lies Teilhard's originality, from which he derives his power, but at the same time it is here that we find his limitation: a limitation in two directions, since he has not a very clear, nor always a very favourable, idea of the field into which he does not enter. No doubt, he has done more in this way to bring interior realities under consideration than if he had simply added his own analysis of them to that of so many others. We know only too well how many really profound books still fail today to make their influence felt, still seem abstract and indecisive, still give many of our contemporarires the impression (even if wrongly) of being purely personal, simply because they neglected the soil in which Teilhard's work is rooted. At the same time, from the converse limitation

[2] Cf. Christian d' Armagnac, *De Blondel à Teilhard*, *Archives de Philosophie*, 1958, pp. 289–312.
[3] Cf. *L'Activation de l'énergie humaine*, *Œuvres*, VII, p. 416; *L'Énergie d'évolution*, p. 385; Les Singularités *de l'espèce humaine*, II, pp. 362–4.
[4] *The Phenomenon of Man*. Cf. *La Pensée religieuse*, Ch. 15.

which we find in the latter, are derived a number of what appear to be converse effects, if not of negation, at least of misunderstanding: and yet all that lies behind it is simply a lack of methodical consideration.

It is thus that the intervention of moral freedom holds a predominant place in his representation of universal evolution; one might almost go so far as to say that it holds an exclusive place: "Nothing truly exists in the Universe except myriads of more or less vague spontaneities, whose close-packed swarm gradually forces the barrier that cuts it off from freedom." [5]. Once the barrier has been forced, Teilhard in no way minimizes the dramatic role of choice that is thereby introduced Starting with man, "evolution has now to make its own choice." [6] Man must choose between revolt and adoration, for his salvation or for his loss: the ineluctable dilemma has to be faced: and does not this mean that at the same time we meet the idea of moral evil with all its formidable specific character? [7] To say that Teilhard refers to "the perils and responsibilities implied by Progress only incidentally and to disarm possible criticism," [8] is to neglect the evidence. He is at great pains not only to justify, but to discover the real basis of "the sense of responsibility", by making apparent to everyone "the true grandeur and gravity of the human condition". [9] Nevertheless, even if Teilhard's doctrine of evolu-

[5] *L'Hominisation* (1923); *Œuvres*, III, p. 103. The whole sentence is italicized.

[6] *Place de la Technique; Œuvres*, VII, p. 168.

[7] Thus it is not the intrinsic ill-will of sin that Père Teilhard overlooks. What he objects to is what he considers the excessive emphasis, in the spiritual attitude of his time, on the fear of evil, compared with the hope and confidence engendered by better action. (In *La Lutte contre la Multitude*, two successive analyses of pain and sin will be found.)

[8] B. Charbonneau, *op. cit.*, p. 120.

[9] *L'Évolution et la responsabilité dans le monde* (1950); *Œuvres*, VII, pp. 214–221. He wishes to hope for a "final convergence", in the unanimity of a free adherence to good: or, at least, he sees this as an "ideal" to which "to orientate our efforts"; he attributes more importance to the converse hypothesis, and he constantly retains the tragic possibility of an evil choice and its consequences. Cf. *The Phenomenon of Man*, pp. 288–90, etc. The first essay he wrote during the

tion leads explicitly to the necessity of an "existential" choice, it is nevertheless true that, in the most systematized part of his teaching, the "objective" consideration is always paramount. In this doctrine, in spite of some pointed references, there is nothing resembling the working out of an "existential anthropology". We may note, and even regret this, but we should not hold it against Teilhard. The "physicist" that he remained until the end in his examination of the "phenomenon" (even if he thought it necessary to invade the field of metaphysics) immediately steps back, and again looks at the development of man's history from the "outside", as he did for the development of natural history. Then, he tells us, "over the world, so marvellously spontaneous, sentient, and subtly differentiated by human relations now appreciated on our own scale, there spreads, from the distance at which we stand, the impersonal, geometric veil of a new Matter".[10] For the "relaxing" of our spirit allows it to sink down towards matter,[11] and this "relaxing" is evidently more important now, in the progress of existence, than the moments of high tension. "The Second Matter", continues our observer from outside, constituted by the "philosophical determinisms" and "social mechanisms" that become paramount in proportion as man allows the vital urge—now transformed into freedom —to subside within him.[12] And it is then that he spoke of the inevitable wastage of evolution; it is in this context that are introduced the notions of the "play of large

---

1914 war (was it ever completed?) consisted of "Reflections on the problem of evil"; this subject was continually in his mind, and he understood that beneath the problem he hoped to solve there still lay a "mystery". Cf. letters of 6 Aug. 1915 and 29 Jan. 1917 (*Making of a Mind*, pp. 61, 174); *L'Hominisation, Œuvres*, III, pp. 106–7.

[10] *The Phenomenon of Man.*

[11] *La Lutte*, I.

[12] *La Crise présente, Études*, 20 Oct. 1937, pp. 163–4. Cf. *The Phenomenon of Man*, p. 94.

numbers", or of "statistical necessity" or "statistical evil".[13]

From the objective point of view, as so defined, evil is considered as an "evolutionary by-product" resulting from "resistances to the spiritual ascent inherent in matter".[14] We see that there can be "no order in process of formation that does not, at all its stages, involve disorder", and, in consequence we see that evil, moral as well as physical, is involved in the structure of a world in process of becoming. All this, however, could be said without, from another point of view, the idea of freedom, of good and evil, and of sin, being thereby impugned. "Statistical necessity does not imply obligation, nor do away with freedom."[15] A "universe that is becoming interiorized" is "by the same process" a "Universe that sins", and already in the animal kindgom we find a distant analogy with what, in man, will be strictly sin, just as spontaneity prefigures and prepares the emergence of freedom.[16]

[13] *Mon Univers* (1924), p. 7; *The Phenomenon of Man*, postscript; *Comment je vois*, no. 30 (1948); *La Pensée du Père Teilhard de Chardin par lui-même* (1948); *Les Études philosophiques* (1955), p. 582.

[14] *Le Christ évoluteur*, p. 7. Cf. G. Crespy, *op. cit.*, p. 130: "Teilhard had the brilliant audacity to include consciousness in the phenomenal world, and thereby was compelled to understand evil as a phenomenon."

[15] "It is statistically necessary that when a large number of letters are posted, some mistakes will occur, stamps forgotten, wrongly addressed, etc. At the same time everyone who sends a letter is free not to make a mistake". (*Études philosophiques*, 1955, p. 581). Cf. *L'Analyse de la Vie* (1945); *Œuvres*, VII, p. 145. Cf. Jacques Maritain, *Dieu et la permission du mal* (1963), p. 5: "It is inevitable, necessary, certain, that in a town full of hot-tempered people, a quarrel will break out, some time, between some two. But it is not inevitable, nor necessary, nor certain that at any given moment a quarrel will break out between any two given people." It will be remembered, too, that both St Augustine and St Thomas have on more than one occasion been accused of reducing freedom and moral evil to mere fictions: for example, by Charles Renouvier, in *L'Année philosophique*, 1897 (1898), pp. 13–15.

[16] Letter of 2 Jan. 1925: "See how the animals behave (monkeys, for example, or even certain insects): we see them doing things that are materially culpable, and only need the emergence of a fuller consciousness to become fully reprehensible."

In these last considerations the two points of view are implicitly brought together.

They come together—but it is still true that it is only the first of the two that is developed for its own sake. Even though we have no right to hold this against Père Teilhard, it is nevertheless important to appreciate that, for that very reason, his thought is still incomplete—much more so, indeed, than he seems to have realized. He never attempted a philosophical synthesis outside the points of view he adopted, and they were dictated by an objective science. Nor did he attempt a similar Christian synthesis. Had he done so, he would have been obliged to allow more room to the drama of sin, and all that it entails. A few scattered passages in his writing, particularly in the *Milieu Divin* show that he would have been willing to attempt such syntheses. However, he took a different view of what was required of him. Thus, to use an expression borrowed again from the scientific field—suggested by a friend who is familiar with Père Teilhard's thought,[17] we can find in him hardly a trace of that "super-natural—or trans-natural—entrophy" which, in the lives of each of us, and until the final consummation, continues to provide a disconcerting obstruction that Christ alone can remove.

At the same time we may say, using, this time, Père Teilhard's own words, that he thereby allows—or rather leads us to recognize—"complete freedom to theology" (but first also, to another Phenomenology than his own) "to work out more exactly and examine more deeply the data or suggestions (which, beyond a certain point, are always ambiguous) provided by objective experience."[18] This remark is of central importance. We should add, that if we wish to be quite certain in our minds about the whole of Père Teilhard's personal attitude to these problems, and are really to get to the heart of his thought, we must, as we are now trying to do, closely

[17] Père Dmitri Michaelides.
[18] Cf. *The Phenomenon of Man*: appendix, p. 311.

examine his spiritual writings and try, in them, to overhear the words of his prayer.

Now that we have seen the nature of the limitation dealt with above, we may well proceed to note that in our "mutating"[19] world, in the course of this "change of era" that Teilhard diagnosed so rapidly and with such force,[20] nothing was more opportune and urgent than the attempt to find a new way to open this new world to the revelation of Jesus Christ that it seems so unwilling to accept. Other forms of thought probe further into the depths of metaphysics or the more mysterious treasure house of revelation. Others again, and these are many, are apparently better balanced, more incontestable, suggest no disturbing prospect to the reader and dig no pit into which he may fall. On the other hand, we should take to heart the wise remark of a German theologian, Fr Karl Rahner: "It is all very well to warn readers of the dangers in Teilhardian teaching and the false interpretations that may be applied to it, but it would be better still to be more concerned to construct a sound view of the faith based on the temper of the modern world."[21]

It may well be, too, that Père Teilhard was often, through circumstances over which he had no control, in an atmosphere

[19] Jean Corbon, *L'Expérience chrétienne dans la Bible* (1964), p. 41.

[20] *L'Hominisation* (1923); *Œuvres*, III, p. 107.

[21] *La Foi du prêtre, aujourd'hui* (Katholikentag, Hanover, 1962). "This does not mean," Fr Rahner explains, "that we must accept without question the ideas of the non-Christian world we live in; on the contrary, this effort can be reconciled with a profound transformation of contemporary ideas." The world of today, he says, is "the indivisibly vast, and continually growing, world of the natural sciences, in which man is still trying to determine his own place, the world of rational and technical levelling, the world of implacable laws, of everything that is precise; the world of community; the world cut off from God, in which the underlying divine activity must be searched for and appreciated in a new way; the world in which the activity of God seems almost always hidden by that of the world itself; the world in which religion is subject to countless terrestrial regulations; the world, finally, that feels the inevitable character and the burden of death with more immediacy than it feels the happiness of eternal life. It is from that world that our faith must arise". Cf. Ferdinando Ormea, *Pierre Teilhard de Chardin* (Turin, 1963), pp. 143–65.

that, if not "rarefied", as on several occasions at Peking,[22] was at any rate too far removed from the intellectual and religious environment in which he might from day to day have found friendly hearing and criticism, and where the normal contacts with specialists in other disciplines could have widened some of his views and given them greater flexibility. Sometimes, again, he may have been the victim of the generosity of his own attitude. One might, in fact, say of Père Teilhard what **Étienne Gilson has written of St Thomas: "No one is more anxious than he to leave open all the doors by which a variety of minds may attain the same truth. He lovingly tends the seeds of truth wherever he finds them."**[23] At the same time, M. Gilson adds—and this again applies to Teilhard as to St Thomas—"a half-truth is never conceded by him except as a step towards the complete truth", as he sees it and wishes others to see it.

One might, too, say of Teilhard what was said of Pope John XXIII, that "he always tried to see anything that was positive in what people thought, even when they themselves did not realize all its implications"[24]—nor, we might add, all that it was based upon. It was this readiness that made Père Teilhard appear sometimes over-optimistic, or to come too close to views that in fact were a long way removed from his own; occasionally, too, it made appear a concession on his part what was, in fact, only the first step in a formal refutation. This applies to some of his criticisms of communism[25] and

[22] Cf. Letter of 15 Aug. 1936: "We are still working in Peking, in a rarefied atmosphere"; and again from Peking, to his cousin: "On the whole we are cut off from any main vital current."

[23] *Duns Scot.* (1952), p. 626.

[24] Jean Aucagne, *Le Monde communiste face au Concile*, in *Travaux et Jours* 8 (Beirut, 1963), p. 3.

[25] Although Père Philippe de la Trinité is forced to admit that "a secular cult of progress cannot ['does not' would be more exact] derive from Teilhardism", he none the less seeks to make the latter answerable for the former, by adding that "the latter fosters, as one of its own fruits, the former" (*Rome et Teilhard de Chardin*, p. 210, note). History is only too easily distorted, but this

fascism.[26] It applies also to his approach to the problem of war and peace, which went much deeper than any trite or pernicious pacificism.[27] Instead of saying that the Christian "destroys" his selfishness, Teilhard preferred to begin by saying, that he "magnifies" it or "expands" it, but making it clear those terms involved destroying it.[28] In short, his was a process of "immanent" criticism or criticism that first entered fully into the statement or attitude criticized. He tried "to give hope to man's work and research".[29] It was in this spirit that, chiefly after about 1936–40, Père Teilhard, without ruling out a further step, of which one generally finds an indication in his work, tried first to distinguish the "homogeneous category" and "common front" that might be formed by Christians and non-Christians who, each from their own angle, were alive to "the march of Humanity".[30] As though he already felt the immediately post-war "existentialist" wave which he was to come up against when he

critic should have known that the "self-styled Catholic pro-Marxist progressivism" insisted on claiming for itself the sanction and support of Thomism—just as Maurras' "self-styled Catholic" traditionalism recently did. In neither case would I suggest that the claim was justified, but it is wrong to try to shift the responsibility.

[26] See, for example, *Universalisation et Union* (1942), *Œuvres*, VII, pp. 96–101, and cf. VI. 99–101, and letter from China, 15 Aug. 1936, referring to the Spanish Civil War: "Although I'm not involved, I tremble at seeing fascism and Christianity being identified."

[27] Letter to M. and S. Bégouën, Peking, 20 Sept. 1940: "Peace is not the opposite of war. It is war carried above and beyond itself in the conquest of the trans-human. Always the same solution, so simple, so radically dependent on synthesis, for the problems that divide us" (*Letters from a Traveller*, pp. 267–8). On this "transformation" of war, see the earlier *Terre Promise* (1919), pp. 1–11; *L'Heure de Choisir* (1939), *Œuvres*, VII, pp. 19–26. Only a peculiarly prejudiced mind could hold that Teilhard was "an ardent supporter of total war" (Charbonneau, p. 152).

[28] Cf. *La Vie Cosmique* (1916), p. 2: "A hidden, intimate call, expanding our selfishness, tells us that, through our immortal souls, we are the unnumbered centres of one and the same sphere."

[29] 10 April 1934, *Letters from a Traveller*, p. 202.

[30] *Sur les bases possible d'un Credo commun humain commun* (1941); *Œuvres*, V, pp. 105–6. Cf. *Letters from a Traveller*, p. 228.

returned to France from China, he would have liked to unite everyone, "against all pessimisms, whether lay or religious", in "a common faith in a spiritual future for the Earth".[31] At the same time he was equally inclined to think that "outside the continually active influence of Christianity, men can only with great difficulty acquire and retain an appreciation of the great universal realities of the present day, and still more of those to come. In other words the "world-citizens" of my dreams can hardly be recruited except from those elements that are by *predisposition christianized*." These words were written in 1932,[32] but again in 1952 he was writing that should Christianity disappear "the presence of a loving God would disappear from the psychological equipment of the world—darkness and cold beyond any we could even begin to imagine".[33] From a very similar point of view, an earlier letter had clearly brought out the dual aspect of his thought on this subject:

> I think that unbelievers are mistaken about the value of these new *human virtues* that they prefer to sanctity; or at least that in imagining that they can cultivate them outside religion they set humanity an impossible task. But at the same time I think that we Christians, for our part, have a great need to "humanize" our sanctity—without, of course, doing violence to the dogmas we hold.[34]

If we are to give a true picture of Père Teilhard, it is important not to pass over or obscure either of these two antithetical but allied aspects of his thought.

[31] Letters from Peking, 11 and 12 Jan. 1941. Cf. 20 Jan: "There will be no real peace, I am sure, until men share a common understanding, at least in general terms about what we should expect and hope from the world's future" (*Letters from a Traveller*, p. 278).

[32] Letter of 13 March 1932. Again, on 4 May 1931: "I have been struck by the difficulty of making certain universalist lines of thought intelligible to men who have never been Christians or who have escaped any deep-reaching Christian influence" (*Letters from a Traveller*, p. 117).

[33] *Letters from a Traveller*, p. 302, note.

[34] 28 July 1918. *Making of a Mind*, p. 222.

Finally, we should note, with Père Smulders, that even if his "fundamental intuition" is valuable and fruitful, it sometimes happens that its expression is at fault, because he was "insufficiently familiar with the methods proper to metaphysics and theology";[35] at the same time, we should remember, with Père Yves Congar, that "to think out a new reality is a difficult task for one who has at his disposal only inherited categories",[36] and must therefore create his own. Nevertheless, with our knowledge of Père Teilhard's thought, based as it was on prayer, and the realness of his inner life, in which we see reflection and practice ("research" and "presence") so closely linked, can we have any doubt but that there was a substantial correctness of orientation (which is much more than correctness of intention) in his work itself—and by his work I mean that part of it that embraces the Christian faith and the spiritual life? It is because of this conviction that even among his intellectual opponents, or those who see grave objections to his teaching, or who emphasize its limitations, you will find many who are ready to recognize his preeminent Catholicity. In so doing they are not simply applying to him the well-known "presupposition" of St Ignatius, often quoted and even more often misunderstood.[37] The case of Père Teilhard, again, they see as one that provides a wonderful confirmation of some thoughts expressed by Newman in his *Idea of a University*:[38]

I still say that a scientific speculator or inquirer is not bound, in

---

[35] *La Vision du Teilhard de Chardin*, p. 27.

[36] *Archives d'histoire doctrinale et littéraire du moyen âge*, vol. 28 (1961-2), in connection with theological problems in the thirteenth century.

[37] *Spiritual Exercises:* "It must be presupposed that every good Christian should be more ready to retain his neighbour's proposition than to condemn it. We should look for every way that may enable us by understanding it to retain it."

[38] I have somewhat condensed the passage (see *Idea of a University*). Newman adds that he always assumes "good faith, honest intentions, a loyal Catholic spirit and a deep sense of responsibility". This is eminently true of Père Teilhard.

conducting his researches, to be every moment adjusting his course by the maxims of the schools or by popular traditions . . . or to be determined to be edifying. . . . Being confident, from the impulse of a generous faith, that, however his line of investigation may swerve now and then, and vary to and fro in its course, or threaten momentary collision or embarrassment with any other department of knowledge, theological or not, yet, if he lets it alone, it will be sure to come home, because truth can never really be contrary to truth, and because often what at first sight is an *exceptio*, in the event most emphatically *probat regulare* . . . it is the very law of the human mind to make its advances by a process which consists of many stages, and is circuitous. There are no short cuts to knowledge . . . moreover, it is not often the fortune of any one man to live through an investigtion. . . .

Great minds need elbow-room, not indeed in the domain of faith, but of thought . . . There are many persons in the world . . . gifted by nature with some particular faculty or capacity; and, while vehemently excited and imperiously ruled by it, they are blind to everything else. . . . Now, these men may be, and often are, very good Catholics, and have not a dream of anything but affection and deference towards Catholicity, nay, perhaps are zealous in its interests. Yet, if you insist that in their speculations, researches or conclusions in their particular science, it is not enough that they submit to the Church generally, and acknowledge its dogmas, but that they must get up all that divines have said or the multitude believed upon religious matters, you simply crush and stamp out the flame within them, and they can do nothing at all. . . .

Every human system, every human writer, is open to just criticism. . . . There is indeed an animadversion which implies a condemnation of the author; but there is another which means not much more than the *pie legendum* written against passages in the Fathers.

14

"DEATH IN GOD"

WE cannot have a complete or accurate idea of the prayer of Père Teilhard unless we understand the part played in it by the thought of death. So far we have had only a glimpse of this.

Of all his thought, even scientific, it would be true to say that it was one long meditation on death.[1] Not, indeed, that he was haunted by a morbid fear of his own individual death, even though at the same time he was as much subject as any man to our natural anxieties. In the first place, he faced, with equal courage and clearness of mind, the overwhelming fact of universal death, which so many others, in their systems of thought or in their lives, seem to try to shut their eyes to. On countless occasions, he insisted on the problem it presents and showed that it is one that cannot be by-passed.[2] The thought of death, "the essence and common basis of all that terrifies and bewilders us"[3] already lies at the heart of his thought, during the war years of 1914–18. "Blessed be inexorable Time and its perpetual mastery. . . . Blessed above all be Death and the Terror of falling back into the Energies of the Cosmos!"[4] It is central, again, in the *Milieu Divin*, a book

---

[1] *La Pensée religieuse*, in particular chs. 5 and 12.
[2] For example in *L'Atomisme de l'Esprit* (1941); *Œuvres*, VII, pp. 50–3. Cf. *Comment je vois* (148), no. 9, on the "twofold problem of Death and Action", *Vie et Planètes* (Peking, 1945; *Études*, May 1946); *Œuvres*, V, pp. 153–6.
[3] *La Foi qui opère*.
[4] *Le Milieu Mystique*, 3. Cf. 19 June 1916, and 13 Nov. 1916 (*Making of a Mind*, pp. 101, 144).

which, if one may put it so, was long prayed before it was
written, and which cannot be understood unless it is prayed as
it is read. And in his last essay (1955), which he called, "The
barrier of death, and co-reflection", he once more undertook
to show that "at the supra-individual level of the Species",
the problem of death and of the loss of heart that it seems
inevitably to entail, loses none of its urgency, but on the contrary becomes "vastly graver and wider".[5]

Père Teilhard looked closely into the meaning of death, that
appears to natural man as a "threat" and a "stumbling-
block".[6] In death he saw a confluence of all the setbacks, all the
obscurities, all the evils that are the portion of our terrestrial
condition. At the same time he believed that "death releases"
and that "if there were no death, the earth would certainly
seem stifling".[7] The "World" on which he then centred his
thoughts and to which he clung passionately, was the World
of beyond death, to which our present World is no more than
the indispensable preparation: death, then, is "the only way
out to the greater Life".[8] Death does not return us to "the
great current of Things" but "surrenders us totally to God".
Thus, in a submissive and loving welcome to death, to "death
in God", he saw the exercise of that supreme passivity which
is supreme activity, and without which he knew that it is
impossible for man to be reunited with God:[9] "I feel, my

[5] *Œuvres*, VII, p. 422.

[6] *L'Atomisme de l'Esprit*, 7; *Œuvres*, VII, p. 49.

[7] 5 Aug. 1917 (*Making of a Mind*, p. 199). *Barrière :* "Tomorrow (I am convinced of this because I am already feeling it myself) a sort of panic claustropho-
bia will possess Humanity simply at the idea that it may find itself hermetically
sealed in a closed Universe" (*Œuvres*, VII, p. 246). According to his brother
Joseph, such thoughts often recurred in his conversation.

[8] *La Grande Monade* (*Cahiers*, 2, p. 47), 13 Nov. 1916.

[9] *Note pour servir*, etc. (Epiphany 1919): third and final period, "cycle of
interior (and apostolic) life"; "to sublimate human effort by making it attain
(by extension of itself) the higher forms of activity—which are purity, contemplation, death *in God*"; 13 Nov. 1916; "Death surrenders us totally to God;
it makes us enter into Him; we must, in return, surrender ourselves to death with
absolute love and self-abandonment" (*Making of a Mind*, p. 145).

God, that by a reversal of forces of which you alone can be the author, the terror that possesses me when I have to face the nameless changes that are making ready to renew my being, is melting into a flood of joy at being transformed by You." [10] Contemplating the crucifix, listening to its call "in the depths of the night", he saw everything reversed. "The outward appearances are the same,—and the material determinisms— and the vicissitudes of chance—and the restlessness of men— and the transit into Death", but "he who *dares* to believe enters a field of the created in which things, while retaining the surface texture we know, seem to be made of another substance. Everything phenomenal remains unchanged, and yet everything becomes luminous, animated, loving." [11]

We should note that this attitude to death, though certainly Christian, does not fully include all that makes up the Christian attitude. The aspect of death to sin is not, it is true, positively rejected, but it is not explicitly present. This, no doubt, is an omission, and it is one of the effects of this omission that we were drawing attention to a moment ago; it is because of this that Père Teilhard's spirituality, however acceptable its positive content may be, cannot be universally applied just as it stands. His language, incomplete though it may be, is nevertheless the language of faith, of a faith that prays: "To accept, to love, every communion with death"; it was that counsel that, in line with what he had so often expressed, he urged on himself during one of his last retreats; [12] and his resolution was continued into an act of trust: "It is death that sets the seal on life: on this point, we must have absolute trust in God, since on him alone depends 'a good end'." [13] A little before, in 1940, when, as he did each year, he was making the exercise of "preparation for death", he wrote: "Whatever

[10] *La Messe sur le Monde.*
[11] See below, pp. 156–7.
[12] 1948 Retreat (*Les Moulins*).
[13] To his cousin, *Les Moulins*, 4 Sept. 1948.

my death may be, grant, my God, that it may glorify you
(*clarificet*)!—You, the You I love so dearly: Omega!"
Earlier, he would ask his friends: "Pray that my life may con-
form with my vision." [14] Now he asks them: "Pray that I may
end well, in conformity with what I have tried to preach:
This I am seeing more and more as the grace of all graces." [15]
This becomes increasingly his chief prayer.[16] A little before his
death, he wrote to a former colleague from his days in Jersey
and at Ore Place, a man as devoted as he was to geological
research and natural science, and whose friendship he had
always enjoyed, Père Christian Burdo: "Sometimes I
feel still quite young, sometimes I have the feeling that
everything in me is disintegrating. May God ever grow
greater in this alteration and combination of 'plus' and
'minus'."

As every Christian, Père Teilhard saw both the cause and
the warrant of the final victory that death can constitute, in
the death and resurrection of Jesus Christ. But there was this,
too, that he lived with an extraordinary intensity the mystery
which others accept with only superficial and insufficiently
concentrated faith. "Have no fear: it is I, the First and the
Last, the Living! I was dead, and lo! I live to centuries of
centuries, holding the keys of death and Hades!" [17] He loved
that text from the Apocalypse, to which he would often return
in his meditations. The prayer, too, for the hour of death that
appears in the *Milieu Divin* has already brought help to more
than one of his brothers in Christ. Beneath its literary expression, they have felt that it was a *real* prayer. I remember
that when the Abbé Francisque Cimetier died in Lyons in

[14] To Père Auguste Valensin, Holy Saturday, 1922.
[15] Letter of 18 Sept. 1948.
[16] 22 Nov. 1953, to his cousin: "To end well, as I have so often told you, is
becoming, so far as I am concerned, my chief prayer and my one great ambition"
(*Letters from a Traveller*, p. 348 note). Cf. to the Abbé Breuil, *ibid.*, p. 359.
[17] Apocalypse 1. 17–18.

1946,[18] he had himself seen to it that all his affairs were in perfect order, and left only one single paper. It was found in a drawer in his table, and contained this prayer, copied out in his own hand:

O Energy of my Lord, irresistible and living Force, since, of us two, You are infinitely the stronger, if is for you to consume me in the union that shall fuse us together. Give me, then, something even more precious than the grace which all the faithful beg from you. It is not enough that I die in communion. Teach me *communion in dying*.[19]

[18] A Sulpician Father (1880–1946). He was a former Dean of the Faculty of Canon Law, and former Superior of the University Seminary.

[19] *Milieu Divin*, p. 90. This prayer was printed by his fellow priests on M. l'Abbé Cimetier's memorial card, Cf. Retreat of 1948: "Communion by death (death communion)." Similarly, M. Blondel, *L'Action* (1893), p. 422: "Is not death itself, the last, the complete, the eternal communion?"

15

THE IGNATIAN TRADITION

OOTED as it was, thanks to the long and sound cultiva-
tion we have described, in the heart of Catholic tradition, this life of prayer almost instinctively, in the
very act of developing the most personal intellectual contribution, discovered in tradition all sorts of overtones, some of
which were generally unappreciated in his day. Earlier, we
noted examples of these. On the "cosmic Christ", the mystery
of the Incarnation, the strength of purity, the sovereign power
of faith—*Beata quae credidisti*—the efficacy of the contemplative life,[1] among other subjects, Père Teilhard spoke in a
way that was in advance of practically all his contemporaries.
Here again, and more clearly than even he suspected, what he
had to say was again an echo of what the Fathers had said.
Sometimes he overdid the rhetorical imagery that sought to
bring home to his readers the urgency of a new idea by an
unqualified contrast with the past. In so doing his own ideas
were grossly over-simplified. On more than one occasion,
however, he followed Tradition more faithfully than he
explicitly recognized. In his exploration of new lines of thought,
again, he appreciated that all questions of a spiritual category
"must be treated in union with the spirit and living tradition
of the Church". In this field, he saw, "facts", by which he
meant the teaching of Jesus Christ, "must take precedence of
theory", and the believer must always bow to facts without

[1] *La Pensée religieuse*, pp. 318–20.

waiting until he has found an "explanation".[2] Even in completely new situations he knew—as he tells us himself—that "it is the practice of the saints, even if we have difficulty in finding a rational basis for it, that is *imposed* on us as the real thing, the solid truth". Even when he was explaining that we should not look to the saints of the past for a ready-made solution to problems that their conscience never had to meet in the form that we meet it, he added that we should always be able substantially to recognize in the "gestures" we now make, the "saints' gesture of perfection"; similarly, he knew the importance of guiding himself, within the Church, "by the immutable axis of sanctity".[3]

Whether Père Teilhard was always completely successful is another question which we must, as pointed out earlier, have some reservations in answering. We should, in any case, note a point that has already been referred to: if he sought, in work so resolutely aimed towards the "ahead", to transmit the echo of the spiritual tradition of Christianity, it was with the particular emphasis that, naturally enough, was impressed on a son of St Ignatius Loyola. Whoever has been through the Spiritual Exercises, will in fact recognize in the *Milieu Divin*, as in much else he wrote, a new but on the whole authentic expression of the attitude they inculcate. The use of creatures,[4] the assumption of human values (so sharply criticized at times by the Society's opponents and a principle that can lend itself to abuse), perfect detachment in a life that is not cut off from the world, the contemplation of God in and

---

[2] 4 Aug. 1916 (*Making of a Mind*, p. 117).

[3] *L'Atomisme de l'Esprit* (1941), *Œuvres*, VII, p. 63, *Maurice Blondel et le Père Teilhard de Chardin* (*Archives de Philosophie*, Jan.–March 1961, p. 156), *Le Milieu Divin*, p. 86: appeal to "what has always been the attitude and practical teaching of the Church on the problem of human suffering". Cf. Père Smulders, *op. cit.*, p. 213–29: "The ancient, or rather the eternal and hence ever-new, truth, is seen in a new light", but is better preserved than by the literal repetitions you sometimes find, and: "the contradiction between Thomas à Kempis and Teilhard is only apparent, even if there is a very real difference of emphasis."

[4] *Milieu Divin*, p. 100 note: "fundamental problem of the use of creatures."

beyond all things, and the acceptance of his will loved "for its own sake",[5] passionate love of Jesus Christ, the desire for his kingdom,[6] the boldness of grand designs to serve him—these are among the principal components of the spirituality that we find expressed both in Teilhard and in the *Exercises*. Père Teilhard left his own mark upon it—such a disciple could never be no more than a carbon copy—by the boldness both of his mystical interpretaiton and of his open receptiveness of the world. In the first place, however, and far more recognizably, it was the *Exercises* that left their mark upon him.

In the reflections suggested to him by Père Paul Dudon's life of St Ignatius, which he read during his 1940 retreat, he notes the two features that seemed to him particularly characteristic of the "kernel of the Society of Jesus" in its early days: "reform of the Church by the 'counsels' *plus* an integration of the human". He then wonders "who will be the new St Ignatius", who we need today to realize the second of those two principles, and who will be "his happy companions" called to serve as our models in applying it; for even if the "counsels" are still with us, substantially unchanged, "integration of the human" must become more conscious and more complete. And this must come not as the effect of less insistence on perfection, nor in order to make the aspostolate less difficult, but in virtue of the acquisition by man of a new awareness of the value of creatures and of his own responsibility in the evolution of the world. "Detachment" "renunciation", then, will be in no way minimized: it will still be, as in the past, total. But there will be this difference, that, more resolutely than in the past, it will be renunciation of

[5] *Le Cœur de la Matière* on "the rapidly increasing importance assumed in my spiritual life by the sense of the Will of God". 11 July 1932: "To be loyal to what God asks of me". (*L'Élément universel*, pp. 6–7). There are numerous similar allusions in the letters, e.g. 29 June 1916 (*Making of a Mind*, p. 106).

[6] He wrote to his superior-general, 12 Oct. 1951, in a letter already quoted: "You can count on me to work for the Kingdom of God, which is the only thing I can see and that matters to me in Science".

personal satisfaction, not of use (assuming, on the other hand, that it is legitimate use); it must take primarily the form of an "emergence" or a "passing beyond". This is because the definitive World, that in which Christ reigns, is constituted rather by a "transformation" than by a "break-up" or an "extinction".[7] Ignatius had written "Exercises designed to conquer one's self' and one's disordered affections. "I dream", says his loyal but free disciple, "of Exercises to shatter the narrowness of one's views, one's desires, one's egoism".

These principles of Christian ascesis are laid down, we must remember, in such a way as to be valid for all Christians, each having to apply them according to his particular situation. Even with this qualification—and we saw earlier that Père Teilhard recognized this—they have to be handled with care. It calls not only for complete moral soundness but also for an informed sense of the spiritual life. From Père Teilhard's correspondence we can see without any doubt that such was the case with him. What he advocates is not so new, perhaps, as he sometimes seems to say, when he is anxious to bring out an aspect to which he attaches particular importance. It is still, as, moreover, he recognizes, a question of "the same victory by man over his egoism and his comforts", the difference being that the victory will have a "different tone". Up to a certain point, as he says again, it will be "another form of sanctity"—but it will still, as before, necessitate "crossing the threshold into sanctity", and this will still have to be done by following the line of that only "concrete truth" which, in this context, is "the practice of the saints".[8]

[7] He had explained this view in Dec. 1919 (*Archives de Philosophie*, 1961, p. 137). Teilhard's renunciation is not "some form of lack of interest", any more than is Ignatius' "indifference" (*La Vie Cosmique*, p. 4). It must derive from "a sort of higher indifference (impassioned indifference) which is born of attachment, in all things, to what is above all".

[8] Letter to Père Valensin, 29 Dec. 1919 (*Ibid.*, p. 132).

Père Teilhard saw, earlier than the majority of his contemporaries, and perhaps more forcibly than any of them, the rapid transformations our age is undergoing; he was convinced that it would be "impossible (fortunately) to stem the irrestistible tide that is carrying human thought of our time along with it".[9] As the supreme danger, accordingly, for present-day Catholicism, he feared a petrifying, sterile, withdrawal into itself, whose effect would be to make it cease to appear what it is in reality for every age and every man: The truth of life, "the long despaired-of answer to the question asked by every human life".[10] More than once, on this point, he even spoke of "transposition"[11] both in spirituality and in traditional Christology. The use of the word is arguable, as is his picture of the procedure to be followed. In his mind, no doubt—at any rate, we may say, in his intention—there could be no question of in any way whatsoever parting with the substance of Christianity: he sought to perpetuate it, to present it more clearly for everyone to see. This, indeed, he says explicitly: if he wants Christianity to be able to "transpose" its precepts and counsels, it is certainly not with any idea of transforming or weakening them—it is in order that we may see to what degree, in the context of a Universe in evolution, "the most traditional human moral teaching takes on a new form, coherence and urgency".[12]

---

⁹ Letter to Père André Ravier.

¹⁰ Lecture to the Marcel Légaut-Jacques Perret student group (Paris, 1940).

¹¹ He wrote, for example, from Peking, 27 June, 1932: "The whole theory of the Supernatural . . . is discussed in a field of thought that most modern people have left behind them. It is essential to *transpose* it into a system where things are represented in a way that is intelligible and living to us". In this he may have been mistaken or may have exaggerated. But to appreciate the correct significance of his suggestions, one should read them in the light of the converse assertion: "I am convinced that a more traditionalist expression of my views is possible . . ." (Tientsin, 15 Aug. 1936). When Père Philippe de la Trinité uses the word "transposition" to justify his conclusion that Teilhard's teaching "leads, without doubt, to what is in fact naturalism" (*op. cit.*, p. 17, cf. p. 28), he is grossly misinterpreting the word.

¹² *L'Atomisme de l'Esprit* (1941); *Œuvres*, VII, pp. 55–6.

Père Teilhard calls for, and himself seeks for, a rejuvenation of the Christianity we know to be immortal, "not by structural alteration but by assimilation of new elements".[13] If he occasionally used the unfortunate term "neo-Christianity", what he meant by it, as he made clear himself, was the "Christianizing of a neo-humanism",—which was not his own invention. In his view, it was "the 'humanist' problem now 'present in a completely new form'". This called for a new and almost unprecedented effort to find a Christian solution to the problem, and for that we must look to the marvellous "power of growth" that is peculiar to Christianity.[14] This effort may be identified with Père Teilhard's own effort to project himself into the future. In itself it was not entirely free from illusion, and we should, I believe, recognize that it involved more serious risks, when exerted by a Christian less firmly rooted in authentic tradition than he was, less afraid of appearing to preach his own private religion and less completely and resolutely loyal.[15] Père Teilhard himself hoped that "his own obedience" would serve to win recognition for his view. He said that he was "deeply convinced, for reasons that derive from the very structure of his lines of thought, that religious thought develops only traditionally, collectively, 'phyletically'"; he declared, too, that he "had no other desire nor hope than to *sentire* (feel) or, more exactly *prae-sentire cum Ecclesia*.[16] He never sought to do more than "preserve by rejuvenating".[17]

[13] *Christianisme et Évolution* (1945).

[14] Letter of 29 Oct. 1949. *The Phenomenon of Man*, pp. 296–7. He also spoke of a "super-human Christianity" (*Réflexions sur le bonheur*, Cahiers 2, p. 70). Even if a few isolated phrases "might make one think that the role of Christianity was played out, the whole body of Teilhard's work points to and proves the contrary" (P. Smulders, *op. cit.*, p. 128).

[15] Loyalty, or fidelity, is one of his favourite words. Cf. *Milieu Divin*, pp. 137–140.

[16] Quoted by Claude Cuénot, *Situation de Teilhard de Chardin* (*Bulletin de la Société industrielle de Mulhouse*, 1963).

[17] Cf. 29 Aug. 1916 (*Making of a Mind*, p. 122).

To the expression of his most personal and contestable views, he explicitly added, "without prejudice to the integrity of Christian tradition". We should continually bear that phrase in mind if we are to judge his ideas without constraint and at the same time be fair to Père Teilhard himself.

Towards the end of 1948 he wrote to me that he wanted to "feel with the world", not vaguely, but "in so far as the world carries within its moving layers the reserves of being it awaits to bring about its complete Christification". In all his work of research and his desire for renewal, he was determined to remain both "in union with the mind of the Church" and "in sympathy with the Earth's present crisis".[18] Only those, I believe, who are quite unaware of this "crisis" would reject his view entirely. He could, as any of us, be mistaken, but, loyal as he was to his vocation—which he knew to be a "special vocation"[19]—he could never falsify it. Whatever just criticisms may occasionally be prompted by his ideas, he lived his vocation, in the presence of God, until his last day.[20]

[18] 1940 Retreat, second day. Cf. *La Parole attendue*, Peking, 31 Oct. 1940). "In the centre of the total crisis the World is going through" (*Cahiers*, 4. p. 22). 9 Dec. 1933: "The problem in which we are now inevitably *caught up*, and whose consequences I am surprised so few realize." Cf. Pope Paul VI on "The world of today shaken by rapid and profound transformations" (*À la noblesse romaine*, 14 Jan. 1964).

[19] 1940 Retreat, fourth day.

[20] 13 Dec. 1952, to his cousin: "Pray to God for me continually that I may finish in such a way that my end may humbly, but unmistakably and worthily, set the seal upon my witness" (*Letters from a Traveller*, p. 335). He makes the same request to several of his friends and fellow Jesuits; see above, p. 114.

16

CHRIST'S SECOND COMING

E have seen that the "World" to which Père Teilhard dedicated himself was essentially beyond our World. It was the World upon which Jesus Christ is to impress its definitive form.[1] Thus, the *expectation of the Parousia* forms the natural epilogue to the *Milieu Divin*. It was on that, until the very end, that his eyes were turned. His intellectual effort was, indeed, embodied in a number of different writings, with what appeared to be different ends in view—and that met with different forms of appreciation. Everyone, let us repeat, has the right (provided he gives his reasons and appreciates the issues involved) to contest their value, to reject their premises, to test their scientific basis, to question the reliability of their method or the cogency of their arguments, and also, indeed, to point out the shortcomings of their expression or of their thought when it enters the field of theology: but the correctness and integrity of the urge that inspired them can never be impugned.

This urge, as I believe we have already seen quite clearly, was sustained and directed by prayer. Both in his *Phenomenology* and in the *Apologetics* that complements it, Père Teilhard sought to show how human effort, exerting itself to forward technical, social, and even mental progress—an effort,

---

[1] Letter of 9 Jan. 1917: "For me the real earth is that chosen part of the universe, still almost everywhere dispersed, and in course of slow segregation, but which is gradually taking on body and form in Christ". (*Making of a Mind*, p. 165).

moreover, that is realized and works towards its goal in a process independent of individual autonomous decisions [2]—how
this effort must produce the natural conditions of maturation
that are the necessary preliminary to the Return of the Lord:
"The unique and supreme event in which the Historic will
be fused with the Transcendent." [3] The necessary, though not
"the sufficient conditions, of course", he adds. [4] If it is true,
as Père Teilhard thought and as we are justified in thinking
with him, that human effort co-operates in the natural fulfilment of the world, his position is in the line of the most generally accepted tradition, which teaches that the natural world
is not to be annihilated but transfigured. [5] At the same time he
shows how the final result must, for each individual, be
a change of mathematical sign, governed by man's free
choice. [6] In the spiritual part of his work, he in no way changes
this doctrine, but completes it. He shows the Christian that
he must both supply the human effort and, by interiorizing
it, Christianize it. If the Kingdom is indeed to come, the
life-sap of the world must be "sanctified", "supernatura-
lized". And a "supernatural consummation" cannot be brought
about by "natural potentialities": it must be "received".

The second coming of Christ, it is true, must be preceded
and prepared by a long process of human development,
which itself has carried on from the whole of earlier evolution.
Such a view, Père Teilhard believes, is "perfectly analogous

[2] Cf. *Comment je vois* (1948), no. 16: "It would be easier to stop the Earth
from turning than to stop the totalization of Mankind." Or, *La Planétisation
Humaine* (1945–6): "As impossible for Mankind not to self-integrate as for the
intelligence not to push its thoughts indefinitely further and deeper". (*Œuvres*,
V, p. 164). *Ibid.*, p. 159: "No power in the World can enable us to escape from
what is the very strength of the World."

[3] *Trois choses que je vois*, p. 7.

[4] *Le Cœur du problème* (1949); *Œuvres*, V, p. 348. Cf. *La Pensée religieuse*,
pp. 173–4.

[5] Cf. St Irenaeus, *Adversus Haereses*, l. 5, c. 36 (P.G., 7, 1221–4), and countless
others.

[6] *La Pensée religieuse*, Ch. 10. *The Phenomenon of Man*, p. 226: "In Man,
Evolution becomes free to dispose of itself".

with the mystery of the first Christmas, which could not have operated (as is universally agreed) except between Heaven and an Earth that was socially, politically and psychologically ready to receive Jesus". [7] It is none the less true of the second coming as of the first, that only divine operation can bring it about. [8] "Nothing attains Christ that he does not take and place within him." [9] And nothing can take the place of, or force, Christ's gesture, nothing can set in motion the "attractive force he exercises directly on his members." This is the gulf—which persists even in union—that separates the natural from the supernatural. Père Teilhard insists on union, on "intimate connection", because it is the aspect of the truth that he thought often neglected, and was anxious to focus attention upon; but, contrary to what has been maintained, [10] he was careful to avoid confusing the two. For him, nature is, as it were, "matter" offered to the supernatural —which is the Christian concept expressed in the very language of the Schoolmen. [11]

Similarly, there is the same gulf between the present World and the beyond-this-World. No sort of "cosmic convergence", then, would suffice to produce the "parousiac spark". No "point of human maturation" can by itself release the "point of Christic parousia". Anyone is perfectly justified in holding that Père Teilhard gives too much weight to his conviction that the meeting of these two "points", or, as he puts it elsewhere, their "concrete coincidence", [12] is

[7] *Le Cœur du problème; Œuvres*, V, p. 34.

[8] *Trois choses que je vois*, p. 7.

[9] *Le Prêtre* (1918).

[10] According to Dom Georges Frénaud, *op. cit.*, p. 18: "In his synthesis, Père Teilhard always confuses with supernatural grace the divine help needed by created nature throughout the ascent of its natural evolution towards the final term of its concentration." This is an arbitrary statement, unsupported by anything Teilhard wrote, and contradicted in many places.

[11] *Le Milieu Divin*, pp. 152–3.

[12] *Le Cœur du problème; Œuvres*, V, p. 348. In *Le Christique* he uses a less simple metaphor, that of the sphere that is more deeply entered into, and of the

indispensable; or in thinking that the type of symmetry he sees in this ascending "maturation" and descending "parousia" is too hard and fast. From a more general angle, we are entitled to think that he sometimes carries to extremes the closeness of the bonds that genetically connect the Kingdom of God and human effort,[13] with the result that there is a danger that some who believe they are following him may concentrate on the latter at the expense of the former. Père Teilhard, however, is careful not to confuse the two.[14] This is why, when he carries this line of thought into the field of natural reflection—this side of Revelation—he uses, to designate the term towards which our species moves, deliberately vague expressions. "Some thing", he says, for example, "awaits us in the depths of time to come" [15]; or, if he puts it more fully, it is rather as a way of suggesting his meaning.[16]

To put it another way, and again to use Teilhardian expressions, the final "concentration" of the Noosphere does not in itself produce the indispensable "excentration" which is to mark the definitive transition "beyond the future"; human "maturation" does not suffice to procure "ecstasy" in God; —any more than the first "fullness of time" could have sufficed to realize the Incarnation of the Word—and that even though the two things may be linked together in fact in God's Design, itself written into the laws of our World.

More generally, even in passages where he most delights in

Centre in process of expansion. A certain kinship with the thought of Fedorov, adopted by Nicolas Berdyaev in his *Essai d'autobiographie spirituelle*, is apparent here.

[13] *Recherche, Travail, et Adoration* (1955).

[14] Cf. *Œuvres*, VII, pp. 289–90: "... the Supernatural not excluding, but rather requiring, as a necessary preparation, the complete maturation of an ultra-human".

[15] *L'Énergie de l'Evolution* (1953), *Œuvres*, VII, p. 388; cf. *ibid.*, p. 387 ("the attractive force of the future") and p. 185 ("in a Christian context ... beyond the the future").

[16] See, for example, below, p. 163 and note. Or, on the cyclotron, *Œuvres*, VII, p. 377.

their "combined play", Père Teilhard distinguishes clearly, on many occasions, "the two curves (or convergences), cosmic ('natural') and Christic ('supernatural')". It is easy enough to say, as does Père Philippe de la Trinité,[17] that "he tends radically to confuse the two orders of natural and supernatural" and that thereby he changes Christianity into "evolutionism of a naturalist, monist, pantheist type"; but it is much more difficult to prove it. The accusation, in fact, is a complete travesty of Père Teilhard's views. In reality, even if he does not always use the specialized terminology of the text-books, and even if one thinks that he sometimes accords a relatively too large or too indispensable a part to "nature", Père Teilhard knew very well that the universe (the universe of persons) is "capable" only of "receiving" Christ and that one cannot "look for the love and kingdom of God and the same level as human affections and progress".[18] He simply maintains that between "the genesis of Humanity in the World" and "the genesis of Christ through the Church", there is a relationship of "coherent subordination".[19] Thus when he speaks, in a reverse process, of "Christifying Evolution", he points out again that such an undertaking involves a twofold programme: "the scientific task, of establishing the 'convergence' of the universe, and the re-ligious task, of bringing out the Universal Nature of the Christ of history",[20]—which is as much to say that the human

[17] Op. cit., p. 98.
[18] Letters of 22 Nov. 1936 and 7 Aug. 1950. Milieu Divin, p. 110 note, etc.
[19] Hérédité sociale et Progrès (1921); Œuvres, V. pp. 50–1.
[20] Letter from New York, 8 Nov. 1953 (Letters from a Traveller, p. 347). On the third day of his last retreat (21 Aug. 1954), meditating on "the essense of [his] vision", he sums it up as "to integrate Evolution in Christification (Nature in Super-nature.)" Integration (even if one may criticize an over-simple mode of that integration) is a way of uniting and subordinating, not of confusing, two things. Cf. Le Cœur du problème: "The Christian 'Above' is incorporated (without being swallowed up in it!—but by 'supernaturalizing it') in the human 'Ahead'. And, in the same process, we see that faith in God, in proportion as it assimilates and sublimates in its own life-sap the sap of faith in the World, assumes its full power to attract and convert to itself!" (Œuvres, V, p. 48).

sense of "convergence" is not sufficient to engender the "centre" necessary to religion,—and that again amounts to distinguishing, within human society (or "at the heart of the social Phenomenon"), the role proper to "the Christian Phenomenon", incarnate in the Catholic Church.[21] Similarly, adds Père Teilhard, if the Parousia is to be realized, the "propulsive force of man" must be combined with a force, different in order and origin, "the Christian ascensional force", which itself depends entirely on the force of the risen Christ.[22] That, speaking to such Christians as he believes need the warning, Père Teilhard often says—putting it the other way round—that the "Ahead" must be combined with the "Above", in no way alters the fact that he distinguishes between the two. As Père Rabut rightly points out, for Teilhard the supernatural action of Christ is distinct from the "evolutionary ascent".[23] "Human, terrestrial, progress is not, as such, supernatural."[24] In consequence, the Parousia must be made to burst forth not by an accumulation of human discoveries, technical advances of achievements, but by a different sort of progress, an "obedience", a "humble fidelity", "an accumulation of desires", invisibly aroused by the Spirit of Christ in the heart of the faithful.[25] Finally, if the

[21] *Comment je vois*, no. 37. *Le Christique* (1955), p. 7. Cf. M. Barthélemy-Madaule, *op. cit.*, p. 450. In the *Christique* passage, Père Teilhard is thinking of his friend Julian Huxley, and criticising his "sort of religion so warmly and brilliantly proclaimed under the name of evolutionary humanism".

[22] *Trois choses* (1948). *Le Cœur du Problème, loc. cit., Making of a Mind*, pp. 142–3, etc.

[23] *Dialogue with Teilhard de Chardin*.

[24] Père Philippe de la Trinité, *op. cit.*, pp. 8–9.

[25] *Milieu Divin*, p. 150. Similar passages are referred to in *La Pensée religieuse*, Ch. II. 6 Jan. 1917: "True progress never makes itself felt, is never realized, in any of the material creations we try to substitute for ourselves in the hope that they will survive our life on earth: it is in souls that the advance is made, the real sparks in which the inner fires of the World are concentrated and embodied, and it disappears with them" (*Making of a Mind*, p. 163). When he was writing those lines, Père Teilhard had already fully conceived the idea expressed in *La Maîtrise du Monde et le Règne de Dieu*, written the year before. In *L'Étoffe de l'Univers* (*Œuvres*, VII, p. 405) the Parousia is described as "more like a matura-

spark is to explode into flame, Fire must come down from Heaven.[26]

Accordingly, as Père Teilhard looks anxiously at our present day, listless and directionless, he asks, "Where is the Christian, whose impatient nostalgia for Christ will succeed, not in submerging (though this is what is needed) but even in only restoring a correct balance to what human love and cares are centred on? Where is the Catholic as passionately devoted (by *conviction*, not by *convention*) to extending the hopes of the Incarnation, as many humanists are to their dreams of the New City?" It was this Christian and this Catholic, that Père Teilhard sought to be. "We go on saying", he sadly notes, "that we keep watch in expectation of the Master. But, to be sincere, we shall have to admit that we no longer look for anything."[27] In himself, in the first place, and then in us, he strove to reawaken and maintain a sense of expectation—passionate, active, expressed in the double form externally, of work, and internally of hope.[28]

It is in this faith that the prayer of Père Teilhard is rooted, and by it that his activities as well as his "passivities" are transformed into prayer. The Promised Land to which his eyes are turned at the end of his days is indeed that which

---

tion than a destruction", but he does not say that this maturation is entirely of the natural order; as he was writing from a different point of view, it is understandable that in *L'Étoffe* Père Teilhard was not so precise as in the other passages quoted.

[26] Cf. Père Smulders' comment, *op. cit.*, pp. 134–43; G. Crespy, *op. cit.*, pp. 97–103. Cf. Yves de Montcheuil, S.J., *Problèmes de vie spirituelle* (1959), p. 205: "The universe is not a meaningless sequence with no eternal significance; at the same time it cannot attain fulfilment without intervention from on high to rescue it from the conditions in which we know it."

[27] *Milieu Divin*, p. 152.

[28] *Mon Univers* (1924): ". . . confident in the word of Christ, passionately awaiting the death of the world, that we may be absorbed, with him, in God". (*Œuvres*, V, p. 402). Cf. Hans Urs von Balthasar, *Glaubhaft ist nur Liebe* (1963), ch. 5: "Freed from the past by the Spirit, Christians, in every activity by which they build up and transform the world, advance towards a radiant figure that beckons to them across all things: Christ who comes again."

comes from the "universal renewal" announced by Peter in the name of his Lord Jesus.[29] This is the "new Earth" which the Return of Christ is to inaugurate—the return of the only "Christ of the Revelation", to whom the Earth "opens at its Summit", and without whom we might well "stifle to death". Already, too, by anticipation—*beyond itself*—it is this present Earth, the World of experience in which we are still immersed, because on the day of the Incarnation, the "radiance of a love" came down upon us.[30]

Our warrant for the Return we await is the Resurrection of our Lord. And Père Teilhard longed to die on that day. His prayer was granted. On Good Friday, 1955, he had opened his conscience to his Provincial, who had not been expecting him on that day. On Holy Saturday he made his confession. On Easter morning, after saying his own Mass, he went to pontifical high Mass in St Patrick's Cathedral, New York. In the middle of the afternoon he was struck down by a cerebral haemorrhage. With the poet, he will have been able to say, but in words that are new and vastly more related to reality:

> I have descended with You into the tomb . . .
> There I have lain motionless, and the
> confines of your tomb
> Have become the confines of the Universe.[31]

[29] Acts 3. 21: "When all is restored anew." "The triumph of Christ is beyond this world"—Père Teilhard believed this as firmly as Père Philippe de la Trinité (*op. cit.*, p. 53).

[30] *Le Christique* (1955), p. 7; *Milieu Divin*, pp. 140, 154. Eloquent appeals not to "dissolve the message of Christ 'in the flux of time and evolution'", and not to "anaesthetize man's sense of the absolute" (Cf. Ch. Journet, *Le dogme chemin de la Foi*, 1963, p. 91), could apply to Père Teilhard only by an obvious misunderstanding of more than one allusion. Cf. *Mon Univers*, p. 3: "As far back as I can remember (before I was ten) I can see that I had one dominating passion, the passion for the Absolute."

[31] Paul Claudel, *La Maison fermée* (*Cinq grandes Odes*, p. 167.)

TEILHARD'S DEFENSE
OF CHRISTIANITY

I

NOTE ON TEILHARD'S
APOLOGETICS

THE term "apologetics" is somewhat out of favour in these days. The science itself is decried, as though it could be no more than a sort of special pleading inspired by prejudice. We must, indeed, admit that examples of this are not infrequent, and that, no doubt, is why many believers allow external pressure to impose this pejorative view of apologetics upon them, and seem to be afraid of being found engaged in such unpopular work.[1]

Père Teilhard was never subject to such fear. His thought, we know, was profoundly influenced by that of Maurice Blondel. Now, Blondel never believed that an apologetic aim must necessarily detract from the rational objectivity of his philosophical work; on the contrary, in his celebrated *Letter* of 1896, he brought out the importance of the "demands of modern thought as affecting apologetics" and tried to determine "philosophic method in the study of the religious problem".[2] No more did Teilhard fear any opposition between such an aim and the rigour of his own phenomenology. Just as Blondel, and, indeed, we may say, following Blondel's

[1] This point was raised by Cardinal Siri, Archbishop of Genoa, in his 1963 Pastoral Letter: "There are some who would like to do away with apologetics and find it offensive to see it in action or even to hear it spoken of. . . ."

[2] On this *Letter*, see Henri Bouillard, *Blondel et le Christianisme* (1961), pp. 29–44, and his *Philosophie et Christianisme dans la pensée de Maurice Blondel* (in *Logique de la Foi*, 1964, pp. 169–92). Cf. Albert Cartier, *Existence et Verité* (1955), pp. 211–13.

example, he endeavoured in numerous essays to conduct his thinking in accordance with a rational process that neither presupposes, nor formulates as it progresses, any affirmation of faith, but "develops by the internal force of its principles",[3] and holds good for every type of mind. Again like Blondel, he never, when he is not speaking as a Christian to Christians, introduces into his premises, avowedly or surreptitiously, anything that we hold by faith. This does not prevent him from openly and frequently proclaiming his apologetic aim— much more so than Blondel, who had some reason to shield himself from the abuse of a term that was used as a weapon against him.[4] Teilhard wrote mostly "for the Gentiles", and he could have said, again with Blondel, who was echoing Descartes, "*Scribo etiam Turcis*".[5] The fact is, he thought, "it is not given to all immediately to appreciate supernatural views of the Incarnation". He sought accordingly to disclose to his readers, in the first place "by following a line that is intelligible to the majority of unbelievers, the value of spirit, of God, and of personality". Without accepting the "least distortion of spirit",[6] he sought to direct minds "towards some divine Meeting-point", to lead them up to "the expectation of some revelation", to communicate to them "the burning vision of a Universe that is not impersonal and closed, but open . . ." In 1948, when he was drawing up a brief summary of his thought, he said that if, in a first period, it was expressed

---

[3] Cf. F. Guimet, on Blondel. *Cahiers universitaires catholiques* (1964), p. 381. Similarly, Blondel speaks of the "chain of intellectual determinism", *L'Illusion idéaliste* (1898), *Premiers écrits*, vol. II, p. 99.

[4] Blondel sometimes accepted and at other times rejected the term, according to the meaning attributed to it. He protested, with reason, when Émile Brehier maintained that "Blondel's work was not philosophy but apologetics", and showed that he had given proof of "an attitude of mind quite the opposite of the prejudice too readily attributed to the apologist". *Le Problème de la philosophie catholique* (*Cahiers de la Nouvelle Journée*, 1932, pp. 150-1).

[5] *Loc. cit.*, p. 6. Cf. *Itinéraire philosophique* (1928), pp. 41-2. *Le Christianisme de Descartes, Revue de métaphysique et de morale* (1916), p. 566.

[6] Marcel Légaut, *Cahiers universitaires catholiques*, Oct. 1956.

in a "Physics" (or "a sort of Phenomenology") this Physics
forms the basis on which he sought to build, in a second period,
an "Apologetics"—itself complemented by, or crowned by,
a "Mystics".[7] Such, in fact, is the most usual pattern of his
thought.[8]

It will often, accordingly, be essential, if we are not to misunderstand Père Teilhard, to bear in mind this approach to
apologetics. This has been well brought out in an important
study by Père Christian d'Armagnac.[9] In November 1912,
Père Teilhard himself, in an article for the *Correspondant* on
the religious ethnology week he had just attended at Louvain,
wrote, "The days have gone when our apologists, timidly
sneaking unacceptable data they had begged from their
opponents, tried to reconcile them with their belief." From
that time his attitude was determined. His apologetics was
always to be *positive* and mastering. It would thus escape
the reproaches customarily levelled against those apologists
who do, in fact, simply "apologise". It could not completely
escape the difficulties that are inevitable in any apologetics:
just as the proofs of the existence of God, if one cannot go
beyond the limitations of the proof itself, seem to place God
at the service of the world, so, in one light, Christ can appear
to be at the service of evolution—heaven at the service of
earth. This, we should be careful to note, is a false impression
that closer attention would soon have corrected.—These,
however, are problems that need not be discussed here. Our
immediate aim is more limited. Leaving aside, at first, the
content of Teilhard's apologetics, so far as we can without
doing injustice to it, or referring to it only to refresh our

[7] *La Pensée du Père Teilhard de Chardin, par lui-même*, for a proposed article on his thought, April 1948. *Les Études philosophiques* (1955), pp. 580–1.
[8] In *Comment je vois*, unusually, the threefold division is Physics (Phenomen-ology), Metaphysics, Mysticism .The apologetic viewpoint is included in the first part.
[9] *La Pensée du Père Teilhard de Chardin comme apologétique moderne*, *Nouvelle Revue Théologique* (1963), pp. 598–621.

memories, we shall instead examine its predominating form or plan. To put it more exactly and narrowly, we shall concentrate on the analysis of a passage in which his programme is outlined, commenting on it with the assistance, when necessary, of any other passages that may help us to understand it fully. We shall thus be able to check some interpretations it has suggested.

This text has, in fact, been quoted and commented on, and criticized, in many quarters. Many have found it objectionable from the point of view of the Catholic faith, and at the same time peculiarly characteristic of Teilhardian thought. It runs as follows:

> If, as a result of some interior revolution, I were successively to lose my faith in Christ, my faith in a personal God, my faith in the Spirit, I think that I would still continue to believe in the World. The World (the value, the infallibility, the goodness of the World): that, in the final analysis, is the first and the last thing in which I believe. It is by this faith that I live, and it is to this faith, I feel, that at the moment of death, mastering all doubts, I shall surrender myself. . . . I surrender myself to this undefined faith in a single and Infallible World, wherever it may lead me.

TEILHARD'S
APPROACH AND METHODS

THE quotation found on page 136 is taken from an
article in the *Osservatore Romano* of 1 July 1962. The
anonymous author follows it with this note of distress,
which makes one fear the worst: "*Tuttavia leggiamo con
vera pena queste righe. . . . Sono parole del 1934, ma quanto
sarebbe meglio che non fossero mai state scritte!*"[1]
We would not deny that there is something over-nice and
paradoxical in the turn which Père Teilhard gives to his
thought, even, as we shall see later, when compared with his
normal way of expressing himself. But it will be well to apply
in our own case what Étienne Gilson recently said of another
writer: "You must see that you are qualified to understand
the text before you comment on it."[2] Had the anonymous
author we have quoted, and some others with him, made it
their first care to "be qualified to understand" the disputed
text, first by reading it in its context, then by noting the type
of literary setting in which it appears, and finally by trying
to form a precise idea of the extremely complex Teilhardian
concept of "the World", then, I believe, they would have
profoundly modified their verdict.

[1] Nevertheless, it is with real distress that we read these lines. . . . True, these
words were written in 1934, but how much better if they had never been written
at all.

[2] *A propos de Rabelais. Rabelais franciscain*, in *Les Idées et les Lettres* (1955),
p. 236. "A considerable modification of method should be introduced." M.
Gilson's hope is far from being universally realized. Cf. *ibid.*, p. 231: "We should
learn Rabelais' language before we read him, and ask ourselves just what the
words he uses mean." This advice is as applicable to modern as to ancient texts.

The passage in question, of which we are told only that it dates from 1934, is taken from an apologetic essay entitled, *How I believe* (*Comment je crois*).[3] Père Teilhard wrote it in China, between September and November, at the suggestion of a theologian friend, Mgr Bruno de Solages.[4] At first he wished to publish it, but when he had finished the draft he was not entirely satisfied, and he does not seem later to have tried to have it brought out. Even so, the essay is none the less a reflection of his thought. We shall see later to what type of reader it was addressed. Here we may note in the first place that it is not simply influenced by apologetic considerations. Like several other of his essays, and perhaps more than any of them, it is essentially and integrally an apologetic writing. To this, more than to all the others, applies the remark he made to one of his correspondents two years earlier, in connection with *L'Esprit de la Terre*: "You must understand that this is addressed *ad gentiles*."[5] The lines we quoted appear in the first paragraph. Restored to their proper place they can be explained, we shall see, in a perfectly natural, and, in my opinion, acceptable sense.

Let us examine this more closely.

The first section of *Comment je crois* is entitled: "The individual stages of my Faith." The first paragraph of this first section deals with *Faith in the World*. The sentences quoted from the *Osservatore Romano* article are the first and last sentences in that paragraph.[6] Here we have an essentially methodological text—even though its scope, as we shall see later, goes beyond a mere indication of the method. The

[3] The title is given (in English) in a letter of 23 Sept. 1934: "I am calling it 'Comment je crois' ('*Why and How*')"; *Letters from a Traveller*, p. 205. (Père Teilhard's English title is italicized.)

[4] He was already thinking about it in April, but was unable to get down to drafting it until the beginning of September. It was finished about 10 Nov.

[5] Letter of 17 Oct. 1932. Cf. 6 Oct.

[6] The final sentence should not, therefore, be run together with the first, with no qualification.

apologist, before beginning his series of demonstrations. states an initial hypothesis, of which at the same time he says, in the very first words he uses, that it is completely fictional. "If, as a result of some interior revolution, I were to lose, etc." Thus, by a process that is the converse of the positive process he proposes to carry through later (in which, throughout the essay, supporting proofs will be adduced), he begins by starting with a clean sheet. By this preliminary operation, he intends to place himself on the same level as his supposed interlocutor, the unbeliever whom he hopes to lead to the Christian faith. In doing so, he indicates in advance, enumerating them in reverse order, the four successive stages of the demonstration he proposes to give, or of the road which he invites him to share.

What he thus announces is no novel approach, but one of the most natural of procedures. It is—seen, of course, in its proper perspective, which we shall soon have to define— the classic procedure of our natural philosophy and of our current apologetic treatises.

In other words, like every honest and serious apologist, Père Teilhard does not propose to assume the very thing he is setting out to prove. He starts, accordingly, by going back on his tracks, dismissing, with a just care for method—first his faith in Christ—then his faith in a personal God—and finally even his faith in Spirit, that is, in the spirituality and immortality of the soul[7]: his faith in what he generally calls, using the technical vocabulary required by his cosmic outlook, the "irreversibility" or "exigence of their reversible"[8]; he has other ways of expressing this: for example, "the human

[7] Cf. to Léontine Zanta, 24 Jan. 1929: "In my view, souls, and the soul of souls, are coming increasingly to take on the appearance of solidly consistent and real things. To dissolve a soul seems to me, in all sincerity, infinitely more difficult than to smash an atom. By survival, no doubt, the soul is introduced into organisms of which we can speak, as of the divine qualities, only by analogy:—but the soul, the more centred it is, is stable, with the very stability of the Universe."

[8] *Les conditions psychologiques de l'unification humaine* (1949); *Œuvres*, VII, p. 182.

spearhead *pierces* the confines of the experiential, *qua* (by virtue of being) charged with irreversibility", or, "the World will never slip back from any peak of consciousness it attains".[9] None of the three things he has surrendered, Père Teilhard thinks, is self-evident, however certain he may be of it himself. None of the three has yet been accepted by his interlocutor. Accordingly, Père Teilhard asks him, as a start, to accept only one thing: this is something more elementary, more immediate, the one thing that the unbeliever he knows and is addressing is ready to grant him since, for the unbeliever, there can be an argument about it. It gives them both, therefore, a common starting-point, or a common basis, for the successive stages Teihard hopes they will cover together. Using this "fundamental adherence" as foundation, he will then try to build up again, while the unbeliever looks on, the complete structure of his own faith. The foundation, Teilhard believes, is well chosen in as much as, unlike the three other objects of belief he has distinguished, some "faith in the World" seems to him initially imperative for everyone. At any rate, even if he cannot define it exactly, he finds it present in many of his contemporaries, particularly among the scientists he is addressing, and is conscious of it himself. "Matter could more easily be independent of gravity than a soul be independent of the presence of the Universe."

Continuing to address his reader, the unbelieving scientist, the apologist then says: "To this faith in the World, the primary faith we both share, I surrender myself, wherever it may lead me—a faith that is not only spontaneous and elementary but 'undefined' or vague, of whose implications (as I know from my own experience) we are as yet unaware."

[9] Quoted by Roger Leys, S.J., *Revue Teilhard de Chardin* (1963), p. 5. Cf. *La Refléxion de l'Énergie* (1952), 4: *Irréversibilité de la Refléxion. Le Rebondissement humain de l'évolution* (1947): "irreversible, that is to say, immortal". *L'Atomisme de l'Esprit* (1941), 7. *L'Étoffe de l'Univers* (1953). *Barrière de la mort et co-réflexion* (1955), 4; *Œuvres*, VII, pp. 347–51, 348, 400, 424–6; V, p. 265. *Sur la loi d'irreversibilité en évolution, Œuvres*, III, pp. 73–4, etc.

Here we have an invitation to the other to surrender himself, as Teilhard has done, with the disinterestedness indispensable to a search for the truth. Where, then, will this initial faith lead him? Teilhard is well aware of the answer[10]: so well aware that it was to demonstrate it that he sat down to write this essay, and if we wish to know it, too, we have only to read on. This initial faith, as it unfolds its implications, leads "successively" to faith in the Spirit—then to faith in a personal God—and finally to the threshold of faith in the personal God revealed in Jesus Christ and adored in the Catholic Church. This, let us emphasize once more, is the whole purpose of *How I Believe*, its whole plan. Père Teilhard writes simply and solely to arrive at that conclusion. We see in it the stages of his apologetic demonstration. This begins immediately, as the second sub-heading indicates: *Faith in the Spirit*, followed shortly by *Faith in Immortality*, then by *Faith in Personality*, until we come to Faith in Christ.[11]

It is apparent, as we pointed out earlier, that this is the classic procedure, as, indeed emphasized by the sub-headings to the successive paragraphs. (We may note, incidentally, that Faith in Christ will not be treated simply in a last paragraph like those that precede it: it will be the exclusive subject of a second part of the essay, differently set out: the reason being that Faith in Christ is not, like the preceding beliefs,

[10] Cf. an analogous passage, in which, however, Teilhard puts it more forcibly: ". . . There is some Absolute that attracts us and at the same time remains hidden. To see its face, to answer its call and understand its meaning, to learn to live more, we have to *plunge* into the vast current of things, and see where the flood carries us". (*La Vie Cosmique*).

[11] Père Teilhard explained this in a letter to the author (15 Sept. 1943): "I want to try and show that there can be no true unification outside a personalizing fusion of the elements with a maximum of consciousness (i.e. of personality). Thus, into 'my universe' are introduced or translated the two notions of divine Personality and human immortality, on which 'Revelation' rests. I'm trying at the moment to express this in a paper for Bruno de Solages: *Comment je crois*." The subject was, in fact, constantly in Père Teilhard's mind. It is the underlying plan, for example, of *L'Esprit de la Terre* (1931), *Œuvres*, VI, pp. 52–7, and *Le Phenomène spirituel* (1937), *ibid.*, pp. 117–39.

derived simply from a process of reasoning. This is a key point to which we shall return later.) Essentially, it is the procedure adopted by St Thomas Aquinas, whose *Summa contra Gentiles* advances from the truths recognized as "natural" by the Gentiles of his day (which in practice more or less means by Islamic thought as known to St Thomas), to those that only Christians profess[12]; or again, as in a celebrated question in the *Summa Theologica*, by an ascent from the World to God: for St Thomas rejects the thesis of some of his contemporaries that the existence of God is *per se nota*[13]; he also, accordingly, "retracing his mental steps" simply as method of proceeding, leaves aside his own faith in God. The same procedure is generally used for instruction in our schools, and it is that recommended, at least as a general plan, by the teaching authority of the Church.

When, however, we said that Père Teilhard adopted the classic procedure we added that he saw it in the light of his own objective, and we should repeat that within this comparatively flexible framework there were certain points of view that he gave new emphasis to. Anyone is at liberty to regard these as more or less illuminating than other points of view; in other words, the utility or cogency of Teilhard's own contribution to the line of argument he puts forward may be contested—just as one is free to have one's doubts, for example, about the validity as a proof of the famous "argument of St Anselm". That, however, is another matter with which we are not immediately concerned. We may confine ourselves to noting three characteristics of Teilhard's approach.

[12] The centuries-old problem of the exact character of this *Summa* has recently been discussed again by M. Anton C. Pegis, *Qu'est-ce que la "Summa contra Gentiles"?* in *L'Homme devant Dieu* (1964), vol. 2, pp. 169–82. See also his *St Thomas and Philosophy* (Aquinas Lecture, Milwaukee, 1964). Cf. M. D. Chenu, *Introduction à l'Étude de S. Thomas d'Aquin* (1950), pp. 249–51. The problem is too complex to be more than referred to here.

[13] Similarly Teilhard, *Comment je crois*, 20: "By this name 'Omega point' I have long designated and shall again here, an ultimate and self-subsistent pole of consciousness . . . such a Meeting-point is not directly apprehensible to us."

In the first place, instead of stating a simple fact, the contingency of the beings that make up our world, Teilhard notes a certain value-content: "faith in the World", in its initial state, is already more than a simple recognition of a reality; it entails a certain attachment to that reality (how understood, we shall be seeing), a certain confidence in it, by reason, at any rate, of a certain appreciation of the "goodness" of created being, or, perhaps more exactly, of its natural progress.[14] It supposes that the intelligence, no longer a slave to first appearances, has rejected the "temptation of the multiple".[15]—Proceeding from that supposition, Teilhard's demonstrations, he intends, will take on an aspect more scientific than metaphysical—even though he here differs more from some modern scholasticism than from St Thomas's; for Père Teilhard's approach consists in linking up again, thanks to our new scientific advances, with the approach of the ancient "physicists" or "natural philosophers", of whom the greatest was Aristotle, and whose general outlook was retained by St Thomas, though rejected by a number of his recent followers. This has been well brought out by Père Jean Daniélou;[16] this, too, explains why some modern scholastics are opposed to Teilhardian philosophy, in which they see not only "confusion" but "retrogression".[17] Finally, a

[14] Teilhard had written on 4 July 1920: ". . . Such a (natural) progress is necessary to explain the present state of the world, and I believe, to provide the foundation stone for our belief in God."

[15] Letter of 27 May 1923.

[16] *Signification de Teilhard de Chardin*, *Études* (Feb. 1962), pp. 147–8.

[17] Père Philippe de la Trinité, *Le Père Teilhard de Chardin, synthèse ou confusion?* in *Divinitas* (April 1959), p. 288: "It is impossible to agree with Scholastics"[i.e. St Thomas in particular] who have followed him [Aristotle] in going astray precisely by methodological confusion, from a failure clearly to distinguish knowledge of ontological type from knowledge of positive type. Such obscurity has been with us too long. It should once again be denounced." For a better understanding of this criticism, one should read an earlier study by the same author (*Divinitas*, 1958, pp. 268 ff.), *Les cinq voies de St Thomas d'Aquin*. See also his *Rome et Teilhard de Chardin*, pp. 49 and 65. Cf. Gaston Fessard, S.J., *La vision religieuse et cosmique de Teilhard de Chardin*, in *L'Homme devant Dieu* (1963), vol. 3, pp. 223–48.

third characteristic: Teilhard's approach is at the same time more "existential", as it is called now, than that of our text-book apologetics. It is not developed completely impersonally, but embodies a personal witness. This comes out in the title, *How I Believe*; and where other writers would speak, for example, of a "chain of reasoning", Teilhard is more apt to speak of "a psychological axis of spiritual progress towards God".

The more unmistakable, moreover, the emphasis of this essay—"a personal confession", Teilhard calls it—the more mistaken one would be to interpret it as a sort of purely subjective confidential statement. In "*How I Believe*", he confided to a friend when he was actually writing the last lines, "I feel that I have succeeded in expressing my personal reasons for believing".[18] At the same time, even though he uses the first person, it is with the conviction, as he himself makes clear, that "man is essentially the same in all of us" and that there is something "deep in his spirit . . . greater than the man himself". He tries, accordingly, to arouse in the other an experience similar to his own, to initiate in him a similar sequence of thought, by showing him "the mark, in [his] heart, of the disquiet and expectation that characterize the religious condition of the World of today".[19] More than twenty years later, in the introduction to his *Le Christique*, he speaks in the same way: he wishes, he says, to bear witness "in all objectivity, to a certain interior event, to a certain personal experience, in which I cannot but see the trace of a general drift of the Human closing in on itself."[20]

He has this in common with all the great apologists: before

---

[18] 11 Nov. 1934. Earlier, on 8 Oct. 1933, in connection with an essay of the same type, *La Place du Christianisme dans l'Univers*, also written "by request", he said, "It is an attempt to distinguish my reasons for believing."

[19] *Comment je crois.*

[20] *Le Christique*, p. 1. See also the whole conclusion: ". . . Might I not be simply the dupe of a mirage within me?—that is what I often ask myself.— But then again . . .." Cf. Pierre Leroy, *op. cit.*, pp. 60-2.

writing for others, he has thought about his own case, he knows the nature and cogency of various objections from having felt them himself, and the solution he offers to others is the solution of his own personal problems: for he knows that his problems are the same as those that face the men he lives among, and that all that has to be done is to help to open their eyes. Here Étienne Borne makes a happy comparison with Pascal. "Both reach their own conclusion only after going through . . . preliminary stages that seem for a moment to merge into the position from which the thought first derived its impulse, just as the tangent at a given point coincides with the curve where we decide to draw it. Thus, both take the risks without which the reasoning lacks authenticity."[21] This may well be some excuse for those readers who mistake the objection Teilhard puts forward for his answer.[22]

On 20 September 1916, Père Teilhard had expressed his longing for "the ideal Christian, the Christian at once new and old" who could solve "in his soul" what he considered the essential problem of apologetics. On the feast of the

[21] *De Pascal à Teilhard de Chardin* (1963), pp. 77–8.

[22] There is still, in spite of everything, too much to distract the student. Remarking on the "distressing confusion" we find in moral science "in its present condition", that is, among many of his contemporaries, Père Teilhard describes it as follows: "What is good and what is evil? and can we even say that there is such a thing as good or evil, so long as no definite direction is attributed to the Evolution that carries us along?—Is effort really superior to enjoyment? Disinterestedness better than selfishness? Kindness preferable to force?—For lack of some guiding point in the Universe, diametrically opposed views on these essential points are plausibly defended. And meanwhile, human energy, with nothing to guide it, is lamentably dissipated on our Earth" (*Le Cône du Temps*; *Œuvres*, V, pp. 119–20). It is hardly excusable to interpret this as meaning that Teilhard "makes his thought perfectly clear" and that he is "undermining moral teaching" and to ask indignantly, "Could one more unjustly cast doubts on the reality of Good and Evil, man's responsibility etc.?" (Dr. Maurice Vernet, *La Grande Illusion de Teilhard de Chardin*, 1964, pp. 167–8). For Teilhard, as, I presume, for this critic, "all this disorder comes logically to an end—all this restless movement is polarized" as soon as we discover that "there is an end to which Life is directed" (p. 120).

Epiphany, 1919, he had written as a colophon to his "Note on the evangelization of our own times": "The great converters (or perverters) of men have always been those in whom the soul of their own time burnt *most intensely*". And to explain and win acceptance for the "reversal of perspective" from which, with his new scientific synthesis, was to result the positive reconciliation between Science and Christian Revelation, he recalled his own interior history:

> First of all, I was impressed, as everyone has been, by the sort of priority enjoyed, in events, by the Lesser and the Past. And then, I was obliged, if I was not to remain incapable of understanding anything in or around me, to reverse the perspective and accord pre-eminence to the Future and the Greater.[23]

This method—if it is indeed a method—was normal with Teilhard. In some cases it can be very largely a style of literary exposition, lending itself to the successive development of various aspects of a problem and of steps towards the suggested solution.[24] Conversely, Teilhard sometimes assumes that a feeling he himself is vividly aware of has been generally shared by his contemporaries rather more rapidly than facts warrant.[25] In most cases, however, the personal angle should be given proper weight. It may repel some readers, but it ensures the apologist a better audience, drawn from a certain number of minds in agreement, even if not openly, with his own. It enables him, too, by dwelling on the "obscurities", the "shadows of the faith", to communicate with more warmth its certainties. And there is a further advantage: in a

[23] From a wedding address (1928). Cf. P. Smulders, *La Vision* (1963), p. 73; G. Crespy, *op. cit.*, p. 71; "*How I Believe* was an attempt at justification presented fictitiously—though where does the fiction begin?—as a description of the birth of faith."

[24] Thus in the *Vie Cosmique*, when he speaks of the "crisis of paganism". In any case, such words as "perhaps" and "just now" are an unobtrusive warning to the reader.

[25] For example, *L'Hominisation* (1923): "It is inadmissible, as we all feel, that two different ways of seeing and understanding things should continue to be current". (*Œuvres*, III, p. 78)

subject such as he is treating, from which any demonstration of triumph over an adversary must be excluded, it enables the apologist to speak throughout with modesty: this does not impair the uncompromising rigour with which he wishes to conduct his exposition, but it means that he can put it forward as the story of a man who has first been a seeker, and is unmistakably anxious to share with his neighbour what he has found, though without wishing to force his agreement.

We should note too, that there is no lack of firmness in his emphasis, and in this, as in many other matters, Teilhard's example as an apologist can be most valuable to us. There are some Christians who are ashamed (and refuse to recognize their shame) of allowing themselves to be persuaded that "we should not sadden nor disconcert those who conceive their whole lives within the limits of this earth".[26] Such people need a tonic, and they could not find a better one than in reading Père Teilhard.

For the same reason, however, certain expressions in the passage we are analysing may at first seem too strong. It is certainly a fact that some people have been shocked by them. Does not Père Teilhard declare that "in the last analysis" the World is "the first and the only thing in which he believes"?

In this passage—and we should remember to what sort of reader it is addressed—there is, indeed, a certain ambiguity. It is, however, we should add, an ambiguity that is initially inevitable. It is an ambiguity inherent in any progress of thought, when one has to make the transition from one order to another. What Père Teilhard is preparing to demonstrate to the unbeliever is that the World, in which both of them, before they even start, believe, in reality presupposes many things which the unbeliever does not yet suspect and would be unwilling to accept. Père Teilhard, accordingly, will try to make him see that, logically, his faith in the World pre-

[26] Cf. a fine and opportune article by Jacques Perret, *Tristesse et action de grâces avec S. Augustin, Cahiers universitaires catholiques* (1964), pp. 373–7.

supposes (or entails) if it is to appear well founded (and by the same token, if it is to be transformed) first of all faith in the Spirit—then faith in a personal and personalizing[27] God—and perhaps even, finally, faith in Christ, through whom God reveals himself in person.[28]

Thus we continually return to the essential skein of thought, whose unravelling will remove all ambiguity. Already, if we have appreciated the initial position, we can understand how it is that the apologist can say, in language that is necessarily ambiguous because he cannot at this point refer to realities whose existence he has not yet established, that the World is "in the last analysis" the first and the only thing in which he believes. The first, in its "confused" and even "extremely vague" form, in as much as it constitutes the natural basis, the starting-point, the logical premise of all the rest; the only, in as much as he can see in advance that everything else is, in some way or another, involved in it. This at the same time is why he can at the start be in agreement with the unbeliever, for whom this faith in the World is equally, though in a more narrow, and restrictive sense, the only certain thing or value; at the same time Père Teilhard hopes ultimately to show him that being "the first thing" it must progressively be followed by the three others, and so be transformed to become in the end "the last".

In other words, in this "existentialist" style of context, and expressed with a personal emphasis, Père Teilhard's basic affirmation once more corresponds to the basic affirmation behind every similar attempt at demonstration: this is, that the World is an inescapable fact, and must be intelligible. Only, the apologist also knows already in his own mind, from

[27] As evolution itself is for Teilhard, the progress of his thought is thus an "ascent into the Personal". *La Montée de l'Autre* (1942), end; *Œuvres*, VII, p. 81. Cf. *La Centrologie* (1944); *ibid.*, p. 124.

[28] On 7 January of this same year, Père Teilhard wrote that he would like to see a book written in which would be shown "the birth of a faith in Christ starting from simple faith in being. . . . Who will give us this *Summa ad Gentiles*?"

mature reflection, where he wishes to proceed: through this World, he can already distinguish the essential conditions of its intelligibility and goodness, conditions which he is keeping to himself, to be revealed step by step to his fellow searcher.— And it is here that it becomes impossible for the disinterested reader *thoroughly* to understand what Teilhard is saying, without distorting or weakening it, unless he makes an effort to share more fully in his "own outlook".

THE COMPLEXITY OF THE COSMOS

WHAT, then, is this "World", which, as our text de-
clares, is the "only thing in which, in the last
analysis", our apologist believes?

This is by no means a simple question, for in Teilhard we
meet the "polyvalence" of the Cosmos.[1]

In the first place, we must point out, as is evident, that it is
not exclusively or even principally—that indeed it is in no
way—a question of the world of appearances (external or
internal), vaguely unified and valorized: nor of the "Universe
in the linked totality of its psychic, temporal and spatial
dimensions" as it can appear to us "for a start", "in a first
period".[2] In short, it is not the "experiential Universe".[3]
It is not "the World closed in on itself".[4] Père Teilhard had
always been conscious of the "irremediable *superficiality*" of
that Universe, "almost to the point of being caused physical
suffering".[5] In itself it offers no permanent interest: far from
it, as long as one considers it in isolation on the supposition
that it is bound to continue as it is. If one were unable to
grasp the law of its evolution, and that means in some way to
unlock the secret of its finality—if one could not ultimately
discover the "centre of attraction that already makes it
lovable"—that World could only horrify us. The world that

---

[1] *La Foi qui opère* (1919), p. 16.
[2] *Esquisse d'une dialectique de l'Esprit, Premier temps* (*Œuvres*, VII, p. 150).
[3] *La Foi qui opère*, p. 13.
[4] *La Conquête du Monde et le Règne de Dieu* (1916), p. 15.
[5] Letter of 12 July 1918 (*Making of a Mind*, p. 214).

imprisons us in our ephemeral individuality, the opaque world that we see blindly weaving "the exasperating veil of phenomena",[6] the world of "agonizing enormity", which makes us die and is itself doomed to death—that world, could we suppose it to be "the only thing", would be entirely unworthy of anything that resembled "faith". For it is a world "desperately frozen and desperately closed".[7] Within such a world a thinking man could only shudder at the thought of being for ever lost in it, immobilized, imprisoned.[8] As for our own world of today, Père Teilhard is constantly saying that mankind must "escape" from it. That, as explained by him, is what matters most intimately to modern man, and the whole question is how to achieve an escape that will not be illusory and will not leave us once again shut up inside the prison: how to "succeed in piercing the temporo-spatial membrane of the Phenomenon".[9] How are we ultimately to find our way out of the labyrinth? The man whose reflective powers are awake tries desperately to "find the way out, to the break through he must at all costs make, from the terrifying cosmic machine in which he is caught up". And Teilhard undertakes to show him the only possible way out, "open at the heart of things"—the only escape that is not a deception; and that is "escape in depth" or "ecstasy".[10]

[6] 20 Nov. 1918 (*Making of a Mind*, p. 256). Cf. *La Peur de l'existence* (1949): "The sensible world disconcerts us by the impenetrable membrane that the Phenomenon stretches between us and all that is above the human spirit"; "The rise of Science" only aggravates this situation (*Œuvres*, VII, pp. 196 and 192–3).

[7] *Réflexions sur le bonheur, Cahiers*, 2, p. 69; *Le Christique* (1955), p. 13.

[8] *Les singularités de l'espèce humaine, Annales de paléontologie*, 1955, pp. 3–4. This, the last of all Père Teilhard's scientific articles, restates, and qualifies more precisely, the idea already expressed in 1918 in the symbolic meditation *La Grande Monade*. Earlier again, in 1917 (Jan. 1) he wrote: "The former cosmic framework no longer suffices to contain (to satisfy) the new activities born with the human soul".(*Making of a Mind*, p. 160).

[9] *Comment je vois* (1948), no. 20. Cf. *Milieu Divin*, p. 140. *Haec est quae vincit mundum, fides nostra*.

[10] *L'Atomisme de l'Esprit* (1941); *La Peur de l'existence* (1949), *Œuvres*, VII, pp. 47, 53, 200. *La Grande Monade* (1943), *Cahiers*, 2, etc.

Thus we take our first step in understanding this World in which our apologist believes. It is the complete contrary of the "World understood in an infantile, confused way", in which some materialist scientists believe.[11] Emerging, by a "revolution in depth" from its material and vital conditions, it is an essentially spiritual Universe, in which "the greatest consciousness" has conquered "Entropy". It is a World, Teilhard says again, in which "the primacy of Spirit" is affirmed, Spirit which he defined as St Thomas does when he says that it is that "which reflects upon itself in perfect reflection".[12] Or we may say, which amounts to the same thing, that it is the primacy of the Future that is affirmed.[13] It is the Universe considered in "its indestructible portion".[14] To put it more precisely, it is ultimately a "personal Universe", a "Universe with a personal mesh",[15] a "Universe of souls", a "World of souls"[16] (this last is a favourite expression with Teilhard). Still more precisely, it is a universe of "inter-personal relationships"—not excluding the relationship to God (Omega) which provides the foundation for all the others; "it is, loaded with the spoils of matter, the individual treasure of souls" which is endowed with a "cosmic consistence" and, being organized around a "supreme Centre, both lovable and loving" is thereby "imperishable".[17] With all its weight, the

[11] 4 May 1931: "Hu-Shih has arrived at a *Credo* . . . faith in the World, but in a World conceived in a childishly immature and imprecise way. . . . He doesn't see that the Cosmos holds together not by matter but by spirit" (*Letters from a Traveller*, pp. 176–7).

[12] *In librum de Causis*, lect. 15. *Summa Theologica*, I, q. 14, art. 2, ad. 1 (quoted by Smulders, *op. cit.*, p. 75). For Teilhard's teaching on spirit, see Smulders, pp. 71–83.

[13] *The Phenomenon of Man*, p. 169. *Le Cœur de la Matière* (1950), p. 9; p. 10: "The bliss that I had sought formerly in Iron, I could find only in Spirit."

[14] *L'Esprit de la Terre; Œuvres*, VI, p. 51.

[15] *Esquisse d'un Univers personnel* (1936); *Œuvres*, VI, p. 88.

[16] *La Vie Cosmique* (1916), p. 42

[17] *Letters from a Traveller*, p. 151. It is impossible to guess what objection Père Philippe de la Trinité can have to this magnificent passage, as to many others which he quotes as "revealing" a perverse "tendency".(*Rome et Teilhard de Chardin*, pp. 39, 40).

world rests upon a centre that lies ahead of it. And, far from souls being fragile and accidental, it is souls, the associations of souls, and the powers of souls, that alone progress infallibly and alone will endure.[18]

Those last words were spoken in 1928. In a letter dated 25 February 1929, five years before he was considering writing *How I Believe*, Père Teilhard gave another explanation of his meaning, not as though his reasoning had just led him to realize a truth that was new to him, but as having just succeeded in pinning down his idea in a more rigorously thought-out structure:

It seems to me [he wrote] that I have almost succeeded in formulating a sort of "Physics of the Spirit", which expresses more completely the suggestions sketched out in my note on the Phenomenon of man. It is a *sort of reduction of the Universe to the spiritual*,[19] on the physical plane . . . that has for me the fortunate corollary of legitimizing the retention of persons (i.e. the "immortality" of souls) in the Universe. I shall try, in this paper, to pin down this prospect of a World whose equilibrium consists in painfully resting on a Consciousness and a Personalization that is continually growing greater—an exact reversal of the World of modern Science.[20]

Again, on 15 April, he writes: "I find now that I can no longer envisage the World otherwise than in the form of an immense movement of Spirit."[21] Only in the direction of the

[18] Wedding address, 14 June 1928.
[19] My italics.
[20] On 29 Sept. 1928, in connection with a note, for the review *Scientia*, on *The Phenomenon of Man*, he wrote: "I believe that the step I am trying to take will be most important for the 'primacy of the spiritual'. God is just the other side of the door. . . ." (The allusion to Jacques Maritain's book, then just published, will be noted.) On 5 April 1927 he had written: "If only you knew how much in spite of (or rather because of) my evolutionist ideas, Man and his spirituality every day take on increasing importance in my eyes!" Cf. *Hymne de l'Univers*, p. 114: "Transformism is, rather, evidence in favour of the essential triumph of Spirit." *Le Cœur de la Matière*, p. 10: "The Universe in gravitation fell forward upon Spirit, as upon its stable form."
[21] Peking, to Léontine Zanta.

Spirit can one find "the open air, the wide road out". And on 20 September of the same year, 1929, he again speaks of this "discovery" which was obviously occupying his mind, and expresses the same wish: "In a roundabout sort of way that I would like to try and describe, I am rediscovering the Personality of God and the immortality of the soul as elements essential to the structure of my Universe." Five years later, no more than a few months before writing *How I Believe*, he wrote to a correspondent that praise of God, the end of creation, should, he thought, be fully expressed in "the realization of an organic *unity*—into which, of course, will be drawn the whole marvellous essence of the inter-personal relationships that characterize the Universe, starting with Man". In consequence, "nothing, in my view, is more spiritual than the consummation of the Universe".[22] Shortly afterwards, again, in a note about *The Phenomenon of Man*, he says, "The Phenomenon of the spirit is . . . the cosmic movement *par excellence*—that on which all depends and which nothing can explain."[23]

This is still not the whole story. We are still a long way from having disclosed the essential component, without which we cannot see it in its concrete and total reality, of the object whose definition according to Teilhard himself we are trying to find. To appreciate Teilhard's thought at this stage, it is not enough to state that the World in which the apologist expresses his faith, is incomparably richer and greater than that accepted by the unbeliever when both apologist and unbeliever set out on their common search. Nor is it sufficient to

---

[22] 29 April 1934. On 24 Aug. of the same year, just as he was starting on *How I Believe*, speaking of a philosopher who had just written to him, "Surely to be the saviour of cosmic Evolution is only a secondary perfection for the Christ who is the saviour of souls?" he remarks, "This distinction knocks me sideways! as if souls weren't the fruit *par excellence* of the Cosmos, supremely 'cosmic' themselves!—I must say, I thought anyone could understand what I meant."

[23] *Œuvres*, VI, 123. Letter of 13 Oct. 1933: "I am working . . . on the lines of a 'spiritual transposition' of the Universe."

say that this World is richer and greater than the ordinary Universe of Science; or that this Universe of personal beings is something quite different from what most men generally understand by "Cosmos".[24] The Teilhardian universe, we must realize again, is richer and greater than that which the Christian himself generally envisages, when by a habitual methodical abstraction, he thinks only of the first result of the creation, adopting only the "natural" point of view of a philosophy of the spirit. The expression "organic unity" we met in one of the passages quoted above, has already served to give us some preliminary warning of this. We should not forget that Père Teilhard's thoughts are always based on the concrete and that his fundamental concepts take on significance and are transformed as the synthesis in their construction progresses. This is particularly true of his idea of the World: this World, when we think we are grasping it, "is always ahead of us".[25]

We must, therefore, follow his example and take the next, and decisive, step, if we are to reach the threshold of the fully concrete "World", which is the World illuminated and transfigured, in the eyes of the believer, by the "fact of the Incarnation"[26]; the World, "introduced and animated by a Christogenesis",[27] "to which Christ, the first and last thought

---

[24] A recent work tells us that Teilhardism is a "theory of the nullity of the human person"; to which the author objects "we are individually greater than the world, which has mass, but neither spirit nor will" (Félix Metra, *Un homme à la recherche de son âme*, 1964, p. 59). This is to forget among other things, that while Teilhard accepts the latter statement, he seeks to give it greater force by establishing it in a new way, in particular by introducing the idea of an "infinite of complexity".—Whether one thinks he succeeded or not, one would have to be blind not to see that the whole of Teilhard's effort is directed precisely to re-establishing the idea of the greatness of man, by overcoming the double critical threat introduced (this, of course, is a simplification) by Galileo and Darwin. Cf. *L'Énergie d'Évolution*, *Œuvres*, VII, p. 383; *Vie et Planètes*, VI, pp. 127–56; *Les Singularités*, etc., II, pp. 367–9, etc.

[25] *L'Esprit de la Terre* (1931); *Œuvres*, VI, p. 42.

[26] *Esquisse d'une dialectique de l'Esprit*, 4; *Œuvres*, VII, p. 155.

[27] *Réflexions sur . . . les consequences religieuse d'un ultra-humain;* *Œuvres*, VII, p. 290.

of the Creator, is to give its definitive form".²⁸ For this last
stage Teilhard seeks, moreover, only to lead us along the
path of light marked out for him by revelation: "Under the
pressure of Christian thought, the agonizing enormity of the
World gradually converges upwards until it is transfigured in a
meeting-point of loving energy." ²⁸ Then, "above us, we see
the gleam of the way out. . . . In a World that is quite certainly open at its summit in *Christo Jesu*, we are now safe
from the threat of suffocation! And instead, there flows down
from these heights not only air to breathe but the radiance of
Love descending upon us." ²⁹

Such, then, "in its last analysis", is the only World, not
that Père Teilhard knows, but that he truly *believes in*: it is a
Universe "charged with love in its evolution"; it is—
embraced in one glance with all its evolutionary preparations
recapitulated and transfigured in it—the Universe of souls
united or destined to be united with God in Christ.³⁰ It
is the Universe, we see again, as revealed to him by his faith:

> Under the transforming action of "operative faith" all the
> natural relationships of the World remain intact: but a principle,
> an internal finality, one might almost say an extra soul is super-

²⁸ Hans Urs von Balthasar, *Herrlichkeit*, vol. I, p. 653; "If the whole cosmos
was created in the image of the invisible God, in the First-born of creation, by
him and for him, and if this latter resides in the world, through the Church of
which he is the head, then the world is in the final analysis a 'body' of God, who
represents and expresses himself in this body, in virtue of a principle of union
that is not pantheistic but hypostatic." Cf. Teilhard to Père Valensin, 10 Jan.
1920: "The impossibility of understanding a Christ who is organically *central* in
the supernatural Universe, and physically juxtaposed in the natural Universe."
²⁸ *Réflexions sur le bonheur*, Cahiers, 2, p. 6.
²⁹ *Le Christique* (1955). Cf. letter of 27 June 1926, Tientsin: "Here I have
found again that sort of clear-minded intoxication, lucid and everlasting, that
so oddly comes to me from the depths—or rather from the Term still to come—
of all that is." [Note: this quote is repeated in the text a little later.]
³⁰ Cf. *La Messe sur le Monde*: "To your Body in all its extension, that is, in
the World that now, through your power and my faith, has become the great,
living crucible in which all melts away, to be reborn . . ." (*Hymne de l'Univers*,
p. 37). To Léontine Zanta, 15 April 1929: "I realize again that we must give
primacy (in the Universe) to the immortal soul and the risen Christ."

imposed upon them. Under the influence of our faith, the Universe is patient, without any external change of characteristics of being made more flexible, of being animated,—of being "super-animated".

. . . Do we believe? Then everything is illuminated and takes on form around us, success attains an incorruptible plenitude, sorrow becomes a visit from God and his caress. But suppose we hesitate? Then the rock is still dry, the sky black, the moving waters are treacherous. And we may hear the voice of the Master, as he looks at our wasted lives, "O men of little faith, why have you doubted"?[31]

To try to set out this concept in all its fullness and complexity would take us too far afield. Here we may simply note that the various meanings we have brought out, are in fact only formal distinctions, defining and seeming to isolate the dialectical stages in the constitution of what is basically one. "For God, willing his Christ (= the Pleroma), willed Man" and willing Man, "He initiated the immense movement of material and organic evolution. Only one thing is willed, and only one thing made, in all the turmoil of the Universe."[32] When Père Teilhard accords to the Universe a value that others find excessive, he is looking at it in "its concrete advance, now actually in progress" whose Term is supernatural. He always positions himself "in real humanity";[33] and, as the last passages quoted show unmistakably, he thus anticipates in his faith, even while enclosed in the opacity of

[31] *Milieu Divin*, pp. 135, 136. Cf. Matthew, 8. 13, 9. 29, etc. Letter (1924?): "I have often told you, if you are to attain peace and never (even when swamped by the worst stupidities) to be stifled by them, the secret is somehow, with God's help, to succeed is seeing the Unique necessary Element that moves through all things, and can be given to us (with its joy and freedom) by every object, provided that it be brought to us by *loyalty* to life, and that it be transformed by *faith* in the divine presence and operation."

[32] Letter of 20 Oct. 1924. It may be apposite to recall that St Thomas Aquinas "saw in the divine plan a sovereign *unity* that we are too inclined to forget. From the creation of the World to the consummation of the chosen in the vision of God, all is a single direct progression." A.R. Motte, O.P., *Bulletin Thomiste* (1932), p. 654. Cf. St Francis di Sales, *Treatise on the Love of God*, Book 2, Ch. 5.

[33] 17 April 1923 (*Letters from a Traveller*, p. 65).

the material world, the state of the world transfigured in God:

> [Man] has hardly given his assent to revealed Truth, before all created Powers are transformed around him, as though by enchantment. Natural forces of all sorts, until then alien, hostile or ambivalent, are straightway charged, *for that man*, with Jesus . . . *Credenti, omnia convertuntur in Christo*.[34]

The Abbé Paul Grenet has rightly said: "The world that fires Teilhard's enthusiasm is a world in which God intervenes."[35] And Père Teilhard's letters are continually developing the teaching of his essays, demonstrating its application in his attitude to life. On 12 February 1919, he writes from his billets in Alsace that "we should foster a great love for Him who, when seen by the eyes of faith, animates the whole complex of exterior events and interior experiences. Is there any better way of understanding and enjoying intimacy with the divine than the knowledge that our Lord is at the heart of all that moves us?"[36] In 1926, he wrote from Tientsin: "Here I have found again that sort of clear-minded intoxication, lucid and everlasting, that so oddly comes to me from the depths—or rather from the Term still to come—of all that is"; and again, "I am still unable to have any appetite for things outside their relationship to the universal Christ."[37] Similarly, at Easter 1927, he notes his "joyful awareness of being in the bosom of a Universe super-animated by our Lord". And in 1926, summing up the main lines of his thought, he explains to a correspondent that "a Universe (1)

[34] *Forma Christi*, 3. This is what Père Teilhard calls "the establishment of the *Divine Milieu*".

[35] *Teilhard de Chardin, savant Chrétien* (1961), p. 87.

[36] *Making of a Mind*, p. 282; cf. p. 106.

[37] 27 June and 21 Dec. 1936. This is another way of putting what M. Jean Mouroux (*Le Mystère du Temps*, 1962, p. 245) says: "The more [the Christian] unifies himself with Christ, the more will he unify the chaotic time of the World, in the enveloping grasp of the time of salvation. . . . In the end, 'all is grace' and the time of the world is already, in the mind of the saint, transformed into time of salvation, because his own being is transformed in Jesus Christ."

THE COMPLEXITY OF THE COSMOS   159

of which the stuff is personal and (2) (which comes to the same thing) that follows a curve of convergence, is the only milieu that is patient both of the Christ we adore, so that it can receive Him, and of the Man we dream of, so that it can matter to him".

It is possible, again, accurately to sum up the Teilhardian concept, by following the governing thread of a short essay, twelve years later than *How I Believe*. In this Père Teilhard wished, he tells us, to cut short any "pantheist" or "naturalist" interpretation of his thought. To avoid "all possibility of ambiguity" he tried to "present, clearly distinguished, the successive stages of his apologetics".[38] In the introduction to this, moreover, he refers explicitly to *How I Believe*. He proposes to develop in it the "law of alternation" he had introduced in the apologetic essay. The second essay, accordingly, serves as a commentary, a retrospective explanation or a theoretical re-drafting of the steps taken in the first. The two correspond to one another rather as prospection and reflection go together in Blondel.

In a first period, Père Teilhard rises from the "cosmic phenomenon" to "the existence of a transcendent God"; he then, in a second period, pursues a line of thought that leads him to the "expectation of a revelation"; and then, in a third, he notes how, "from right within the human phenomenon, there stands out and demands our attention the Christian phenomenon".[39] This is because, "starting from the Man-Jesus, a phylum of religious thought appeared in the human mass", outside which "the idea of God and the gesture of adoration have never assumed such richness, such coherence and such flexibility. And all this sustained and fostered by the conviction that it answered to an inspiration and revelation come from

[38] He adds: "or, if you prefer, of my dialectic". *Esquisse d'une dialectique de l'Esprit* (1946); *Œuvres*, VII, p. 149.
[39] *Esquisse . . . loc. cit.*, pp. 150–4. (The printed text reads, in error, "Christian problem".)

on high". This "unique" phenomenon, still observed from outside, impels us to recognize in its origin "the spark that leapt between God and the Universe *through a personal milieu*". In other words, it makes us recognize the personal divinity of the Man-Jesus. This is the crucial and unavoidable choice that faces us all:

> If we refuse to recognize the Christian fact, we shall see the vault of the Universe, that for a moment opened above us, once again hermetically sealed.
> But if we take the step, that is, if, as reasonable probability demands, we are ready to see in the living thought of the Church the reflection, adapted to our own evolutionary condition, of divine thought—then, our spirit can again move forward. And, climbing a third time [40] to the summit of things, we see not only some centre of consistence, not only some psychic prime Mover, nor even only some being that speaks, but some Word that is incarnate. If the Universe ascends progressively towards unity, it is not, then, only because impelled by some external force, but because the Transcendent has made itself to some degree immanent in it. That is what Revelation teaches us. [41]

Thus, too, at the same time, is defined the humano-divine World, or, as Père Teilhard calls it here again, borrowing St Paul's word, the "Pleroma", to which he declared in *How I Believe* that "in the last analysis" he adhered, recognizing in it the twofold note of "unity" and "infallibility". All that now remains is, in a fourth and final period, to proceed from, and by virtue of, the living Church, to "Christ-Omega", in whom the Pleroma is to be definitively consummated on the day of the "Parousia"; for then all the "stuff of the cosmos"

[40] The first time, it found "transcendent Omega, the Collective Centre, the irreversible". The second time, "God the mover and revealer". This time it is "God incarnate" (*ibid.*, p. 157). Each time, knowledge of God becomes more complete, and, correlatively, the idea of the world is more perfected. Each ascent is preceded or followed by a descent: this is the application of the "law of alternation" recently alluded to. It is the same plan as that of *How I Believe*.
[41] *Ibid.*, pp. 154-5.

through which the Pleroma was prepared will have mysteriously passed into Christ.[42]

In the last lines of the last piece he wrote, Père Teilhard gave it the title *The Promised Land*. It was already the title of one of his earliest writings, dating from February 1919. In neither—and still less in parallel passages in *Dialectic of the Spirit* and *How I Believe*—is he speaking of a visible land.[43]

There is, then, no subjectivism in the continual recurrence of the Teilhardian soul to the Faith that transfigures everything in the World—that transfigures the World. What the Faith brings to light, from the deepest layer in which it lies, is indeed objective reality. Nor is there any naturalism: this final reality, anticipated in the Faith that allows Man, if we may be allowed the expression, to share the point of view of God—a thing which no experience can do, no science, no natural reason—this reality, at the heart of all things, is the Love revealed in Christ, *Forma Christi*.

From this we can obtain an idea of what Père Teilhard was proposing to do when he was considering writing *Le Sacrament du Monde*. In this he intended to return to the idea behind the *Milieu Divin*, no doubt with a more explicit doctrinal basis. There is no great difficulty in reconstructing that basis, provided we read him with some attention. It is, however, the fruit of an effort of thought operating at different degrees of depth. Thus it is important, if we are not to give it a bald and crude interpretation (which could be an occasion of scandal) continually to apply, as Père Teilhard did, "correction by analogy". This, he tells us, "is the essential correction all our views must be subjected to whenever we try to follow any line of Reality through a new circle of the Universe. From circle to circle the World is metamorphosed. It

[42] Thus for Père Teilhard the only "definitive World" is "Christ", and only that World matters to him. Note of Dec. 1919 (*loc. cit.*).

[43] Cf. M. Barthélemy-Madaule, *op. cit.*, p. 491. The repetition of title was probably intentional: he wished to show once again his loyalty to his first inspiration.

undergoes internal enrichment and re-casting. Each time, in consequence, it appears in a new state in which the sum of earlier properties partly subsists and is partly renewed.[44]

Several other essays are less directly apologetic than reflections on the conditions necessary for apologetics in our day. They are addressed not only to Christians but to all who are directly or indirectly concerned with the direction of the Church, to ecclesiastical authorities, that is, and to theologians. Far from wishing to escape the vigilance of the former, it is to them that Père Teilhard addressed what may seem his boldest and most disconcerting remarks, for he was anxious to make them see the urgency of the problem as he saw it,[45] and did not need, writing for them, to develop the arguments aimed at those whom he sought to lead to the faith. Thus, in such papers, he brings out, with the energy he drew from his apostolic zeal, the necessity to accept a certain "faith in the World", which was coming more and more to mean to him a "human, propulsive faith, directed towards the "Ahead".

[44] *The Phenomenon of Man.* From this we can see by what an improbable sequence of misrepresentation (and hence of confusion) it was possible to sum up Teilhard's teaching on the relationship of God and the world as follows: "His pantheism considers God as the soul of the world—God all in all things and persons—the world being as though the body of the Divinity" (M. Vernet, *op. cit.*, p. 19). The same author would have it that Teilhard "divinizes the universe at the expense of the human person", that he assigns as our final end "fusion in the great All", i.e. an "identification with matter", "in anonymity and absurdity" etc. (pp. 196, 199, 214, etc.). Who, I wonder, is suffering from the "great illusion"?

[45] Thus, speaking of a "new note" he is thinking about, on "plurality of inhabited worlds", he writes to his Provincial (7 June 1953) that it would be part of a "collection I should like some time to be shown to 'all concerned', not for general publication, and not in a maliciously critical spirit, but because it deals with questions *that cannot be avoided*, that already have to be faced, and that will certainly be answered by general human thought (more or less on the lines I indicate) within the next hundred years. . . . On these various points Mankind is already making up its mind. . . . Christ must, through us, be at the 'head' of the movement. Otherwise, the world of tomorrow (in its Weltanschauung and Ethics) will be built up without us; and that means it would be lost. . . ." This problem had been in his mind for a long time: he speaks of it in a letter of 28 Feb. 1920. Cf. *La Centrologie*, no. 33; *Œuvres*, VII, pp. 133–4.

We find this again in 1919, in the note on evangelizing our own times quoted earlier; and again, thirty years later, in a "short report" drawn up for his superiors in Rome under the title *The Heart of the Problem*. In the years between, we find the same concern: for example, in his answer to an enquiry conducted by *La Vie Intellectuelle* in 1933[46] into present-day reasons for unbelief, or in his *Reflections on the conversion of the World* (1936) which he had been asked for, he tells us, "for someone pretty highly placed in Rome".[47] Another example is *La Parole attendue* (1941) for which he was thanked, in encouraging terms, by Rome. If, then, he notes, for example, that "the religious aspirations of Mankind today are distressingly vague and aimless" at the same time he urges that we should be inspired in our attitude to them by the words of Jesus, "I have not come to set them aside but to bring them to perfection."

On the other hand, in his apologetic writings properly so-called, when he is addressing an unbeliever and assuming in him at least an embryonic form of this Faith in the World, however ill-founded and ill-understood it still may be, he uses it as a lever to move the unbeliever to the point where he discloses to him "the Christian faith in a personal Transcendent, ascending towards the Above". "However effective", he says, for example, "may be man's faith in some Ultra-human, I do not think that its urge towards Some Thing ahead can succeed without being combined with another still more fundamental aspiration, one that comes down from on high, from *Somebody*."[48] On another occasion, reflecting on

[46] *La Vie Intellectuelle* (1933), pp. 218–22.

[47] Peking, 22 Nov. 1936. Cf. Letter to *La Pensée catholique* (1946, 2, p. 4): "The paper in question had nothing clandestine about it, seeing that I had written it at the direct instance of ecclesiastical authority (and in fact had sent it to that authority), to pin-point, for the Propaganda, various ideas developed in conversations at the Apostolic Delegation in Peking." Similarly, *La Place du Christianisme dans l'Univers* (1933) (which became *Le Christianisme dans le Monde*) was written "by request" (Letter, Tientsin, 8 Oct.).

[48] *Comment concevoir ... l'unanimisation humaine* (1950).

"the present crisis" of our civilization, he begins by explaining that we have entered "a dangerous phase that threatens the existence of 'souls'", and he tries to bring home to his readers its gravity: "confronted by the cosmic immensities that Science has disclosed to it, and the collective power seen in the organization of society, Mankind, 'on its present tack', is in danger of ending by forgetting the one essential thing". Then, faced by this mortal danger, he tries to make everyone see that only Christianity can effectively "intervene to restore human aspirations to the only line that conforms with the structural laws of being and life". He holds up before the world "the figure of Christ", "Centre of total convergence" that alone, today as of old, can "save the World".[49]

In each case, though the perspective may be reversed, the same concern animates Père Teilhard: he wants to establish the solidarity of the two sorts of faith, however they may differ in nature. He sets about showing that the irrespective objects are not only linked by an external relationship of condition and conditioned, but are also intrinsically united at their term in Christ—Omega—subject always to the final transfiguration. This, he believes, will put an end to the extremely grave conflict that seems to him the main obstacle that, on the intellectual plane, hinders the conversion of his contemporaries: "a conflict which seemed as though it must set against one another the majesty of the Universe and the primacy of God in an ever more dangerous opposition".[50]

To return to the passage quoted from *How I Believe*. In this we do not find the refinements of theory we get from the later writings. Anyone who took it for something that it neither is nor aims to be, might complain of the vagueness of this "faith in the World" that the author professes: he would not

[49] *La Crise présente*, *Études* (23 Oct. 1937), pp. 163–4.
[50] *Esquisse d'une dialectique*, end; *Œuvres*, VII, p. 158. In *Le Christique* he sets out to show the convergence of "the consummation of the Universe by Christ" and "the consummation of Christ by the Universe".

be entirely at fault. Père Teilhard, maybe, was a little too ready to be astonished that in some particular contexts the meaning he attributed to the words "World", "Cosmos" and "cosmic" could be misunderstood. He did not, perhaps, always distinguish with sufficient care, if not in his own mind, at least for his readers, the different senses, dialectically governed, in which he used them. Like many real thinkers, he sometimes was too ready to believe that he was "using words that are immediately intelligible". At the same time, we should beware of generalizing. His style of writing, in the opening passage of *How I Believe* is philosophically unsatisfactory until it is explained by what follows, but this is exceptional in Teilhard. Normally, however intent he may be on affirming the unity of the whole (the Pleroma), the final object of his faith and hope, he specifies its two components (if we may so express it), as being as distinct in the unity realized as the two natures in the unique Being of the incarnate Word;[51] sometimes, again, the context is sufficient explanation. Even in the final union, the adorer is, for Père Teilhard, always one, the adored another; before their union the desirer is one, the desired another. "Love God", he says in *Le Christique*, "with all the Universe-in-Evolution", just as he had written in *La Messe sur le Monde*: "Christ of glory, . . . it is you to whom my being cries out with desire as vast as the Universe!"[52]— Here, at the very beginning of his apologetic task, he finds himself obliged to use language that is still elliptical and involves a certain ambiguity. He sometimes writes in a way that shows he is perfectly aware of this. Thus the explanations to be found in other writings serve the reader as a

[51] On many occasions. *La Vie Cosmique:* " Incapable of being in any way mixed with or confused with the participated being he sustains, animates, and holds together, God is at the birth, the growth, and the term of all things " (*Œuvres*, V, p. 396). *The Phenomenon of Man*, p. 298; *La Conversion du Monde*, p. 18; *L'Ostensoir*, p. 32; *La Mystique de la Science*, p. 12; *Le Groupe Zoologique humain*, p. 162, etc.

[52] *Hymne de l'Univers*, p. 3.

clarification of Teilhard's thought rather than as a development of it, properly so-called. They introduce no change of thought on this point.

The apologist in *How I Believe* sees, in fact, that the "primordial intuition" on which "the whole structure of his faith is based" is both one and many: one, in itself, many in the explanations prompted by reflection. It cannot, therefore, be absolutely identical both in the apologist himself and in the unbeliever—and that is why, again, he speaks of an "*apparently indeterminate*" concept of the World or of the Whole.[53] It even varies greatly according to whether it is taken simply as a starting-point from which we cannot yet say whether further advance will be possible, or as being already big with all that methodical reflection may extract from it. Père Teilhard, then, is quite right to speak, as we saw earlier, of this "faith in the World" as being a "vague" faith. He speaks again of faith "in its most wrapped-up form", and his very concept of faith, like his correlative concept of World, is markedly similar, as we shall later see more clearly. Of one thing, however, we must be careful, if we are not grossly to distort his meaning, and that is not to stop reading when we come to the end of the paragraph. We must beware of taking the starting-point, which he has clearly indicated as such, for the destination. It is from this point onwards that we shall see unfold all the varied richness of what the first "intellectual synthesis" implies but has not yet made apparent. This is the point at which the whole process begins; and all that follows in the essay will supply the key to these opening sentences. If we want to find in it, as we are entitled to do, evidence of the author's personal faith, we must look for it in all that follows.

Here, then, we have a methodological affirmation prefacing a document, entirely devoted to guiding minds towards Christ: one which, even if open to criticism, is at least proof

[53] Our italics.

of the author's apostolic zeal. It seems to me incredible that such a document could be taken (as we see from the pained comment of the anonymous critic quoted earlier) as some sort almost of defection, of semi-apostasy, or at any rate of a disconcerting dilution or dangerous blurring of the Christian faith. It is no doubt true that method and content of thought cannot be completely dissociated, and that the expression "faith in the World" that appears in Père Teilhard's affirmation carries a meaning that he will stand by, an extremely "Teilhardian" meaning; but we should not conclude too readily that we have determined that meaning. Moreover, if we weigh the whole of the passage quoted and criticized, we must surely realize that the apologist is expressing himself through a hypothesis of an "interior retracting of steps" as unreal as (since his method demands this) it is meant to be total by methodological necessity. If there were no other consideration to be taken into account, how could one possibly not feel that so damning an interpretation, ruled out by the context, and wildly at variance with its subsequent development, is, moreover, contradicted by countless passages written about the same time, in which Père Teilhard gives overwhelming evidence of the firmness of his faith in the personal and transcendent God [54] and his absolute loyalty as a faithful Catholic? [55]

[54] See again, for example, L'Esprit de la Terre (1931), Esquisse (1936), Œuvres, VI, pp. 52–7, 110–14; or again La Mystique de la Science, ibid., p. 223. Cf. Le Groupe Zoologique humain, (1949): "If it is not to be incapable of forming the keystone to the Noosphere, 'Omega' can be conceived only as the meeting-point between the Universe at its limit of centration and another even deeper centre,— this latter the self-subsistent Centre and absolutely ultimate Principle of irreversibility and personalization: the one true Omega".(1956, p. 162). We should note, too, how at the very end of a strictly scientific article, Les Singularités de l'Espèce humaine, Père Teilhard, tempering zeal with discretion, is at pains to suggest at least, "without leaving the plane of the Phenomenal", by a side-glance at the "singularity of the Christian Phenomenon", the existence of a "real Centre, already existing" revealed in Christianity.(Œuvres, II, p. 374).

[55] This, of course, is only a general statement. It does not follow that one cannot discuss Teilhard's thought equally well from the theological as from the

"I have never felt myself more integrally, soul and mind, dependent on Jesus Christ" (1948). "I feel myself today more ineluctably bound to the hierarchic Church and to the Christ of the Gospel than at any other moment in my life" (1951). These are categorical assertions, borne out by Père Teilhard's behaviour until his last day. They are not in themselves a guarantee of the impeccability of all Teilhard's ideas. They still leave it open to us to criticize, but no captious interpretation can stand against their testimony.

We may safely, then, apply to Père Teilhard what a recent writer has said of every true apologist. His explanation will complete our understanding of the initial step in *How I Believe* that we have been analysing:

> It is not despite his Faith, or outside it, but in virtue of it, and within it, that the Christian finds the power and "blessed audacity" to break off his explicit adherence to his own creed, certain as he is, with a supernatural certainty derived from that Faith, of meeting it again, richer still and deeper, when he has "reopened the Christian parenthesis".[56]

scientific or rational point of view. But intellectual discussion is one thing, and impugning the personal faith of the person you are discussing is quite another. Père Teilhard was always most anxious, both in his own life and in his writings, to remain "theologically and traditionally" in agreement with the faith of the Church.(*Le Cœur du Problème*, p. 6).

[56] J. A. Cuttat, *Fait bouddhique et fait Chrétien*, in *L'Homme devant Dieu*, vol. 3, p. 24.

4

FAITH AND ANALOGY

ASED on this same passage from *How I Believe*, another objection has been levelled against Père Teilhard's apologetics, and with particular reference to the supernatural character of Faith. The critic is Dom Georges Frénaud. Having said that Père Teilhard distinguishes a scientific faith, psychological in nature, and a "Christic" faith, and having recognized that "in itself, the mere assertion of these two faiths contains nothing to offend orthodox thought" he continues:

> The same cannot be said of the relationship between the two that Père Teilhard affirms. In his view, in fact, psychological or scientific faith is more fundamental and more certain than faith founded on divine revelation: the former is even the condition of the latter.

This might at first seem a reasonable criticism; for example, on a first reading of *How I Believe* so well-informed a theologian as Père Smulders [1] admits that he was tempted to make a similar judgment. But in proof of his assertion, Dom Frénaud

---

[1] *La Vision du Père Teilhard*, pp. 129–30, in connection with the postscript to *How I Believe* ("I believe that the Universe is an Evolution—I believe that the Evolution proceeds towards the Spirit—I believe that the Spirit is fulfilled in some Personal—I believe that the supreme Personal is the Universal Christ"). Père Smulders writes: "When I first read Teilhard, this passage worried me greatly. It seemed to me to reverse the order of values, by placing 'faith' in evolution before the most sacred and most precious centre of the Christian faith, faith in Christ. In reality, the words are unobjectionable. They are a summing up of the apologetic considerations by which Teilhard, etc."

quotes the now familiar passage from the *Osservatore Romano*.
He adds, in a long note, his own comment on this:

> This passage goes so much too far that we are forced to wonder
> what would happen to an enthusiastic reader who took these
> statements literally and adopted them himself. In basing his
> religious faith on his faith in the World, would he not end by
> abandoning it? What in fact constitutes faith, as such, is not so
> much factual adherence to some particular truth as the motive
> for accepting it: and in the context of theological faith this is the
> word of God revealing and attesting the truth in question. As
> soon as the adherence is based on some other motive—faith in the
> world or the postulate of evolution—it may coincide with the
> Church on the object accepted, but the belief is no longer based
> solely on the word of God, and there is no longer any faith. Any
> over-hasty admirers of Teilhard's apologetics would do well to
> think this over.[2]

We must be grateful to Dom Frénaud at least for hinting
to his reader that the passage in question comes from an
apologetic essay and should be understood as such. As a
result his criticism cannot be so radical, so "distressed" (or
scandalized) as that in the *Osservatore*. Dom Frénaud's
criticism is more technical and its direct conclusion is confined
to condemning the basis of Teilhard's faith—although at the
same time it does not minimize the consequences of a faulty
basis. I believe, nevertheless, that while Dom Frénaud's
initial assertion is justified, he has not realized the considerations it necessarily involves. Thus, although his criticism has
a different character from that in the *Osservatore*, it is still, in
my view, unfounded. According to Dom Frénaud, Père Teilhard destroys the very idea of supernatural faith by neglecting
the only valid motive for it. For this Teilhard is alleged to
have substituted human motives. Thus true faith is already

---

[2] *Pensée philosophique et religieuse du Père Teilhard de Chardin* (1963), published and recommended by the "office international des oeuvres de Formation
civique et d'Action doctrinale selon le droit naturel et chrétien" (Headquarters
at Sion, Switzerland). (Dom Frénaud is a monk of Solesmes.)

killed at its roots in the very process by which the apologist seeks to stimulate it.

This accusation seems to stem from a double *ignoratio elenchi*, and a close reading of *How I Believe* will show that it must be rejected.

It might be a good plan to precede any seminary course of apologetics by the exposition of a dogmatic thesis on the nature of Christian faith and its "formal cause". However that may be, such a plan would be out of the question in an essay in practical apologetics addressed directly to an unbeliever which takes him as is and speaks to him in his own language; and Père Teilhard was quite right not to have done so, provided, of course, that in his preliminary explanations or in anything that follows, the apologist does not put forward any principle that tends to confuse divine faith and human faith, that is, to reduce the former to a modality of the latter. This Teilhard does not do: in fact, he does quite the contrary.

The formal cause of divine or supernatural faith is the testimony given to us by God about himself. Père Teilhard was perfectly aware of this. But in addressing the unbeliever, he is speaking of something quite different. He sets out various "reasons for belief" by which he hopes to lead him, starting from some human faith they both have in common, to the threshold of supernatural faith. We need dwell no further on that approach, which is that of any sound apologist.

Further, so that there may be no question of ambiguity, Père Teilhard begins by explaining, quite unmistakably, what he means by the word "faith". From this it emerges that his concept of faith is essentially analogical. This is the first point that Dom Frénaud seems not to have appreciated, and from this arises his first *ignoratio elenchi*.

Analogy, we should recall, plays a great part in Père Teilhard's thought. He realized this himself. Not only did he have recourse to it as an indispensable category, but on more than one occasion he spoke of it in the most explicit terms. Thus, in connection with a sort of "anthropo-centrism" that some might be inclined to accuse him of, he said: "The whole difficulty lies in applying 'corrections by analogy'. That is the old Scholastic truth—but rejuvenated in the perspective of Duration." And again, emphasizing that perspective, "I believe that one can push the theory of Analogy further in an evolutionary Universe than in a static World-structure."[3] In 1916, he remarked that "in accordance with our World's particular order, everything is formed by transformation of a pre-existing analogue".[4] He explains this again, in 1928, in the essay on the *Phenomenon of Man* quoted earlier. He warns his reader against a tendency to over-simplify and so attribute an "univocal value"[5] to physical reality. In the present case, it is not a question of "physical reality" nor of an "evolutionary Universe" but it is just as much a matter of analogy. Teilhard sees the life of the individual spirit in a dynamic perspective, and at each stage of the demonstration he is developing, a type of faith must emerge that is not an exact reproduction of the model found in its predecessor. In other words, his idea of faith involves so many analogical applications.[6]

"To believe", he says, "is to formulate an intellectual synthesis." Thus one can distinguish as many types of belief as one distinguishes successive types of "intellectual synthesis". More exactly, the meaning of the word "faith" will assume increasing fullness and loftiness as the formu-

---

[3] Letters of 29 April 1934, and 20 Oct. 1949.

[4] *La Maîtrise du Monde*, ch. I.

[5] *L'Atomisme de l'Esprit* (1941); *Œuvres*, VII, p. 37.

[6] Similarly, it will be noted, St Thomas sometimes uses the word "believe" in an analogical sense. In his commentary on the *Ethics of Aristotle*, 1.5; "*Subjungit quod juvenes sapientalia quidem, id est metaphysicalia non credunt, id est quod non attingunt mente, licet dicant ore*"; quoted by Étienne Gilson (*Sur l'âge de la maturité philosophique selon Saint Thomas d'Aquin*, in *L'Homme devant Dieu*, vol. 2, p. 157), who comments, "The act of 'believing' in this context, being the giving of assent to the truth of a judgment."

lation of the intellectual synthesis becomes vaster and loftier. From this will follow profound differentiations, not excluding the transition *ad aliud genus*. Here Père Teilhard suggests (though without stressing it) a comparison that enables us to proceed further: the comparison with the *phylum*. Every belief is born of a preceding belief. We know, according to the Teilhardian idea of the evolution of living beings, that it must in principle be possible to follow the ascending line of a phylum, distinguishing in it a series of innovations produced by orthogenesis, from which a higher living being results each time, more or less radically irreducible to those that preceded and prepared it. This obliges us to speak at the same time of "homogeneity" and "synthetic transformation".[7] It is this that enables Père Teilhard, in the picture he draws of human origins, to bring it all back essentially to "Man's being *rooted* in the Universe and the remarkably pronounced RENEWAL in him, on a new and higher plane, of all earlier life".[8]

Here, let me repeat, he is only making a comparison, but it is a suggestive one, drawn from one of the central and most constant sources of Teilhardian dialectic. Referring again on one occasion to what he called the "principle of creative transformation", he said that this principle explains, though without our thereby having to envisage any break in the cosmic framework, "life after matter, thought after instinct, Revelation after rational effort, the New Land after the old, etc." This is

---

[7] On the notions of orthogenesis and the phylum in Teilhard's philosophy of science, see Barthélemy-Madaule, *op. cit.*, pp. 156–65. "The phylum [is] a succession of mutations in additive sequence in the same direction". *Une défense d'orthogenèse; Œuvres*, III, pp. 381–91. Letter of 16 March 1952 (Barjon-Leroy, pp. 101–5).

[8] Letter of 23 June 1935. Note the contrast, or increase, between the two shades of emphasis. While insisting on the "roots" Teilhard insists even more strongly on the renewal.

what he calls, again, the fundamental principle of "discontinuity in continuity", a translation into dynamic terms of the general principle of analogy. He again explains it well in a note of 1951, when he says that "all this confused and disconcerting medley of contacts and differences" we see "between the Living and the Human is readily explained as soon as we have the law of transposition and transformation to carry us from one domain into the other".[9] He had once found a striking formulation of this principle in an article by his fellow Jesuit Père Maurice de la Taille on contemplative prayer, and had been delighted by this coincidence of thought.[10] "That contemplation", wrote Père de la Taille, "is transcendent in relation to the means proper to natural man, and to his characteristic notions, even assisted by grace, is manifest . . . from its character of being free from origination in either the senses or any abstractive property. From this admission, however, it does not follow that it must therefore be included among the phenomena that are exceptions to the divine law and hence miraculous. On the contrary, given the law of Providence on the growth and development of grace, we may say that there can be no regular and normal progress for a given subject, once it has passed the point it can attain by the human exercise of the virtues and the supernatural gifts, except by the passive way."[11] In other words, to adopt again an expression of Père de la Taille's noted by

[9] *Transformations et Prolongements en l'Homme du mécanisme de l'Evolution; Œuvres*, VII, p. 323.

[10] Letter of 21 Dec. 1919.

[11] *L'Oraison contemplative* (1919), pp. 287–8. Père de la Taille, Teilhard says in the same letter, "tries to reconcile the two extreme mystical schools by a solution 'of the future',—and conceives that ordinary active prayer leads the soul progressively to a point where the *logic* of the sanctifying divine operation demands more immediate, 'extraordinary', intervention by God. Thus, contemplation is really a heterogeneous form of prayer, compared with the other, to which the other does not necessary lead *sua virtute* (Poulain . . .), but, at the same time it succeeds organically, vitally, to ordinary meditation, by virtue of a more general law of spiritual development, which associates them both in the same 'creative' process (Saudreau)."

Teilhard, and much akin to some of his own, there can be a "point of fusion", which ensures continuity between two successive states, or between two beings, or again between two acts, two sorts of intellectual synthesis, all *heterogeneous*.

"This passage", writes Père Teilhard, "interested me greatly because it contains an exact application of the principle that seems to me fundamental in the whole history and understanding of the real." In fact, *mutatis mutandis*, in *How I Believe*, when Teilhard is speaking of faith and its different meanings, he reasons just as Père de la Taille reasoned when speaking of two sorts of prayer, or as he himself reasons elsewhere when speaking of the succession of biological syntheses. His constant aim (as he says himself) is "in all things to demonstrate and reconstruct the foundations"; in this case, the natural foundations from which, as a starting-point, access to spiritual faith will normally be possible. This, however, does not amount to a relationship of cause and effect: it in no way means that the ulterior reality, whatever in each case it may be, is reduced to the basic reality.

In the present case, as the essay continues, it invites us to distinguish, following an ascending line, three sorts of faith, that, in one context, seem to be in continuity—the two first serving as a preparation for the third—but whose characteristics are very different.

First of all there is the "initial belief", constituted by some "faith in the World". It can already by given the generic name of "faith", by analogy, since it already assumes the intervention of a first act of intellectual synthesis, this being the "adherence of our intelligence to a general view of the Universe, however "vague" and "elementary" that view may be. But, on the part of the man the apologist is addressing, it is a semi-spontaneous faith, an "inevitable" [12] faith, akin

[12] We have, says Teilhard, "first to verify the solidity of an initial, inevitable faith". This will be the "launching platform".

again to what others would call immediate evidence.—Then comes faith in spirit, in immortality, faith that culminates in faith in a personal God, transcendent and present in the World. This faith is attained, stage by stage, as the result of a series of rational steps, always based on reflection on experience but assuming, where necessary, the very precise form of a syllogism.[13] It is thus a process of reasoning.—Finally, at the end of a last stage, there must emerge, as the apologist intends, but in a quite different way, Christian, supernatural faith.

Did Père Teilhard confuse this last with either of the two preceding?

Certainly not. The whole structure of the essay is evidence of this, as no attentive reader could possibly fail to see. Once it has been established that there exists a personal God present in the world, the whole picture changes; and, the better to emphasize this complete change, the apologist, instead of adding no more than a final paragraph modelled on the earlier ones, tells his reader that he is moving on to a *Second Part*. This is the cardinal point in the essay.

He is not proposing, starting from the "faith in the World" (or, as Dom Frénaud puts it, from "the postulate of evolution") that has led him to "faith in God", to arouse in his reader (or in the first place in himself) "factual adherence to some truth" of the supernatural order. Nor is he proposing to prove by way of reasoning any of the Catholic dogmas, either individually or *en bloc*. The object of divine Revelation is for Père Teilhard, as for every Catholic, one indivisible whole, which no premise of the natural order can contain.[14] The assumption of the contrary is the second of Dom Fré-

[13] Thus, in the paragraph on faith in immortality, "... Let us in turn examine the major and the middle term of this reasoning ... But then ... I am justified in concluding ...."

[14] In a letter of 15 Sept. 1934 he explains how he introduces into his Universe "the two notions of divine personality and human immortality, on which revelation rests".

naud's *ignorationes elenchi*. In reality, Père Teilhard, starting from faith in God (or, if you prefer, with this faith in God as foundation) invites the reader to take a new step, quite different in character, that we must now proceed to analyse.

5

REVELATION AND CREDIBILITY

THE first part of *How I Believe* ends with these words: "Since I can distinguish in the Cosmos a higher sphere of the Personal and of personal relationships, I am beginning to suspect that there may well be forces of attraction and guidance, intellectual in nature, enveloping me and speaking to me. A Presence is never dumb."

Here again, if we continue to observe the *form* of his exposition, his *plan*, we recognize the most classic of procedures. God exists—not any Principle, any axiom, abstraction, or any vague and impersonal Unity-of-the-multiple, but a real, concrete (super-personal) and present being. He can speak. He can communicate with man. Revelation from his side is possible, even probable. As Teilhard said in a later essay: "Once we have admitted the personality of God, the possibility and even the theoretical probability of a *revelation*, that is, a reflection of God on our consciousness, not only involves no difficulty but is eminently in accordance with the nature of things." [1] It will, indeed, be a revelation in the full sense of the word, as understood by the Catholic Church, a Word come from on high, from the "Beyond", with the twofold character of being intellectual and supernatural. It will be a personal manifestation, and it will be a teaching.

[1] *Introduction à la vie chrétienne* (1944). Cf. *Esquisse d'un Univers personnel*, which ends with the word "Revelation". Similarly, *Esquisse d'une dialectique de l'Esprit*: "The expectation of a revelation" (*Œuvres*, VII, p. 152). *Comment je vois* (1948), nos. 21 and 22.

"The fact of the Incarnation", Père Teilhard wrote later, in 1946, "cannot be known by the way of pure inference", but only by "adherence to an affirmation received from above."[2]

In this there is nothing of the immanentism or anti-intellectualism of which the modernists had recently been accused and which, as history abundantly shows, are a permanent temptation to the human mind. On the contrary: Père Teilhard had been in a position to observe the last phases of the modernist crisis. He had often heard it discussed, and had been moved by the tragic case of George Tyrrell, once a Jesuit, who died while Teilhard was studying theology in England; he kept up with the literature on the subject. As for his basic attitude to modernism, he generally took a very severe line. He freely criticized its short-sighted historicism, which he designated as "fragmentation", and its undisciplined mysticism, divorced from any intellectual viewpoint and with "no axis of progression". As such, in particular, he stigmatized the thought of Alfred Loisy.[3] In 1919, that is, at a time when the two words "modernism" and "integrism" had still all the novelty of their contrast, he had even chosen as a definition of his own teaching "a term that a narrow use has made offensive: *Integrism*".

> Integrism in its purity: certainly. Meaning, in the first place, the authentic Christ, Christ in his truth and supernaturality. In this form alone has Jesus the power to conquer the World and incorporate it with himself—But integrism, also, in Universality. May no element, I pray, of created force, may not one iota of the redeemable World be lacking to the Plenitude of Jesus![4]

[2] *Barrière de la mort et co-réflexion; Œuvres*, VII, p. 427. *Esquisse d'une dialectique de l'Esprit*; VII, p. 155. Cf. to L. Zanta, 25 Jan. 1924: God manifests himself "to the minds that await him."

[3] This was his reaction to Loisy's *Mémoires*, lent to him by a friend in Peking.

[4] *L'Élément universel*, end. Blondel has also at times spoken of his own "integrism"—before the word was compromised. He then substituted "maximalism". Cf. *L'Itinéraire philosophique de Maurice Blondel* by Fr. Lefèvre, p. 68.

Later, he preferred to speak of "Integralism". What he meant by that was his determination, in opposition to all forms of minimism, to accept and maintain "Christ in his integrity" as he is given to us in revelation. However modern or even "ultra-modern" his thought may be called, it is only by an abuse of language that it can be described as "neo-modernism".[5] He was always careful, in particular, to distinguish, with the consequent effects of such distinction on attitude and method, between "the Truth elaborated on Earth" and "the Truth come down from Heaven".[6]

But how is the latter to be found? How are we to set about looking for this divine revelation? Here we immediately come up against the radical difference in method from that which we found in the earlier stages, a difference dictated by the radical difference of the object in question. No longer are we concerned in this new and final stage, with immediate experience, nor with purely rational demonstration, nor with any sort of individual reflection on evidence we have already acquired. Once again as in classic apologetics, history comes into play. For it is not a question of making a religion for oneself, a completely interior religion, but, when the time comes, of adhering to the word that will have echoed somewhere, for all of us, in the heart of Mankind. It is a question of "integrating" ourselves to the social organism, if such exists, through which the word comes to each one of us. In short, although the word has hardly yet been mentioned, of entering some Church.

To this end, Père Teilhard now asks us to join him in a vast inquiry into the fact of religion, taken in all its collective dimensions throughout space and duration. On other occasions, he offers the "Christian phylum" more directly for

[5] Luc. J. Lefèvre in *La Pensée catholique* (1963), p. 2: "Modernism, from which, in a new form, stems the Neo-modernism of Teilhard." Even a single supporting reference would be desirable. Cf. *Milieu Divin*, p. 117.
[6] *La Maîtrise du Monde et le Règne de Dieu.*

our observation (as he later did in the epilogue to *The Phenomenon of Man*, where the element of comparison is only implicit). But in this year 1934, his recent experiences in traversing the continent of Asia has shown him the value of a wider confrontation.[7] In *How I Believe*, he has indicated some broad lines of approach, so that the inquiry may not be lost in an endless mass of detail.[8] Now, in this "testing of religions", what we shall have to look for will no longer be just a proof, inductive or deductive, but a "sign". However the sign may be obtained—we are not at the moment concerned with the particular content of this stage of the apologetic—it will be, to each person who receives it, an instigation to belief. Faith, however, will not come automatically as the result of an intellectual inquiry, any more than it will depend on individual examination of each article. Not only are "faith in the World" or "the postulate of evolution" incapable of engendering it (as Dom Frénaud alleges that Père Teilhard maintains), but any form of proof is equally incapable of doing so. It is something quite other than a mere conclusion or a mere assertion. It is infinitely more, and belongs to another order. It can only be an answer—an answer to a sign. To believe, we must, in a personal act, "give ourselves" to the God who is here present, manifested in his Word.[9]

[7] He had given much thought to the problem of missions. He wrote to me from Peking (7 Jan. 1934): "Everyone in the Far East is waiting for a book on the essence of Christianity, or on the Christian point of view (as opposed to Buddhism or Confucianism). It would be translated into all languages. But it would have to be something with the scope and serenity of Bergson's last book. . . . Who will give us this *Summ ad Gentiles?*"

[8] The same sort of inquiry, more schematic, was again undertaken in an essay of 1950, *Pour y voir clair*, in which he severely criticized Eastern "identification" mysticisms. This does not prevent Dr. Maurice Vernet from writing that Teilhardian doctrine is a doctrine of "identification", and, again, "the Christian theologian is shocked . . . by the pantheist vision that identifies all the forces of the universe" (*op. cit.*, pp. 214, 221). See below, p. 192.

[9] *How I Believe*, Parts 2, 3, p. 24.

This is developed later in the *Esquisse d'une dialectique de l'Esprit :*

> As soon as we accept the reality of an *answer* coming to us from on high, we in some way enter the order of certainty. But this comes about as a function, not, as before, of mere confrontation of subject and object, but of contact between two centres of consciousness: it is no longer an act of knowing but of *recognition :* the whole complex interplay of two beings freely opening and giving themselves to one another—the emergence, under the influence of grace, of theological Faith.[10]

Since Père Teilhard was addressing a reader who was still an unbeliever, he was not concerned to develop as he does in the passage just quoted the implications of the process he is describing to him. Still less was it appropriate to build up a whole theological theory of Faith. The final act to which he leads the reader of *How I Believe* none the less answers without any doubt the conditions of the act of "theological faith", of supernatural faith.

Does that mean, as Dom Frénaud would seem to exact, that no motive of the natural order, that is "no reason for believing", should serve to lead him to that faith? Was Père Teilhard wrong in speaking, in his conclusion, of "reasons for [his] faith", as though in so speaking he had affirmed that those "reasons" were its "formal cause"? If that is so, I find it impossible to see how the same objection could fail to be raised against anyone who speaks, as sometimes he must, of "reasons for believing". To be supernatural must not faith be all the more rational? And for the supernatural itself to be authentic, does it have to be without any "connection" with our nature? Is Christianity in no way to be seen as the truth of life? If there is some confusion here, the fault does not lie with Père Teilhard. On this point we must recognize that his thought seems perfectly balanced and, to put it in a word,

[10] *Œuvres*, VII, p. 155.

theologically exact.[11] As every believer who subscribes to the Catholic faith must do, anyone who contradicts Teilhard must ultimately himself admit that, in a sense, his own "religious faith" is founded on some "faith in the World" (if it is true that it is from the world that human intelligence starts its ascent to God)—even though it does not result from that "faith in the World" and even though it be of a different order. This initial "faith in the World" is differently understood by each party; on the one hand it concerns no more than the existence of a world recognized as contingent, and on the other the evolution of a world in process of becoming: but this difference does not essentially affect the plan of argument in the stages preliminary to the act of faith: on both sides, the intelligence derives its impulse from an equally natural basis.

There is, then, a sense in which one may, and even must, speak of a natural "foundation" or a natural "condition" for adherence to supernatural faith. Dom Frénaud can no more escape this than can Père Teilhard. To maintain the contrary would be to condemn all apologetic effort, and succumb to the irrational. We may indeed, agree with Père Philippe de la Trinité that "no induction or deduction, of a natural ontological type, will ever lead to *faith* in Christ. Knowledge, supernatural in order, of the Incarnation and of grace cannot be objectively reduced, even indirectly, to no more than natural reasoning and intuition". We may agree that "supernatural faith in Christ cannot be dictated by a process of the natural order, even though it be a process of cosmogenesis".[12] On the other hand, we have just seen that, in the process that is to lead to faith, Père Teilhard in no way minimizes the importance of transition through revelation and through "recognition" of that revelation. As G. Crespy has seen, he

---

[11] Cf. René d'Ouince, S.J., *loc. cit.*, p. 337: "The theologians who advised the authorities in Rome certainly underestimated the theological competence of their colleague".

[12] *Rome et Teilhard de Chardin*, pp. 57, 78–9.

does not "disguise the 'transition to another type' that constitutes the act of faith",[13] and when he says that "only the Christian faith is capable fully of embracing (by amorization, i.e. impregnating with love) a Cosmogenesis of convergence",[14] he does not thereby imply that this Cosmogenesis of convergence in itself demands Christian faith and is capable of engendering it in the intelligence of anyone who has grasped the idea of it. Must our faith, to be supernatural, be incapable of shedding light on anything?

Later, in the *Phenomenon of Man*, he used an extremely careful and exact expression to describe his intention, and one that fits well with his approach in *How I Believe* and similar essays: he wants, he says, to disclose "the rational invitations to an act of faith".[15] Apologetics can do no more, and should not be satisfied with less. Christian faith, we must insist again, is rational, even though it goes beyond and is too much for reason; and the great Newman, whom Père Teilhard read eagerly, was not putting forward any naturalist thesis when he referred in one of his university sermons[16] to the great comfort a Christian feels when he realizes that Revelation is deeply rooted in the natural order of things. No more does Teilhard when he wonders at "the profound harmony" of the idea of the Incarnation[17] and sees in it a sign of Christian

[13] *La Pensée Théologique de Teilhard de Chardin*, p. 107.

[14] *Un sommaire de ma perspective phénoménologique du monde* in *Les Études philosophiques*, New York, Jan. 1954.

[15] In its immediate context this applies only to faith in the meaning of the Universe and "survival", but it includes all that follows in consequence and, *a fortiori*, applies to the acceptance of revelation. Père Teilhard wished, says Père d'Armagnac, to show "the roads that lead from a vision of the world to religious faith". Those to whom this vision of the world seems too hypothetical and arbitrary may not find this a very cogent apologetic argument, but it does not follow that it is not sound; and it may be helpful to others.

[16] *University Sermons*, 2 (13 April 1830).

[17] *Œuvres*, VII, p. 169. To Père Philippe de la Trinité, "such an apologetics is valueless, and that *a priori*" (quoted in *Nouvelles de Chrétienté*, 21 May 1964, p. 19). This is a personal opinion, to which another, with better support in tradition, may well be preferred.

truth, or when he seeks to show Christianity as "the great direction, the great regulator of this vast thing that surrounds us and is the world".[18] Much as the teaching authority of the Church is opposed to any naturalization of faith, it equally rejects the fideist temptation. It would, of course, be absurd to accuse Dom Frénaud of fideism, but we are justified in saying that his criticism of Père Teilhard is based on too one-sided an interpretation of the Church's teaching. In the heart of controversy he has, I fear, gone too far.

[18] Lecture to Maurice Légaut group, 1930.

6

THE AXIS OF ROME

DOM Frénaud already had a precedent when he formu-
lated the criticism we have been answering, and, on our
side, the essential points of the answer were already at
hand.

The same criticism, in fact, has already appreared, under
the name of Père Garrigou-Lagrange, in 1946; it could be
read in the periodical *Angelicum* under the provocative and
arbitrary title, "Whither the new theology?"[1] This "new
theology" which, according to the writer, "was leading to
'scepticism', 'fantasy', and 'heresy'", was deduced from a
mixture or juxtaposition of scattered quotations, sometimes
cut down to a single sentence, drawn from a number of
different writings, often of doubtful origin. Père Teilhard
appeared in this witch-hunt, in virtue of the same *How I
Believe* in which Dom Frénaud, in turn, claimed to find a
fatal naturalism.

"In these pages", wrote Père Garrigou-Lagrange, "the
act of *Christian faith* is not conceived as a supernatural and
infallible adherence to revealed truths *propter auctoritatem
Dei revelantis*, but as an adherence of the mind to a general
view of the Universe." A little later, still referring to the same
essay, "Dogma is no longer considered from the point of view
of the faith infused in divine Revelation, interpreted by the
Church in her Councils. . . . The point of view adopted is

[1] *La Théologie nouvelle où va-t-elle?*, *Angelicum* (1946), pp. 135 ff.

that of *biology*, complemented by highly imaginative flights reminiscent of Hegelian evolutionism."

As though the apologist's work could be identified with that of a theologian expounding Conciliar decisions. . . . As though, again, as soon as one begins to think and ceases to be content with a purely interior analysis, one could dispense with any "general view of the Universe". . . . As though the Teilhardian view in any way resembled Hegelian evolutionism . . . As though to be recognized as a theologian excused one from studying with any care the thought of another writer before dismissing it as a flight of imagination. . . . As though, finally, Père Teilhard had ever confused his "basic general view" with Catholic dogma. It was not long before Père Teilhard, in an unpublished letter, answered this accusation:

> Père Garrigou-Lagrange is completely mistaken about the meaning of my Note (*How I Believe*). In this—which, moreover, was intended for a very special public and not for general circulation—I confine myself to describing a psychological advance, in the order of *causes of credibility* (the effort to find God through reason: *first* session of the Vatican Council). At this preliminary stage, subordinate to supernatural adherence to what is revealed, the act of theological faith is not denied, for it has not yet come up for consideration.[3]

Here, we see, Père Teilhard distinguishes the two essential stages in his apologetic advance, as already analysed above and as they clearly emerge from his own exposition.[4] At the

---

[3] March 1947.

[4] These two stages, similarly distinguished, occur again in the *Phenomenon of Man* and *Comment je vois*; he invites the reader who has already followed him so far as to accept with him the great truths relating to the World, Man and God, to turn now to an examination of the Christian Phenomenon. Teilhard had also planned to complete "the Special Properties of the human species" with an appendix on "the Special Properties of the Christian Faith" (5 Jan, 1954), *Letters from a Traveller*, p. 349. This is the very short passage, published only in the *Œuvres*, on "the special property of the Christian Phenomenon" (see above, p. 167, note 54).

same time, without going into unnecessary detail, he clearly distinguishes the causes of credibility, which are natural, and of faith, which is supernatural. Similarly, he is ready to concede that his starting-point and his causes for credibility, in so far as they are personal, may have little solidity or probative force for many minds, including that of his critic: they may, if they wish, regard them as "flights of imagination". He does not, however, believe that he is thereby excused from trying to say something that will weigh with other minds —the "special public" he refers to. He considered that he owed this to the scientists he mixed with, and who more or less shared his initial "general view of the universe", even if they were incapable of discovering a solid basis for it. It was among these men that God had placed him, and it was of them that he once exclaimed in his missionary zeal, "These are the Indies that call me with even more urgency than St Francis Xavier's."

However, the second part of *How I Believe*, in which, starting from belief in God, Teilhard seeks through the whole extent of the religious fact for the sign of any possible divine revelation, is no more acceptable to Père Garrigou-Lagrange. He levelled against it a second accusation, similar to the first. In it he claimed to find the idea that "the world of spirit naturally, so to speak, evolves towards the supernatural order and the plenitude of Christ"; and he took particular objection to the following sentence, the opening words of which he italicized: "*A general convergence of religions* towards a universal Christ, who, fundamentally, satisfies them all: that seems to me the only conversion possible for the World,[5] and the only way in which a Religion of the future can be conceived."

[5] Père Teilhard's text reads "conversion of the World" (*conversion du Monde*) and not (as quoted in *Angelicum*) "for the World" (*au Monde*). A misprint, or an indication of a preconceived idea?—as we find elsewhere when Teilhard is discussed (Cf. the misquoted title of *Hymne de l'Univers* referred to earlier).

To this, in the same letter, Père Teilhard replied:

Why should the idea that spirit evolves "so to speak naturally towards the supernatural order" be attributed to me? I have neither said nor implied anything of the sort in anything of mine that has been published with my full approval, indeed in anything I have written, whether published or not. Doesn't the apparent error arise from an unwarranted transposition of my phenomenology into the order (carefully excluded in the pages criticized) of theology?

When I speak of convergence of religions the context abundantly proves that in my thought this convergence must be *on the Christian axis*—the other creeds finding in faith in Christ the proper expression of what they have been seeking as they grope their way towards the Divine.

A mere reading of Père Teilhard would have been sufficient, if not to put an end to any discussion, at least to quash the objection which he answers in the above passage. Had the objector underlined, besides the word *convergence* the word that follows it, *conversion*, he might have realized that there was a better interpretation. It might have made him understand that, if ever an idea, since St Paul's "*Si forte attrectent Eum*"[6] was basically traditional, then this idea of Teilhard's was. A distinguished Patristic scholar has expressed the philosophy of religion developed by the Fathers of the Church as follows: "The Logos *sarx* fulfils the Logos *spermatikos*. But he does not fulfil it without repulsing it, without fighting an ally turned hostile: the parts of the Logos have set themselves up as so many absolutes and then range themselves against the true Logos. Such is the dialectic of St Augustine in the *City of God*; such, also, in the main, the dialectic of the Fathers."[7] Such again, we may add, though closer to Clement of Alexandria than to Augustine, is that indicated by Teilhard—

[6] Acts 17. 27: "Would they somehow grope their way towards him?"
[7] Hans Urs von Balthasar, *Glaubhaft ist nur Leibe* (1963), p. 8. The author holds, rightly in my view, that this position is incomplete. I am not claiming here any agreement between his thought and Père Teilhard's.

and if it is comparatively optimistic in principle,[8] it is equally severe in its application to particular religious forms: some of his judgments on Buddhism, for example, and Islam are sufficient proof of that.[9] At the same time only supernatural revelation "can preserve from fatal misdirection the powers accumulated at the heart of the individual, of societies and of the World itself".[10]

The "tactics" defined here—to use one of Père Teilhard's own words, though excluding from its meaning, as he did, any suggestion of ruse or artifice—were constantly applied by him, It was this tactical sense that made him on one occasion exclaim to a friend, whose wisdom he had no doubt of but whose mental attitude he thought too negative, "Don't simply refute—assimilate!" One might, if one wished, call this boldness or put it down to *naïveté*, but in any case, in Teilhard's mind, it proceeded not from a weakened or watered down faith, or a faith somewhat tainted by naturalism, but from a tremendous confidence in the converting and assimilating power of his faith. It never shook the firmness of his judgments: an example that might well be studied by some thinkers today whose sudden mistaken enthusiasm for "dialogue" seems to have gone to their heads.

We see an application of this method in the conclusion of "Reflections on happiness" of 1943, which points out the shortcomings of all the "human mysticisms", whether "social

[8] Christ is for Teilhard, in Tertullian's phrase, "*magis extruens quam destruens*" (*Adv. Marcionem*, l. 4, c. 7).

[9] Cf. letter of 8 Oct. 1933: "The Buddhist denies himself in order to kill desire (he does not believe in the value of being). The true Christian does the same from excess of desire and faith in the value of being. It is one of those cases where an external resemblance disguises contrary realities." See also, letter of 29 April 1934. Père Teilhard, who was a good observer and familiar with such orientalists as René Grousset, Jacques Bacot and Madame Solange Lemaitre, was less liable to misunderstand the complexity of the question than some of his summary statements might lead one to believe. Cf. *Letters from a Traveller*, pp. 92–3.

[10] *Esquisse d'un Univers personnel; Œuvres*, VI, p. 89.

mysticisms" or "scientific mysticisms", and that claim
acceptance by "Christian mysticism". We see it again in 1945
in "Christianity and Evolution", where it is made clear that
the synthesis required is not a mere confluence: "For the
synthesis to be produced, Christianity must, without modify-
ing the position of its summit, open its axes to embrace the
whole totality of the new surge of religious energy welling
up from below and seeking sublimation". We find an even
more definite statement in 1947, in a short essay on "Faith
in Man": here, after stating that "the rise of human faith
we are witnessing is a vitalizing phenomenon and in consequence irresistible" he immediately adds, "This does not
mean that we have to abandon ourselves passively and un-
conditionally to that flood: the more powerful and youthful
an energy is, the more is it ambivalent and dangerous in its
effervescence." This, again, is the inspiration (in 1948) behind a whole paragraph in *How I See*, in which the Catholic
Church is presented as the "central axis of universal convergence and exact point at which blazes out the meeting of the
Universe and Omega Point".[11]

Later again, we see the same ideas expressed in some of
Père Teilhard's last writings. In July 1950, he wrote "to clarify
ideas" a short "essay in basic classification of religions". It is,
in fact, somewhat summary in style, and in it is emphasized
a tendency to schematizing that characterizes a number of
pieces written in his last years.[12] In this, I believe, he
oversimplified a great deal, in particular when he speaks,

[11] No. 24 (end of part 1). Earlier, in 1925 (letter of 12 June) he wrote about
someone who had misunderstood him: "He doesn't seem to be able to conceive
an assimilation (animation) of science by Faith that is not a reduction of Faith to
Science."

[12] *Pour y voir clair; Œuvres*, VII, pp. 233–6. In my opinion such schematizing
impoverishes the thought in the process. As so often happens with increasing
age, Père Teilhard's vision, still keen, was growing more narrow. He interpreted
this as meaning that his thought was more rigorous: this was only partly true.
Familiarity with his earlier writings is necessary to an understanding of the
later schematic statements.

historically, of "Christian mysticism of the 'juridical' type".[13] A few strongly marked features suffice for his characterization of the three "religious currents that at this moment are rivals for the adherence of the Earth": the eastern, Marxist, and Christian currents. He then tries to bring out the "spiritual potentialities" of Christianity, which alone can and must be the religion of the future.[14] The essential idea, nevertheless, is still clear, and is in no way "syncretist".[15] This he was to express forcibly in a letter to Père d'Ouince, "Nothing can associate except on the axis of Rome".[16] We find the same again in an answer (4 October 1950) to an occasional correspondent who thought he saw in the recently published encyclical *Humani Generis* a sign of the decline of the Church of Rome:

> Only in the Roman stock, taken in its integral unity, can I see biological support sufficiently wide and sufficiently variegated to operate and maintain the transformation we await. For half a century I have seen at too close range the revitalizing of Christian life and thought—in spite of any Encyclical—not to have immense confidence in the re-animating powers of the ancient Roman stock. . . .[17]

Surely such a view anticipated the present Council?
Another example of this same idea is to be found in a note

[13] This passage illustrates the gaps, which indeed he recognized, in his historical knowledge.

[14] In defining the great non-Christian mysticisms as "identification", he anticipated the similar view of Fr. von Balthasar, *Herrlichkeit*, vol. I, when he explains "what *inevitably* happens in all extra-Christian mysticisms: the finite is absorbed by the infinite, the non-identical stifled by identity". See above, p. 181, note 8.

[15] See also on this, Jacques Bacot, *Autour du congrès universel des croyants* (*Cahiers*, 2. pp. 143–9).

[16] In *L'Homme devant Dieu*, vol. 3, p. 343, note 16 (Dec. 1950). He speaks also of "The Roman stock" (4 Oct., in M. Gorce, *Le Concile et Teilhard*, p. 198).

[17] Quoted by Maxime Gorce, *op. cit.*, p. 198; on page 183 the author exaggerates the undoubted Romanism of Père Teilhard, when he makes him say of the Pope what he said of God himself, "Personal Centre of the Universe"! Cf. *Pensée religieuse*, p. 277.

concluding a study (November 1950) on "the appetite for living", in which he deliberately takes his stand on natural reason and ethics. That there may be no doubt about his personal position, he ends:

> These lines were deliberately written from a strictly neutral point of view. Had I spoken as a "Catholic" I should have had to add that the Church, not by arrogance but at the dictation of her very structure, *cannot but* consider herself as the *very axis* on which can and must be effected the movement we await of association and convergence.[18]

Next year, Père Teilhard summed up in a few lapidary sentences his intellectual position in a report to his General. Once again he uses similar terms to express himself. He believes in "the unique value of Man as the spearhead of life", "the axial position of Catholicism in the convergent fascicle of human activities".[19] Finally, in 1952, "The Christic" studies the place of the "Christian Phenomenon" in the religious history of mankind, and again compares it with the place of the human phenomenon in natural history. Here Père Teilhard notes that Christianity after, like man, suffering an eclipse, again like man "is winning back and consolidating its axial and directive place as the spearhead of human psychic energies".

If we have spent some time in dealing with this last misconception in the attack on Père Teilhard, it has not been, you may be sure, with any idea of reopening a dispute that is now a thing of the past. It has been because a similar interpretation of his thought is still tending to be widely advanced: it comes, indeed, from a different quarter but it is based, sometimes explicitly, on the accusations dealt with above; with this difference, however, that Père Teilhard is now praised for what earlier was held against him. Because he spoke—in what a legitimate and exact sense, we have just seen—of a

[18] *Œuvres*, VII, p. 249.
[19] Leroy, *op. cit.*, p. 57.

possible and desirable "convergence of religions", there are
some who, neglecting his continual insistence at the same time
on the "transcendence of Christianity",[20] seek to make of
Père Teilhard a prophet of a universal syncretism. With no
text to support the assertion, without ever expressing it with
sufficient precision to allow contradiction, they link him with
a "new era" that will see the establishment of a "cosmic
religion". "The expectation of a new religion", it is claimed,
can be perceived, and the implication is that Père Teilhard
will prove to have been its herald. By taking his "Hymn to
Matter" out of its context and cutting out passages that
bring out its full and real meaning, it is quoted in such a way
as to make it the theme-motif of a "ritual dance". Because he
spoke of "the fantastic increase in scientific powers of discovery",[21] or of "the fantastic vistas opened up for science"
by his views—that is, the escape of part of the *Weltstoff* from
Entrophy[22]—he is associated with "fantasy" of quite another
sort. Giordano Bruno reappears as a "sixteenth-century
Teilhard". "Omega Point" is associated with the second
surrealist manifesto's "point beyond infinity" and with the
achievement of the *magnum opus* of the alchemists,[23] etc.
These, of course, are wild fantasies, but at the same time they
can do a great deal of harm. Such an abuse of Père Teilhard's
name could never have occurred so readily, had not, unfortunately, some churchmen first helped by the ill-founded
accusations they heaped on him. Even during his lifetime a
number of "legends" and "tendentious intepretations" were
circulating, against which he was obliged to protest—and he
had every right to believe that the explanations he had from
time to time given of his works would definitely scotch such

[20] *L'Étoffe de l'Univers; Œuvres*, VII, p. 406.
[21] *L'Énergie de l'évolution; Œuvres*, VII, p. 391.
[22] *Les singularités*, etc.; *Œuvres*, II, p. 362.
[23] See various allusions in the review *Planète*. J. Bergier, *Le Matin des Magiciens*, p. 476, quoted in *Cercles catholiques d'Angers* and *Nouvelles de Chrétienté*, Nov. 1963, p. 8.

rumours.[24] Even so, in some circles, they reached a "delirious pitch",[25] fostered from time to time both by serious organs (the sort that have grand Latin names) and by the wildest science-fiction magazines. As anyone who has read the earlier part of this book with attention will have realized, we are far from saying that Teilhard is never open to criticism, but we cannot fail to recognize how justified and apposite is the wish expressed by Père Jeannière in the article on Teilhard already referred to: "If only the time would come when I could just talk with Teilhard instead of having to keep on saying that he never said what people want to make him say!"[26] We may at least hope that the sober clarity of the two short hitherto unpublished explanations, so much to the point and so in accordance with countless other passages, which Père Teilhard wrote in answer to the *Angelicum* charges, will re-assure any who have been anxious and distressed. In any case, they are one more assurance that Père Teilhard could distinguish perfectly, without losing himself in unnecessary refinements of thought, the two orders of the natural and the supernatural.[27] They are an assurance, too, that particularly in matters of faith he was well able to avoid the gross confusions some have charged him with.[28]

[24] For example in the two works quoted above: *La Pensée du Père Teilhard de Chardin par lui-même* (1948); *Esquisse d'une dialectique de l'Esprit* (1946).

[25] Abel Jeannière, *Teilhard de Chardin, Sur le Mal et le Point Oméga, Esprit*, March, 1964, p. 365. Cf. p. 363, "delirious interpretations", and p. 360 on "bastard offshoots of Teilhard". See also Adolf Haas, S.J. in *Scholastik* (1964), p. 527.

[26] *Op. cit.*, p. 366.

[27] Many other passages confirm this. Cf. above, pp. 124-9 and *La Pensée religieuse*, ch. 11, *Nature et Grace*.

[28] He himself once pointed out one of the general causes of such misunder-standings, remarking with regret on the "fundamental inability" even of re-putable theologians "to know their way about outside their own terminology". The opinions we have had to discuss show the wisdom of one of the rules laid down by Benedict XIV for the authorities concerned with the Index, and how desirable it is that theologians should always apply it to the publication of their private opinions. We quote from the summary in D. Bouix, *Tractatus de curia Romana* (1880, p. 164): "He should base his judgment on a diligent examination

of the whole work, and not on individual passages taken without reference to their context. If often happens that a proposition, on its own and without the context, may bear an objectionable meaning, and yet at the same time the author elsewhere clearly and *ex professo* defends the contrary doctrine. It thus becomes evident that the proposition was stated by the author in a correct and orthodox sense but with insufficient accuracy of expression."

7

SOME OTHER INTERPRETATIONS

SOME other writers have commented on the passage from *How I Believe* quoted at the beginning of this study, or have at any rate expressed their opinion of it.

We may mention first, simply to note it, what M. Ernest Kahane has said, even though he seems to be as careless a reader as the author of the article in the *Osservatore*. In Teilhard, he tells us, he admires "a rich nature, with an unrivalled sense of the reality of the World and the power, on occasions, to proclaim an eloquent profession of faith in which Christianity completely succumbs to pantheism. . . . One might very nearly add that pantheism itself succumbs almost completely to materialism." [1] This is so wild an interpretation, though more excusable in that it comes from a writer with little knowledge of Christian teaching, that we may well disregard it.

Père Roger Leys, S.J.,[2] has defended the passage in an article (in French) that appeared in the Flemish review *Bijdragen* :

> All this passage does is to state with great emphasis that with the world everything else is given. If we accept it, and weigh it and search into its depths, we must find that it depends only from on high, through the Spirit and through God. Teilhard could write the words objected to, because he knew that his fidelity to

[1] *Teilhard de Chardin* (1960), pp. 67–8.
[2] Professor of dogmatic theology and patristics in the Jesuit Faculty of Theology, Héverlé, Louvain, and the author of a number of publications on Père Teilhard.

the world would give back to him what, according to the hypo-
theis he put forward, he had progressively lost.[3]

Any reader who refers to the context or has followed the
explanation given in this essay cannot fail to agree with Père
Leys, who thus sums up the whole of the first part of *How I
Believe*. He will realize not only that Teilhard's hypothesis
has no basis in fact but also that his concept of the world is, in
this case, pregnant with the essential truths relating to the
spirit and to God that he proposes to extract from it.

However, Père Philippe de la Trinité cannot admit such
straightforward evidence. His preconceived notion of Teilhardism makes it impossible for him to adapt himself to it.
Quoting Père Leys' opinion, he adds the following reflections:

> Consider this extraordinary interpretation: Teilhard says black—
> that means white. . . .
>   In other words, according to Père Leys, if Teilhard *lost* his
> faith in Christ, in a personal God and in the Spirit—well, he has
> not lost it . . . he has simply mislaid it temporarily and no doubt
> will find it again. On such an exegetic principle there is no diffi-
> culty in making any author you please say the opposite of what
> he has written.[4]

Père Philippe de la Trinité has obviously not understood
Père Leys. Such a failure would be quite extraordinary if he
had read the context of *How I Believe*, on which Père Leys'
opinion is based, and which completely justifies the latter's
interpretation. It may be, indeed, that he did read the context,
but in that case he must have forgotten it, for nothing in his
criticism gives any indication that he has had it in mind.
Perhaps, on the other hand, this eminent theologian is a little
too assured in his reliance on his own preconceived interpretation. He would have done better to listen for a moment

---

[3] *Bijdragen* (1963), pp. 1–20. This explanation agrees, in the particular case
of Père Teilhard, with the general explanation given by J. A. Cuttat, quoted
above, p. 168.

[4] *Rome et Teilhard*, quoted in *Nouvelles de Chrétienté* (21 May 1964, p. 24).

to someone else's opinion, rather than immediately to attribute a ridiculous or unorthodox meaning to a man who does not reflect his own view. It is for this reason that we find him gaily piling up his accusations of confusionism, contradiction, illogicality (and these are simply some of his more kindly judgments)—"puerile concordism", he adds, "gimcrack apologetics", "height of confusion", "mythology", "poison". For this reason, too, that he relies on his wholly personal theory of "the five planes of abstraction", as though this were an evangelical principle or a definition of faith, and uses it to condemn the whole Teilhardian effort.[5] Here we have an unwarranted confusion of order which a theologian should be most careful to avoid.

We find a similar pejorative interpretation in an article by Henri Rambaud in *Tradition française*.[6] It is unfortunate that a talented writer, normally moderate and fair, should have allowed himself to be so influenced by earlier criticisms of the passage from *How I Believe* as to write that "it has a certain air of impudence". M. Rambaud claims to have "read Teilhard a great deal". However that may be, he certainly does not seem to have read *How I Believe* or at any rate to have studied it with any care. He treats the disputed passage simply as a "declaration"; had he formed his own judgment of it, a writer who ordinarily uses words with such skill would never have spoken of it as impudent, the most inappropriate word he could have used. It is difficult not to wonder just how closely he has looked at Teilhard's other writings, when we see him finally sum up "Teilhard's

---

[5] *Loc. cit.*, pp. 8–25. We may note also a misquotation by the Abbé Joly, of my *Pensée Religieuse*, p. 295, which makes nonsense of what follows (and allows him to attribute an objectionable meaning to it.) Mgr Combes had already, by an obvious misunderstanding, criticized this same passage in my book. Is this just a coincidence? Is it again simply a misprint, and if so, is *Seminarium* responsible or the *Nouvelles*? However that may be, "terrestrial *and* transcendent" is something very different from "terrestrial *or* transcendent".

[6] Jan. 1964. Quoted in *Nouvelles de Chrétienté*, 27 Feb. 1964, pp. 23–4.

master thought" as "the temporal fulfilment of the world
being nothing more nor less than the progressive manifestation of God". On the other hand there can be no doubt that
M. Rambaud has faithfully studied Dom Frénaud's booklet,
which he recommends to his own readers.[7]

Quite a different interpretation has been put forward by an
Italian writer, Carlo Bo. In an article for the review *Europeo*,[8]
entitled *Il Mondo e la mia fide* (which reached a more permanent public by its inclusion in the widely read *Il Gesuita
proibito*)[9] he set out to show that the anonymous contributor
to the *Osservatore* was needlessly distressed. Signor Bo had no
objection to the passage in question. However, just as the
Osservatore critic whose opinion he contested, and as Dom
Frénaud, among others, he did not bother (or perhaps had no
opportunity) to study the context. Thus, from what he knew
or thought he knew of Père Teilhard's mentality, he conceived
a most inaccurate explanation of the passage, inconsistent and,
frankly, equally arbitrary.

After remarking that we must "make allowances for the
author's romanticism", Signor Bo explains that Père Teilhard
tried, using paradoxical expressions as a "poetic stimulus",
to "bring out the active character of the World, and the
possibility of reading the secrets of matter that elude our
grasp or are still hidden from us". What this enigmatic sentence implies is "basically, an extension of our act of faith";
there can, he adds, "be no doubt that the scientists' ability in
this direction lies at the base of this profound penetration into
the unknown and mysterious". He then introduces the
image of the "priest-scientist" which, though essential to
Teilhard, has not, he believes, been sufficiently emphasized.
"Thanks to Teilhard," he concludes, "what yesterday seemed

[7] *Loc. cit.* p. 24.
[8] 29 July 1962.
[9] Giancarlo Vigorelli, *Il Gesuita proibito, vita e opere di P. Teilhard de Chardin*
(1963), pp. 364–5.

an untenable contradiction has become a symbol of colla-
boration, or what is even more, a symbol of a new and loftier
task."

Signor Bo was quite right to distrust an ill-considered
accusation, and there is no doubt that there is some valid idea
hidden in his remarks; but they have little relevance to the
passage he is concerned with. One has only to go unhurriedly
through the first pages of *How I Believe* to obtain a much
more precise and objective appreciation of the disputed statement.

There remains one more interpretation, somewhat similar
to Signor Bo's. This appeared, again without reference to
the context, in Maryse Choisy's recent booklet *Teilhard et
l'Inde* (1964). This maintains that Père Teilhard wished to
affirm his "love of the earth" and "to give value to the earth"
by "bringing it back to God"—so coinciding, "without realizing it" with Indian thought, as do St John the Evangelist,
St Catherine of Siena and St John of the Cross.—We need not
linger over this rapid and remarkable "summit meeting".
That Teilhard loved the earth in his reattachment of it to God
is undeniable, and we must be grateful to the author for
reminding us of this. It does not, however, follow that that
assertion is any key to the meaning of the passage we have been
trying to explain.

Already in 1961, Pastor Georges Crespy, had analysed
How I Believe in his *Pensée Théologique de Teilhard de Chardin*.
In it he saw "the manner of the great apologists". He did not
devote a great deal of attention to the opening methodological
paragraph, but he quoted the last sentence. Teilhard, he
said, "surrenders himself to this undefined faith in a single
Infallible World, wherever it may lead him". And he follows
up the sequence: "Once we have this first certainty, another
point unmistakably emerges", and so on. Then, after developing, as we did, the whole process of Teilhard's demonstration, he continues:

Teilhard's method of exposition is obviously much akin to that of the classic apologists: the search for a rational basis, the proposition of faith, establishment of coherence between the rational foundation and the hypothesis, demonstration of the absurdity of the contrary thesis, etc. In the procedure itself there is nothing novel: deduction, syllogistic chain, *argumentum a contrario* . . .; even the initial certainty that the particular conclusion is germinally contained in the premisses recalls the plan characteristic of this theological method."

Finally, returning a little later to "faith in the World" as expressed by Teilhard on his first page, Pastor Crespy concludes: "Teilhard had the courage to rely throughout on his initial intuitions; in his own mind he saw that the term would justify the whole." [10]

This is, substantially, exactly the same explanation as that given by Père Leys and put forward in this essay. Not only is there nothing improbable in it, but it is, in fact, imperative. Not for one moment does Pastor Crespy give any indication of having been tempted to interpret the words in question as an admission that might disconcert, distress or shock the believer. He read it without prejudice and looked for its meaning in its context. Had the theologians and writers who were shocked or distressed done the same, they would have been the better for it.

*   *   *

To conclude, we may note a characteristic of Christian faith, as described by Père Teilhard in *How I Believe*. We have already drawn attention to the passage. It is the subject

[10] *Op. cit.*, pp. 71–2, 77–8, 105. Similarly, though he cannot have seen the letters quoted above, pp. 41–2, Fr Prendergast, S.J., has appreciated the importance of Teilhard's concept of the cosmic Christ without being misled by any deficiency in its expression. Cf. his *Terrestrial and cosmic polygenism* in the *Downside Review*, July 1964, pp. 188–9. For other aspects of Teilhardian apologetics, besides Père d'Armagnac's article (quoted earlier), see *Pensée religieuse*, pp. 332–41.

of his epilogue, entitled "The Shadows of Faith". These shadows in no way impair certainty. ("No one has ever doubted the strength of my faith", he once wrote). But their impenetrable obscurity continually envelops the believer, so that, since he too is in the shadows, he is close brother to all men. Indeed, the obscurity overlies not only specifically Christian truths, and supernatural mysteries, properly so called, but everything that impinges on belief in God. "To believe is not to see. As much as anyone, I think, I walk in the shadows of faith". Fourteen years after *How I Believe* Père Teilhard repeated:

> . . . Certainty of hope, since Christ is already risen. At the same time, that certainty, in as much as it is derived from an act of "supernatural" faith, is of the supra-phenomenal order; and that means that, in one sense, it allows all the anxieties of our human condition to subsist, at their level, within the believer.[11]

Could anyone take offence at such words? Could anyone contradict them?

---

[11] *Les Directions et les conditions de l'avenir* (1948); *Œuvres*, V, p. 305. Cf. Maurice Blondel. 17 July, 1894 (*Carnets intimes*, 1961, p. 519): "You leave me with a very lively and very distressing feeling of the darkness of your road, the difficulty of your faith and, (forgive me) the uncertainty of your very existence and revelation. Blessed be you for this. It is this suffering that is to prevent me from remaining in the shadows or in a false light, which is to unite me with so many saddened souls and enable me to arouse them from the darkness in which they lie. I shall have to meet this agonizing obscurity even in the hearts of those who are vowed to you. Where, then, shall I find again your presence and your action and your charity, O God so fearfully hidden? In the security of faith, I feel for ever the doubts, the anguish of search. . . ."

NIHIL OBSTAT: DANIEL V. FLYNN, J.C.D. CENSOR LIBRORUM. IMPRIMATUR: ✠ TERENCE J. COOKE, VICAR GENERAL. NEW YORK, AUGUST 25, 1965. THE NIHIL OBSTAT AND IMPRIMATUR ARE OFFICIAL DECLARATIONS THAT A BOOK OR PAMPHLET IS FREE OF DOCTRINAL OR MORAL ERROR. NO IMPLICATION IS CONTAINED THEREIN THAT THOSE WHO HAVE GRANTED NIHIL OBSTAT AND IMPRIMATUR AGREE WITH THE CONTENTS, OPINIONS OR STATEMENTS EXPRESSED.

INDEX